The Bre

Cycling the Mc
Tour de

ROLF RAE-HANSEN

In memory of my father,
Derek Selkirk Rae-Hansen.

With thanks to Markso.

CONTENTS

AUTHOR'S INTRODUCTION

What follows are extracts from the diary I scribbled during a 19-day attempt to cycle up a few too many Tour de France (and Giro d'Italia) mountains. The name of my, now estranged, fellow traveller has been changed to protect the innocent but otherwise the events recounted are exactly as I saw them unfold.

Our (mis)adventure took place at the tail end of the Armstrong era, that period in cycling when athleticism blended with medicine to form a brash, fantastical fairy tale. Whilst the sporting hero's story seemed too good to be true, events in my own, comparatively inconsequential existence were patently less impressive. My father had recently succumbed to cancer and in the wake of his passing I floundered. Through the trip I sought catharsis — a decisive escape from my troubles. On a less maudlin note, this once-in-a-lifetime experience was also intended to deliver the thrill of following in our sporting heroes' wheel-tracks. At the very least it would provide a break from riding the same old, relatively flat roads around our Edinburgh home town.

Of course, not everything in life goes as we hope it might. My friend and I soon realised that we had bitten off more than we could comfortably (or uncomfortably) chew. Our levels of physical and mental endurance were tested well beyond their shaky limits, before being dragged outside and beaten to a pulp. However, (and I'm still not entirely sure why), it was on the friendship itself that the mountains seemed to exact their heaviest toll. By the end of the trip we were barely on speaking terms; within months, the shreds of our alliance had destructed in spectacular and upsetting style. From then on, consideration of our on-the-bike achievements brought nothing but disappointment, the many positives obscured by thoughts of the friendship's failure. The A4 notepad that had constituted my diary was placed atop a high shelf and left to gather dust.

As the astute reader will have discerned, the story doesn't end there. I'd lost a best mate, slipped free of my grief and left the mountains behind — but the mountains hadn't finished with me. At least once a month I would wake in a sweat having endured a vivid, inspiring and often frightening dream in which I was back on a road high above Italy or France. I would watch bicycle races on TV and recognise nondescript corners of cols I'd ridden, recollections that couldn't have been more alive had the bends been part of a treasured daily ride. Moments of laughter, sadness, anger, exhilaration and exhaustion had been branded onto my psyche by the tarmac twists and turns of cycling's infamous mountains. No matter how hard I tried, there was no escape from their clutches.

The friendship remained irreparably broken but once sufficient water had passed beneath the proverbial bridge I felt compelled to reclaim and re-evaluate the trip's legacy. I reached to the high shelf and that, by then, very dusty diary. Instead of denial, I would embrace and even boast about all that I had experienced — turn those Biro scribbles into a book, a tale to entertain, perhaps to inform and, hopefully, to inspire.

One day my father and I will reunite and the memories that follow here will fade into the ether. Less fleeting will be the mountain passes upon which my former friend and I suffered and soared: the likes of the Stelvio, Mont Ventoux and the Tourmalet. Those names will endure for centuries to come, as rock and tarmac monuments to the cyclists who have faced their challenge — the glorious winners and the nameless others who were brave or daft enough to follow.

DAY 1:
GETTING THERE (JUST)

First off, let's get things straight: I am no great traveller, not Marco Polo, not even VW Polo. I didn't leave the shores of Blighty until I was twenty-five. I'm thirty now, have yet to venture beyond Europe, to undertake the clichéd backpacker's odyssey, discovering the world by drinking and screwing in as many ports as possible. Travelling isn't an experience I enjoy; spending time in foreign climes is great, it's the practical bit at either end I dislike, the getting there and back.

Bleary-eyed and a little nervous, Drew and I checked in at the airport sensibly on time (around 7am), a full two hours before our flight's scheduled departure. The airline staff perused our documents, coughed up some vapid chat and maintained their saccharine smiles — right up until catching sight of our bike bags.

Golf bag? Why, yes, sir, golf is a wholly respectable pursuit and it would be an honour for our airline to transport your clubs. Bike bag? Bike bag! Cycling is the last resort of the weirdo. We'll take your disgusting bicycle but only because we are compelled to do so.

An unnecessarily shameful detour via the Oversize Baggage Desk and we headed to Edinburgh Airport's "Food Village", to waste time and money on something that vaguely resembled breakfast. At the end of a queue that was longer than the one at check-in I found the menu's "giant bacon roll" — a doughy offering that was colossal on the roll but microscopic on the bacon. Ordering and waiting proved less of an experience than paying for said oversize delicacy. The girl at the cash desk lolled uneasily, eyes swivelling in opposite directions to her hips, pursed lips emitting a series of whistles, squeaks and assorted bird sounds. A brief pause to announce that I owed £3.95 for the gluten overdose and she continued with the show. She was insane in the way that a third-rate drama student might be if their assignment for that week's class was to "*act crazy, man*". She made Mad Murdoch from *The A Team* look truly mad, and he wasn't in the least. His lunacy never stretched further than the occasional wacky noise or wearing his cap at a jaunty angle — he didn't even self-harm. Now that would have been something, tuning in every week to see which part of his own anatomy Self-Harming Murdoch had maimed and mutilated.

I presumed Cash-Desk Crazy was merely trying to communicate the fact that she found her soulless employment in a soulless café in a soulless airport far below her actual abilities, that the deep nothingness of it all had driven her obvious intellect into a downward spiral.

"I am more than my job," she said in a whistle and a squeak, "the simple act of adding up your bill has pushed me over the edge."

I waited for the pantomime to reach the point where she handed over my change, cast an eye out the window to a hand-painted mural, which announced that Edinburgh is a, "21 Century Airport". I wondered if they had meant 21st Century, or if this was the same spot upon which visionary Scots had queued for 2000 years, eagerly anticipating the Wright brothers' invention.

After an inordinate amount of time chewing and getting nowhere, I gave up on the baker's challenge and, with a cursory glance at my watch, suggested to Drew that we head along to the departure lounge. We had half an hour or so until take off; best get there as soon as possible, maximise the time spent sitting and staring blankly into space. Drew was still suffering the effects of a particularly nasty chest infection but determination to feed his cold was insufficient to overcome his disgust at the food. He grunted, snorted, swallowed a lump of phlegm and shovelled the sloppy remains of a deep-fried dog's breakfast to the edge of his plate.

We detoured via the bookshop, so Drew could get something to read on the plane. As I nervously checked and re-checked my watch, he wandered in and out of the displays, apparently unimpressed at the thought of books per se, but keen to look at them all, just in case one leapt from the shelf to alter his opinion.

"What are you looking for?" I asked, hoping to hurry him on.

"Dunno," he grunted, snorted and swallowed.

"What about *The Princess Knight*?" I suggested, rummaging through the children's section.

"There's a new Stone Roses book out, I'll see if I can find that," and he wandered out of sight.

Book browsing took far, far longer than anticipated, left me at Defcon One on the Nervous Traveller Scale. I always aim to be at the flight gate/train platform/bus stop on time (better still, inconveniently early), just in case — the eternal just in case that's never required but one day might be — and Drew was either playing it cool or playing it tardy. He reappeared and then quickly disappeared, hunting in the cookery section for a book on The Stone Roses that probably didn't exist. Finally, we departed, book-less and only so Drew could pop in to a pharmacist, "for deodorant, and shit". I was struggling not to nag but time was truly ticking.

Don't look at your watch, Rolf. Just be calm and cool. Take a deep breath and act like flying is something you do every day, something taken for granted, like riding your bike.

The woman at the till decided to try my patience by demanding that Drew present his passport in order to validate the debit-card payment — the same passport he had held in his possession an hour previous but had since misplaced. From there I skipped Two and went straight to Defcon Three, itching to grab Drew and drag him speedily toward the departure lounge.

His "shit" safely stowed, re-discovered passport between his teeth, we finally ambled along, only to hit a lengthy queue at the security desk. I could no longer resist and a peek at my watch led directly to Defcon Seventeen: our plane was due to take off in about seven minutes and we still hadn't passed through the metal detectors at the wrong end of the airport. Only then did Drew cotton on to my panic and — grunt, snort and swallow — muster some of his own.

In that alarm we were not alone. No sooner passed the security guards and we encountered the small army of staff that had been running around the terminal trying to locate the two muppets who were holding up the flight to Venice. We were dragged and we ran, stumbling, mumbling, grunting, snorting and swallowing, red-faced toward the gate. Only then did I hear our (final) boarding call, the exasperated announcer's mispronunciation of my name only adding to the embarrassment.

"Last call for a Mr Drew Henderson and a Mr, eh …[reading the name off the sheet, for the umpteenth time, still struggling with his colleague's bad handwriting and to believe it wasn't a weirdo cyclist's nom de plume] … a Mr Hanse-eh? Mr Rae Hand, Rae-Hank … is that *Hanser?* Mr Rolf Rae-*Hanser?* Or maybe it's Panzer? Yeah, that must be it, Mr Panzer Tank Commander."

At the gate, a riled, rotund woman snatched our boarding cards and demanded an explanation for our lateness. We were back in school, stood before the headmistress, ready to bend over and take what was coming. I wanted to interject but dared not speak up: this scolding session is wasting the few seconds we have left before the flight leaves us behind. All that effort, all those staff running round the airport, only for us to miss the plane because Ms wanted a decent explanation — *and there will be no back chat from you, Tank Commander!*

We were the exact opposite of all those idiots on that horrifically banal Airport programme, the ones who turn up late and aggressively blame their stupidity on some entirely innocent orange-clad minion. We were at fault and we knew it, readily admitted the crime. *It's a fair cop, guv', just let us on the bleedin' plane!* Finally, she let us go, the engines already revving as we fell embarrassed and sweating into the only two empty seats on the packed 737. Our journey had begun, but just and only just.

***

My problem with air travel is being afforded too much time to think. After the blushing had subsided, and my skin-tone returned to its normal pasty white, I switched to dwelling on what lay ahead. For much of the flight, "what lay ahead" translated into thoughts of screaming and panic, bleeping alarms, dangling oxygen masks and death upon impact. A short spell of meditation, a look out the window and I managed to shift my thoughts onto what would follow from a safe landing, tyre-side-down on the tarmac at Venice airport: mountains, lots and lots of mountains. It was hard not to think about mountains given that the aforementioned look out the window had revealed a vast swathe of jagged planet Earth, rocky ranges reaching high to slice the white, candy-floss cloud. I guessed at our flight path, presumed I was looking down upon the Alps, then edged back toward panic — their challenge looked daunting even from 20,000 feet. How were they going to look when we were down there, on the road?

In 16 days of riding we were to attempt the ascent of 33 mountain roads, and not just any old mountain roads. Our schedule read like a roll call of cycling's greatest climbs (in chronological order according to the "plan"): Monte Zoncolan, the Sella Ronda (Sella, Gardena, Campolongo & Pordoi), Passo Fedaia, Alpe di Pampeago, Passo dello Stelvio, Passo di Gavia, Passo del

Mortirolo, Cime de la Bonette, Col de Vars, Col d'Izoard, Col Agnel, Mont Cenis, Col du Lautaret, Col du Galibier, Col du Télégraphe, La Plagne, Col de l'Iseran, Col de la Madeleine, Courchevel, Col du Glandon, Col de la Croix de Fer, Les Deux Alpes, Alpe d'Huez, Mont Ventoux, Col de Peyresourde, Superbagnères, Col d'Aubisque, Hautacam, Col du Tourmalet and Plateau de Beille. Just reading the list left me out of breath, giddy and nauseous.

We'd begin in Italy with the Dolomites, jump across-range to the Alps before heading into France. If we survived their Alps we'd scoot south-west to the Franco-Spanish frontier for the Pyrenees, having slain Ventoux, the Giant of Provence, along the way. The majority of our travelling would be done by car, allowing maximum time to ride up mountains, and removing the need for what Drew and I saw as the two-wheeled purgatory of cyclo-touring — carrying all your possessions, tent, clothes, food and kitchen sink on the back (sides and front) of your bike. We wanted to experience the climbs "as the pros" would, on racing bikes, sans panniers. Difference was we'd probably, well, *definitely*, be a whole lot slower than the pros.

We'd thought it through, in our own special way, and it all looked perfectly feasible, even after the scribbled Post-It notes had been transcribed into type and printed onto paper. Time would tell where on the sliding scale our feasible met with the real-world's version.

I glanced over at Drew — pale legs protruding from khaki shorts, fidgeting hands flipping the safety information card over and over and over, the anguished expression of a man who regretted not having read one last Stone Roses book before death by horrific plane crash — and a glance was all I could take. I turned back to the window. In a matter of days we'd be down there, him and me against all those mountains. Only on that thought did the fear subside, excitement finally seeping in to fill the negative space. It really was happening, hard to believe but true; for once our talk had turned to action.

***

A half-hour argument with the staff at Marco Polo Airport, a spell on the phone to the booking agents in England, we finally got the keys to the hire car and staggered into the blazing Italian sun. Just pushing the baggage trolley from the terminal left me parched, perspiring and seriously concerned: how the hell was I going to cope with cycling up mountains in such heat? (Due to the timing of our trip we were to face the full ferocity of the European summer — we had tried but been unable to arrange it otherwise. Even in June many of the high passes can still be blocked by snow and our work schedules had ruled out waiting until later in the year.)

As part of our trip preparation (I use the p-word lightly. Our preparation had involved little more than excitedly shouting out and then writing down the names of every famous climb we could think of) I had printed out a map and a list of directions for every leg of our journey, (sat nav, you say? Whatever newfangled technology it is you're referring to probably won't work in the mountains, and besides, do you know how much they want to charge us to hire one for three weeks?), including the first leg north to Trento, our Dolomite base-camp. (This information I had filed in a black ring-binder known innocuously as, "the folder".) On paper it all appeared relatively straightforward; trying to actually follow the driving instructions was an experience best forgotten.

The text read like a series of bizarre mathematical equations. Deciphering them whilst travelling at Italian speeds would have challenged Sébastien Loeb and his co-driver, even if his co-driver had been a cross between Daniel Elena and Matt Damon's character from *Good Will Hunting*. (How do I like them apples? I hadn't even worked out that they were apples, and it was all going by so fast that it kind of blurred into a big green undecipherable nothingness. Please pull over, I'm scared!) In our case Drew was Loeb and I was the unnamed, mathematically, geographically challenged passenger.

I still hadn't got round to taking driving lessons, let alone sitting my test, and so Drew would be the sole driver for the entirety of the trip — not that this was in any way an issue. That beery-night back in Edinburgh he'd cheerfully volunteered for said joyful task (and had later reconfirmed the offer when stone-cold sober). We'd been in the pub, had got to talking about bikes, having been off the topic for all of five minutes, back to moaning about there being nowhere exciting or inspiring to ride around Edinburgh. We'd discovered all there was to discover (so we thought), had grown bored of the same old routes. Even worse than the perceived lack of novelty was the very real lack of mountain roads. There were hills aplenty but nothing of the kind we drooled over when watching bike racing on Eurosport, nothing like Alpe D'Huez, which we'd ridden up during a previous, three-day visit to watch the Tour de France (and once we'd had a taste of the pure, class-A hard stuff there was no settling for inferior substitutes).

The two fat, middle-aged blokes at the next table had also been deep in conversation — about breasts (not their own, which were ample, but the female variety), about how they couldn't get them big enough, juicy enough, meaty, beaty or bouncy enough. Edinburgh was just so flat, the four of us agreed, but for different reasons. Another couple of drinks and the fatties had sloped off in search of female body parts to ogle, whilst Drew and I wrestled with the slippery fish of an idea. We'd conceived a foolish notion that involved us riding up the crème de la crème of Europe's mountain roads, a whistle-stop tour during which Drew — no, *really* — wouldn't at all mind being the sole driver.

And so I tried to interpret the instructions, reading being one skill I had accrued over the years:

Depart Marco Polo Airport on Viale Galileo Galilei (North) for 0.6 mi.

"Okay, easy enough."

Bear RIGHT (North) onto Local road(s) for 54 yds.

"Exactly 54 yards? Did you remember to pack the yardstick?"

Bear RIGHT (North-East) onto SS14 [Strada statale Della Venezia Giulia] for 0.5 mi.

"There aren't any road signs but this looks about right."

Bear LEFT (North) onto Local road(s) for 54 yds.

"I will rue the day you forgot to pack the yardstick!"

Bear LEFT (North-West) onto A27 [Autostrada d'Alemagna] for 3.2 mi.

"North-west? Did you remember to pack the compass?"

"No, you said you'd packed it!"

"No, I didn't!"

"You did!"

"Watch out for that moped! And the lorry!"

We drove around in ever decreasing, ever more frustrating and frightening circles, until eventually deciding to head in a guessed compass bearing for Trento. After doubling back on ourselves and successfully negotiating some roadworks and the one-way system of a nondescript village, our reward was to stumble upon the autostrada: lorries hurtled along in the fast lane with one indicator permanently blinking, cars roared by us on both sides, the traffic in front doing 140kph one second and then 4kph the next — brake lights blazing, hazard lights blinking as we all somehow swerved around the school bus that had, rather inconsiderately, crashed and blocked two lanes. The road's excessive speed (and price) left the impression that the red Ferrari spirit had infused an entire nation's driving habits.

We careered north toward the Dolomites, through the Soave vineyards, so hot in the car I dreamt of plunging naked into a giant vat of chilled plonk. The first ground-level glimpse of mountains came just north of Verona with the Monti Lessini. With peaks up to around 1700 metres, they left us feeling even more inconsequential than we already felt, worrying about how we would react when the "real" mountains showed up. Even the vast quarry that scarred the nearest slope was minute in comparison to the mountain's greater whole: those tiny dots in the distance were men and machines futilely hacking at the massive bulk, just as we would soon attack far bigger prey armed only with bicycles.

Two hours up the road and we landed at the outskirts of Trento, capital city of the autonomous province Trentino. Our first port of call, the Via Torre Vanga, and the hostel that would be our home for the next five nights, lay in reach, just across the river. According to the map, our destination was just a little further up the road along which we were already driving, over the bridge and second right — the same bridge that was closed by cones and a line of yellow signs emblazoned with the word *deviazione* (a word that would come to haunt us).

We duly followed the crazy yellow signs, on a journey that took us round the outskirts of Trento and back again in one hundred and one different ways, never once taking us over the river or anywhere near the hostel. We stopped locals to ask for directions and, having limited Italian between us, vainly hoped some of the copious body language would reveal an answer. It did, only the answer always seemed to take us right back to square one, to the closed bridge and that damned deviazione.

They say that if you give a monkey a typewriter and an infinite amount of time it will eventually bash out the complete works of Shakespeare. Well, leave two Scotsmen in a car, set them off around Trento and eventually, one day, they'll find a way over the river that hasn't been cordoned off by workmen. An hour of frustrated driving later and we somehow stumbled upon the park our map suggested was adjacent to the hostel. Thirty seconds on and I was leaning out the window yelling, "Via Torre Vanga, Via Torre Vanga!", like I'd just discovered the secret that would cure all the world's ills and make me its richest man.

***

With stomachs rumbling to the point of *Alien*-style explosion, we dumped our bags, held off exploring the immediate surrounds and headed out for a very early dinner — only to find that Trento appeared to be a city with a shortage of restaurants. Edinburgh has approximately three cafés or restaurants per square metre, that's two members of waiting staff for every man, woman and child in the city. (My data may be the result of over-exaggeration for emphasis.) We expected the same culinary choice from Trento but our expectations were not to be met, and so we eventually settled for an al fresco pizzeria, the affordable one of only two restaurants we could find.

After some sub-Pizza Express fare, we wandered around the centre of town, trying hard not to look (and feel) like a honeymooning couple.

"We are here for the mountains!" I wanted to shout. "To cycle up those mountains and not to skip hand in hand through their idyllic pastures."

Because of its geographic position, between northern and Mediterranean Europe, the Trentino region has long been a land of new encounters and cultural exchange (so the Tourist Board leaflet said). The Romans, French and Germans have all left their mark, making Trento a city with a rich history and many amazing historic buildings (the Tourist Board pointed us toward the 15th Century Gothic Cathedral, or Duomo, by which we gaily promenaded). Despite the distraction of our surroundings, a degree of homesickness had already manifested itself in the shape of Drew's constant time checks and maudlin pronouncements such as, "it's twenty-past eight here, twenty-past seven back home." (A habit he would repeat almost each and every time he checked his watch for the entirety of the trip, always correcting to British Summer Time in an unconscious attempt to reconnect with the Motherland.) He had also begun to pass such comments as, "wonder what they're doing back home without me? Watching *Terry and June* repeats and enjoying tea and biscuits, I suspect," as if we were POWs who'd been away from their families for years and not holidaymakers barely half a day in.

We eventually gave up trying not to look like pining/loved-up honeymooners and returned to the hostel to settle in. If the prison guards appeared none too happy to have us staying (they couldn't have looked more disappointed had they tried) then the rest of the inmates were even less impressed. Neither of us had stayed in a hostel before but we'd both been forewarned that they were great places for making new friends, of all nationalities. Everyone in our wing was Italian and male, and if they weren't loitering menacingly at the front door, arguing with one another and the passing polizia, then they were in the TV room, engrossed in a seemingly never-ending Rai Tre documentary about Popes past and present.

First impressions of our room were unanimous: it resembled a prison cell minus the bars. The three-metre-square box was sparsely furnished: a set of bunk beds, a small table and a wardrobe. In around those facilities we packed our bodies, our holdalls and our bike bags. The remaining, highly restricted airspace swarmed with mosquitoes, aka our evening's entertainment. The free hire-car map came in handy for swatting and squashing, and we'd soon created an interesting polka-dot effect upon the once-pristine whitewashed walls.

Resigned to our outsiders' status, we headed to bed, intending to sleep on Drew's suggestion that we give each other prison tattoos. Not that sleep was immediately forthcoming. The effortless act of lying still left me perspiring like a feverish fat man running up stairs, back to worrying about how I was going to cope with cycling in the cruel heat of day. Turning my two pillows over every five minutes until they were both soaked through with sweat, I eventually succumbed to the sandman's advances, the sound of Vespa scooters and hungry mosquitoes buzzing angrily in my ears.

DAY 2:
THE GOONIES REDUX

Monte Zoncolan
Start point: Sutrio | Height: 1735m | Height climbed: 1203m
Length of climb: 13.5km | Average gradient: 8.9% | Maximum
gradient: 23%

The far-from-intrepid travellers started the day in appalling and
embarrassing fashion. Michael Palin would have laughed in our
faces; Ray Mears would have pulled out his foraged axe, chopped
us up, eaten the paltry flesh and used our bones for kindling. All we
had to do was locate the prison's dining hall and go in there for
breakfast, but even that simple task surpassed our capacities. The
signs were all in Italian, none of the guards spoke English and all
the other inmates seemed intent on beating us down with a
suspicious, distinctly unwelcoming glare — and who could blame
them? We were beyond pathetic.

"Do you think it's in this room?"

"Might be."

"Assuming it is, how will it work when we get in there? Will it
be self-service or should we sit and wait to be served? How do you
say, *self-service* in Italian?"

"Selfo-servicio?"

"Isn't that Spanish?"

"Should we just walk in or should we stand outside and wait to
be called?" I asked Drew in a hungry panic.

"I dunno, I'm scared," was his calming advice.

"You go in first," I bravely volunteered.

"No, after you," came the gallant reply along with a push
toward the door.

Just as it was all about to go to pot, a few of our fellow inmates
ambled by, pausing outside the mystery room to observe the
Scotsmen's bumbling antics. Rather than be laughed out of town,
we bowled bravely into the lion's den, tumbling toward a table like

66.6% of The Three Stooges. Prison breakfast quickly relinquished all of its alien mystery and we realised that on offer along with the intimidating atmosphere were one roll, one small pot of jam, one even smaller portion of butter and a plastic mug of tea or coffee. Slap-bang onto your plastic tray — all that commotion and confusion for a jeely piece and a manky brew.

It was an in ignominious start to the day on which we were supposed to tackle our first mountain, the mighty Monte Zoncolan. A few words from that last sentence, namely, *mighty*, *Monte* and *Zoncolan*, clashed hideously with the way Drew was feeling. The previous day's travelling and the lack of sleep hadn't helped to clear his chest infection, if anything he appeared to have suffered a relapse — grunt, snort and swallow. He was keenly playing the brave solider part to my concerned mummy but the virus was obviously still kicking around in his system, and kicking him around in the process. Poor wee lamb barely had the energy to contemplate the drive to the Monte, let alone actually drive there and then actually cycle up it. Sutrio, the village at the start of the climb, was three hours away, even at Italian speeds, a bad enough prospect for Sickboy without the knowledge that the climb was said to have a section as steep as 23% (almost a one-in-four gradient), and all that (presuming he survived) to be followed by a three-hour drive back to Trento.

Post-slops, we sat out back of the hostel, squinting into the morning sun, poring over the map, as if hoping to discern some short cut from Trento to the top of the Monte. All the while Drew emitted noises that clarified he wasn't up to either the drive or the ride, and suggested that he might be about to drown in a pool of his own phlegm. I sighed an exaggerated sigh of disappointment, ensured that my protestations were noted and put on the record, then duly capitulated. Zoncolan was our first (and I hoped *only*) missed appointment; one challenge in and already we had failed.

***

Located in the remote north east of Italy, close to the Austrian border, Monte Zoncolan enjoys a fearsome reputation. Thanks to gradients like that positively inhumane 23%, the twisting and turning single-track road accrues over 1200 metres of elevation in just 13.5 kilometres travelled. (That would have been some way to open our account, by tackling the kind of climb you might normally hold in reserve for a grand, show-ending finale.) The Giro d'Italia first had a stage finish there in 2003, won by Trentino local-boy, Gilberto Simoni. Whilst most of the attention that day had been on Gibo and his race-winning move, our eyes had been a little further down the road, hopefully observing the comeback (slight return) of Marco Pantani — Drew's cycling inspiration and über-favourite rider, and my third-favourite (yes, I realise how childish that sounds) after Laurent Fignon and Robert Millar. Pantani did his best not to disappoint, put in a series of his once customary attacks, teased us with glimpses of the climbing technique that had carried him to cycling's pinnacle (in past seasons he'd won the general classification and multiple mountain stages in both the Giro d'Italia and the Tour de France). It (all too briefly) looked good (he finished the stage in fifth place, a respectable 43 seconds down on Simoni), but ultimately failed to deliver on the promise. Instead of being the first pedal strokes up the road to a sporting comeback, his efforts were little more than a last hurrah. Pantani finished (what was to be his last race) in 14th spot overall and died of acute cocaine poisoning on Valentine's Day the following year.

Monte Zoncolan would have allowed us to ride where our hero had most recently and so finally shone. Its insanely steep slopes would also have been the first chance to decide whether our choice of gearing had been a little ambitious or startlingly naïve. The standard, shop-bought, top-end road bike usually comes fitted with similar gear ratios to those ridden by the pros: at the front a 53-tooth big cog and a 39-tooth small cog, and at the back a spread of sprockets between 11 and 25 teeth. However, many recreational riders now choose to ride on "compact" gearing, which offers much smaller cog sizes at the front (usually 50/34 teeth), giving much lower gears with which to comfortably pedal up steeper slopes. (Put simply, the smaller the front cog and bigger the back cog, the easier, or lower, the gear.) Some leisure and touring riders heading to the high mountains will even opt for a triple chainset, which can provide front cog sizes down to 28 teeth, making for a *very* low first gear.

For months before the trip Drew and I had deliberated over which spread of gears to run — standard racing doubles, compacts or triples? In the end, our naïve spirit of experiencing the climbs "as the pros" won out and we plumped for sticking to the tougher, higher spread of gears. Our only concessions had been to fit a slightly smaller 38-tooth chainring at the front and a slightly larger

27-tooth cog at the back. We had made that decision despite knowing full well that Zoncolan stage winner Simoni had used a 38 x 28 gear for his successful ascent, and even then he had struggled to keep the pedals turning. As to whether or not Drew and I would be able to pedal all the way to the top of our first climb, we would have to wait another day, and for another mountain, to find out.

***

No Zoncolan was certain, but what to do instead? Drew still fancied a ride of some sort but only "a tootle around", something easy, a warm-up for the coming day — which would *not* be cancelled. We returned to the map and soon settled on a spin around the shores of nearby Lake Garda. It sounded as twee as we had felt the previous evening when promenading around the city square, but I'd read that the area around the lake was the stomping ground of both Francesco Moser (former Giro and multiple single-day classics winner) and the aforementioned Gilberto Simoni, so at least we'd be twee in good company.

Before departing on our restorative jaunt we had the joy of unwrapping the bikes from their travel cocoons. Doing so in the cramped confines of our prison cell was no laughing matter. It was a right royal pain in the arse, a sweating buckets, grease all over the bedsheets and floor, cursing and swearing kind of affair.

For the flights our steeds had been packed into special bags — basically giant holdalls that fit a bike with the wheels, seat and pedals removed, and the handlebars turned round. Most bike bags are slightly padded but insufficiently to withstand the delicate attentions of your average airport baggage handler. So, to ensure that we wouldn't spend our trip crying over cracked frames and bent spokes we had encased the bikes in a layer or three of bubble wrap before stowing them in the bags. Drew had gone a touch overboard on the wrap and his layer or three had turned into six. By the time we'd unpacked, the cell was full of bubble wrap, like a cartoon when the washing machine explodes and the house fills with suds. Somewhere in amongst it all were two bikes and two skinny Scotsmen, one of whom was very sweaty, the other coughing, cursing and wondering what they were doing back home without him.

Next task was to negotiate our way out of the city, trying to follow the deviazione in reverse order and worrying that we might not be able to find our way back. We searched the skyline for a suitable landmark and settled on the monument to Cesare Battisti (an Italian patriot who was executed by the Austrians in 1916), sitting high on the hill above the hostel. Off we went, purposely avoiding the autostrada but onto equally crazy (i.e. Italian) roads.

***

We arrived at Riva del Garda (situated at the northerly end of the lake) in something resembling one piece, and headed down the western shore, from where we hoped to cut up into the hills for a short loop. So we ambled out of town — very slowly, Drew still coughing, both of us grinning manically — weaving our way through the hordes of tourists, glad to have escaped the prison, proud that, despite missing the Monte, we were still actually cycling in Italy (a first for either of us).

It took a tunnel through the lakeside rock to interrupt our excitement. I panicked, recalled having read in *Rough Ride* (the memoir of ex-pro cyclist Paul Kimmage) of hideous experiences had whilst riding through unlit tunnels during the Tour de France. Kimmage described scenes of chaos and near-carnage as riders collided with one another in the pitch black. Thankfully, ours was a far happier encounter, this tunnel equipped with giant strip lights and offering nothing more discomfiting than a dose of shade from the baking sun. I was still struggling to cope with the heat, temperatures easily 20 degrees higher than the Scottish "summer" we had departed, and so the tunnel's cool air came as a blessing.

We ambled through and on, along a road that hugged the rock-face to our right, nothing on the left but a sheer drop, open air and the sparkling azure water.

"This is lovely," I thought. "One day I will be able to tell the grandchildren — or someone else's grandchildren — that I have ridden along the shores of Lake Garda and that it was very lovely and very beautiful indeed."

Then, a few kilometres later, we hit another tunnel, once again cool and shaded, but this time minus the giant strip-lights. The instinct to panic (are you spotting a theme here?) quickly subsided as we noticed open archways on the side overlooking the water, the patches of light they cast sufficient to guide our way. Tunnels? Easy!

We rounded the next bend and suddenly there weren't any archways, suddenly no light whatsoever, suddenly it was entirely pitch black. Panic? Moi? Kimmage might have panicked but I didn't. Unlit tunnels were no problem when you had the full-beams of a passing car to light the way.

Then the car sped off round the corner, taking its headlights with it, leaving us completely and utterly in the dark.

Kimmage? Are you there? If you are then I'm so, so sorry for having doubted you.

Stupidity, bravery, uncertainty at what was the best thing to do caused us to keep pedalling. When I finally decided it was advisable to lift my shades, a look around revealed not a blind bloody thing. I heard Drew, who had been a few bike lengths ahead, shout in alarm. Then I heard my own shout, before Drew's eerie echo, my own reverberation running scared and screaming behind. Just as Drew skidded to a halt, I too hit the brakes, narrowly avoiding a collision with his back wheel. The last thing one would want to do in such a situation is panic.

Panic ensued.

I could hear Drew, he could hear me but the solid black was so disconcerting and disorientating that it sent us stumbling around in bewildered circles. Within seconds we'd lost track of where the road was, which way forward and which back. I reached out and found the tunnel wall to my right, damp and gritty, my sense of touch heightened by the lack of sight. A brief calm was provided by the solidity of that structure — a landmark in the otherwise empty void — but it was a moment short-lived. What sounded like an express train was bearing down upon us.

"Quick, get against the wall," Drew shouted from somewhere nearby.

We pressed ourselves as close to the stone as possible, as headlights rounded the corner, and the noise — like a million jet engines — bounced off the brickwork, screaming out our names, death at the wheel and coming to claim.

"It can't see us!" I yelped, holding my bike up like a shield, as if a few kilograms of carbon fibre were going to save me from the speeding tons of steel.

Could the cycling trip of a lifetime really be about to end in such ignominy? Had we forsaken a slow death upon Monte Zoncolan only to be swatted like mosquitoes against a tunnel wall? Thankfully, the answer to both questions was a shaky no. The speeding express-train from hell turned out to be a small pick-up (its threat had been exaggerated by a dodgy exhaust and the tunnel's amplification) and it somehow — just — missed us, shaving off my grimace with its wing mirror.

"Quick!" We panicked some more, realising we still had something left to live for.

An extremely hurried debate ensued, the rough gist of the agreed outcome being that we had to turn back. (*We can't go forward seeking light at the other end, because any ride we do from there will be ruined by the ever-present knowledge that the only road back comes through this bastard Tunnel of Doom. I agree, let's go back now. Yes, but which way is back? I think it's this way, but if it's not then we'll start new lives at the other end of the tunnel.*) We fumbled our way across the road and scrambled onto what felt like a narrow ledge about a foot up from road. From there we side-stepped along, pressed to the wall's damp, greasy surface, dragging our once proud racing bikes behind us like spoilt kids grown tired of their toys.

Just then a lorry came round the corner. I knew it was a lorry because by the time it had fully passed our position I had unintentionally licked each and every one of its eighteen wheels. Dribbling, shaking wrecks, we carried on, and as the tunnel curved back round we could just about discern a faint glimmer of hope.

"Quick, toward the light!"

We made it to the rough archway we had passed pre-panic, its illumination leading perpendicular from the road, through another short tunnel and on to a huge chunk of blue sky.

"We're saved!" Came the overly optimistic cry.

We climbed over a fence, ran toward the light and then skidded to a halt — just in time, swaying gently back and forth like the bus at the end of The Italian Job. We had reached a sheer drop, a route of "escape" that involved either a jump or a climb down into the water 100 feet below — a prospect so awful to these two non-swimmers that it made the tunnel appealing. We turned back toward the road, tiptoeing by the giant spider-webs that littered either wall of the faux escape route.

"Hang on a second, did you just say, *giant spider-webs?*"

"Yeah, I did. Look, over there, and there, and there too."

"Oh shit! Are they funnel webs?"

"The webs are certainly funnel-shaped, but they're *huge*. I thought funnel webs were much smaller than that."

"So they're *huge* funnel-webs?"

"Which means inside them there'll be ... ."

"Huge funnel-web spiders!"

"Look! There's another one over there!"

Drew and I had been friends for about six years. We'd met when working for Royal Mail. I was a temp amongst a thousand postie lifers, the majority of whom viewed me as an unworthy outsider. Drew was one of those lifers but one who dreamt of escape, whose tunnel-digging/file-inside-a-cake plans had yet to be realised or relinquished. One morning break I was sitting reading a cycling magazine, my pale-blue Royal Mail shirt unbuttoned to reveal a Stone Roses t-shirt — the magazine and the t-shirt being twin badges of my difference to the lifers, and to society in general (neither the band or the sport were particularly popular at the time). Drew strolled over, commented on my good taste in music and struck up a conversation about a mountain bike he'd just bought. That was the first at-work, non-work-related conversation I'd had in six months on the job. Within days we were cycling together, smoking dope together, talking, laughing and generally, genuinely bonding. It was an unexpected but truly welcome friendship, one that seemed likely to last, one neither of us had imagined would end with us being crushed by a lorry or killed by a swarm of super spiders inside an Italian tunnel.

We'd escaped from *The Italian Job* and stumbled into *The Goonies*, one of Drew's favourite movies, and a very funny one too, but far less funny when you are actually living it, for real. I wanted some popcorn and a comfy seat. I didn't want a long, dark tunnel filled with giant spider-webs, with certain death at one end and almost certain death at the other.

"Where's the treasure map?"

"What treasure map?"

"Isn't that why we're here?"

A couple of cars roared by, their blazing headlights teasing us with glimpses of the escape route, images we set to memory in order to imagine the way out. Over the fence, onto the road, and we made a last-ditch bid for freedom. We'd hobbled and shuffled about twenty yards back along the main tunnel when a car came up behind us, its lights seeming to snake round the corner and lick our backs like a giant yellow tongue. We jumped onto the bikes, vaguely aware of the road ahead.

A few frantic pedal strokes later and the car was upon us.

Drew slammed it into the bike ring, bellowed, "go for it," over his shoulder, like I wasn't already doing exactly that.

We were both out of the saddle and sprinting, hoping to keep in front of the car until the end of the tunnel, hoping the driver had seen us and wouldn't roll right over the top of our flailing, skinny bodies.

The noise was deafening, amplified by the tunnel walls and shot after shot of adrenaline. I could almost feel the heat of the engine against my calves when Drew shouted again, this time a yell of excited, joyous relief. The light was in sight, and at that frantic speed it was coming fast. (The car was surely sitting in our slipstream, coasting along with the engine off.) We emerged, newborn into the sunshine: *oh feel the sunshine, kiss the sunshine!* My thoughts came like the lyrics to a Dodgy song. Exhilarated, we were the Goonies only just escaped from the Fratellis' clutches, bright smiles dripping from faces blackened by exhaust residue and tunnel grime.

***

We freewheeled back down into Riva del Garda and ensconced ourselves outside a café, celebrating a return to light, life and freedom with omelettes and copious liquid refreshment. A gaggle of German mountainbikers sat around the neighbouring table, smug at having ridden up and over, and not through, the mountain, with being far less grimy than their neighbouring, on-road brethren.

The clear, blue waters of Garda, Italy's largest and most spectacular lake, are backed by the wooded slopes of towering, craggy mountains, a perfect picture-postcard scene that has long drawn hordes of tourists. I tried to come up with a Scottish equivalent but the best I could do was Drumnadrochit at the head of Loch Ness — an equal in terms of scenery, a lesser in terms of weather, and a poor cousin when it comes to visitor amenities. Drum', as the locals call it, is wholly reliant on the mythological monster said by many, but surely believed by none, to inhabit the amazing Loch. Like Riva, Drum' could trade upon the truth that lies all around, on swathes of the most beautiful scenery and landscape to be found anywhere on earth. Surely better to have foreign cyclists lingering to spend their Euros in classy cafés, in the local hotels and restaurants, than a quick coach stop to photograph the water, grab some plastic Nessie-themed tat and bugger right off again?

As our second round of Cokes arrived, the heavens opened, making way for the thunderstorm that had brewed whilst we'd been trapped inside the mountain. Glad of the rain's cleansing shower, we sat back and took in the view, gazing out across the cobbled plaza, passed the sailing boats and onto the sparkling, raindrop-speckled water. We didn't care about the missed Monte; at that moment we were just glad to be alive.

***

Friday night in Trento: on holiday, bored and trying not to dwell on the disappointment of the missed climb or the daunting prospect of the coming-day's four. We returned to the restaurant from the night before and, unwilling to live on pizza alone, opted for spaghetti and risotto. The waitress took the news of our anti-pizza decision badly and tried to change our minds by intimating that it would take thirty minutes for those other dishes to cook but only ten for pizza.

"Don't care how long it takes," we told her, "we're on holiday in Italy and we want to try some authentic pasta and risotto."

She decided we must have misunderstood, concluding wrongly on twin counts that we were both English *and* stupid, before entering into a primitive form of communication using gestures and numbers scribbled onto the paper tablecloth.

We understood; we weren't for shifting.

"Ah, but you see," she seethed through gritted teeth, "those dishes will take thirty minutes, *you understand?* Only *ten* for *pizza*, get it?"

"Yeah, we get it, but we'll wait."

I decided to try a bit of Italian, as far as my limited skills and a quick glance at the phrasebook allowed, followed it with a big smile, an attempt to pacify our worried waitress. My efforts were rewarded with a dramatic wince, as if she was suddenly in great pain, my Italian so bad that it hurt her like acute appendicitis.

You insult my language you insult me, my brother, my sister, my parents, my old frail grandmother, my entire family! Most importantly, you insult Uncle Antonio, the chef who only likes making pizza and is already in the kitchen coughing up phlegm to thicken your spaghetti sauce. You ignorant English bastardi!

She indicated all that non-verbally, and then minced off to the kitchen to break the bad news.

A quick scan of the surrounding tables revealed not a single pasta or risotto dish, each and every fellow diner "happily" tucking into pizza, all succumbed to the waitress' charm offensive (or were they offensive charms?). Twenty nervous minutes later (ten less than the "horrific" thirty she had predicted), our pasta and risotto arrived. The waitress appeared to have partially forgiven my lingual indiscretion and the food (rather tasty and no obvious signs of phlegm) was wolfed down in less time than it had taken to order.

We finished up and headed through the piazza in search of a gelato stall, keeping a safe distance apart, only to end up looking like an embarrassed, not quite out-the-closet honeymooning couple, or a honeymooning couple who'd recently had a lovers' tiff.

Apart from bolstering one's (clearly diffident) masculinity, what does a tourist do at night in a place like Trento? We spotted a couple of bars but, with a full day of cycling to come, weren't really up for drinking (Drew certainly wasn't, his symptoms improved from the morning but still evident — grunt, snort and swallow). If we'd been on a lads' holiday, whatever that might be, things would have been hideously different. For starters, we wouldn't have been in Trento. We'd have been somewhere far less salubrious, puking into the gutter, winking manically at unlucky local lassies. Somehow I didn't feel that Trento was ready for two skinny Scotsmen puking into its gutters, so we returned to the cell for a photographic review of the day and our trip's first laptop slide-show. (My new occasional nickname would henceforth be Slide-show Bob.)

Shortly before lights out and we lay down to sweat, I mean, sleep, Drew asked to borrow a pen and some paper then disappeared into his bunk. He emerged ten minutes later with "Minxy", his hand-drawn, "Trenthouse Magazine Playmate Pet of the Week". He taped her gory glory to the wall and invited me down to ogle the 34-37-44TT figure. A horrifically disfigured line-drawn creature, Minxy had two horrendous, misshapen breasts, a wild, bramble-bush crotch, and potatoes in place of hands. According to the small biog included, she was 22 years old, from Hicksville, Utah, and her likes were fast tractors and men with beards.

Finally, we shut our eyes, to dream of less disfigured girls back home, cool Scottish nights and the mountains we'd yet to encounter.

DAY 3:
SMELL THE FEAR

Passo di Sella
Start point: Canazei | Height: 2244m | Height climbed: 769m
Length of climb: 11.4km | Average gradient: 7% | Maximum
gradient: 8.9%

Passo di Gardena
Start point: Plan de Gralba | Height: 2121m | Height climbed:
250m | Length of climb: 5.9km | Average gradient: 4.2%
Maximum gradient: 7%

Passo di Campolongo
Start point: Corvara | Height: 1875m | Height climbed: 307m
Length of climb: 6.1km | Average gradient: 5% | Maximum
gradient: 6.7%

Passo Pordoi
Start point: Arabba | Height: 2239m | Height climbed: 637m
Length of climb: 9.4km | Average gradient: 6.8% | Maximum
gradient: 9.7%

We awoke to the theme tune from *Chariots of Fire* blaring from
the alarm on Drew's mobile phone. In place of inspiration I had
nausea — a heavy, acidic stomach and churning guts. I put it down
to nervous anticipation of the climbs ahead, all the while trying not
to consider how Uncle Antonio might have expressed his dislike at
being forced to cook pasta instead of pizza. A peek through the
curtains revealed a grey and murky day cowering beneath a leaden,
foreboding sky, a day I wasn't yet ready to meet. Where was my get
up and where was my go? Where was the dazzling Italian sun, the
cloudless azure sky? Was Mama Natura trying to tell us something,
her warning sent in meteorological code?

As we drove north toward Bolzano, the heavy skies burst,

rattled open by the roar of thunder and cracked wide by lightning. Rain turned road into river — easily three inches of water up around the car tyres — and the pitch-black heavens made Trento's grey soup appealing in hindsight. Drew was still coughing and spluttering but, unlike the weather, at least his cold appeared to be clearing, lungs doing their best to remove the remnants of that infection. He turned his head away from the windscreen to glance at the lightning, gobbed out the window like a seasoned sea dog spitting into the storm. He spat, and splat! Old sea dog had forgotten to open the window. The thick green blob slipped due south, streaking a snail trail that would still be visible when we returned the hire car.

Not only were the clouds foreboding (for at some point we would have to exit vehicle and pedal up into them), they also obscured the mountains to which we headed; the Dolomites we expected to loom upon the horizon were lost amongst that gloom. I began to chatter nervously, going over the details of an epic cycle, during which we would discover the Sella Ronda, a circular route with four great passes: Sella; Pordoi; Campolongo; Gardena. We were going to stumble upon them through breaks in the cloud, dodging lightning bolts, eardrums resounding to the rumble of thunder. It would be an adventure, definitely exciting but hopefully not petrifying like a ride through Garda's unlit tunnels.

Any discovery would, of course, be purely personal. Tackled by cyclo-tourists on a daily basis (weather permitting), the Sella Ronda is a 50km circuit around the Gruppo di Sella, a rocky massif whose sheer walls rise to over 3000 metres above sea level. Clearly, it can be ridden in either a clockwise or an anti-clockwise direction, and opinions vary on which is the best or indeed the hardest way round. For no particular reason we had settled on riding clockwise, to begin and end at Canazei, and kicking off with the Passo di Sella. The descent from there would lead us onto the Passo di Gardena, over and down onto the Passo di Campolongo before a final slog up the Pordoi. All in all not bad for a day's biking, missing a climb one day but making up for it in spades the next.

Half an hour up the road, the windscreen wipers couldn't compete with the deluge, and the crazy Italian drivers seemed to think higher speeds and shorter stopping distances were the best way to cope with torrential rain. It had gone from looking like we were driving up a river to feeling like we might be fully submerged (hopefully in some kind of James Bond super car), visibility about as good as it had been in Garda's unlit tunnel. How to waste a rainy day in Italy? Take a drive into aquatic oblivion.

Afraid of another day senza montagne, I forcibly adopted a tenuous Mr Optimism persona: "sure I'm sure those are blue skies ahead. Oh yeah, of course it's clearing."

And it was clearing, but only in my imagination. We had come to ride mountains, couldn't exactly return to Trento and spend a day in the cell under siege of the weather. What would we do back at the prison? Challenge the Italian mob to a table-football tournament and wait until the Pope Channel kicked-off? Even Playmate mutant Minxy was insufficient to keep us in the cell for a whole day.

The further north we drove the more Germanic our surroundings became. Road signs were in both Italian and German, many of the towns and villages to which they welcomed us having distinctly Germanic names. The Trentino-Alto Adige region (or Trentino-Südtirol as it's known in Deutsch) consists of two distinct areas: the Italian-speaking Trento, and the largely German-speaking Alto Adige (South Tyrol). The latter was part of Austria, hence the German, until its annexation by Italy in 1919. The region covers a large part of the Dolomites and the Southern Alps, its population of some 900,000 people split between two main ethnic groups: Italian-speakers based around Trento; and Bolzano's German speakers. The two cities alternate biennially as the site of the regional parliament and the autonomy of both provinces elevates them de facto to the status of autonomous regions — all living happily together along with the rest of the EU. It hasn't always been sweetness and light. The strategic mountainous frontier was the scene of bitter and bloody fighting throughout the First World War, suffered a spell under Nazi rule during the Second, and it took the ratification of an Italo-Austrian treaty in 1971 to settle matters, hopefully once and for all.

Austria: what does that name conjure up in one's mind? Apart from Eurotrash oddities in lederhosen — mountains, of course, and those mountains reached high above the clouds, growing until they filled the windscreen like a drive-in Imax movie on steroids. I wanted to open the window and shout, "stick!" Quite how much bigger they would get I was afraid to hazard a guess.

***

"Just take a right here," I instructed as we passed through Bolzano, still no sign of our actual, intended turn off, "according to the map" — oh, how that phrase would come to haunt me, eliciting flashbacks and cold sweats long after the war, er, I mean, trip, was over — "this road runs parallel to the one we should be on and connects with it in about ... I reckon it's about three to four thumb-lengths, which can't be more than twenty miles."

Thirty miles later, and where the hell were we? We had turned off in the vague proximity of Cornedo all'Isarco, almost as the map suggested, but instead of being on the main road that followed the base of the Valle D'Ega, found ourselves instead upon a scenic little single-track. This almost-road climbed up and onto the top edge of the valley, might have been headed in the right direction but was doing so rather drastically, almost vertically. The sinuous stretch of tarmac snaked through the woods like a secret code hidden within the pages of a novel, the kind of route I would have cycled as a youngster certain that an adventure of some sort lay at the other end (not realising until later that the adventure was all in the journey).

We were sorely tempted to forget about the Sella Ronda, park up, get out and ride, down to the bottom and back to the top. It made us think, if this is how good Italy's insignificant roads are, then how amazing will the famous passes be? Unfortunately, we had a schedule to follow and the detour was seriously eating into the day's allotted hours, not to mention being what Drew delicately described as a "ball-ache" to drive. The road was so narrow, the drop off the edge so severe, we dreaded meeting a car coming the other way. The standoff would only have been resolved by one car ramming the other over the cliff or through a lengthy period of U.N. mediation.

Once again we had followed the printed advice contained within the folder, but perhaps not followed it exactly, the truth of its message lost in translation. Somewhere deep within the instruction to turn right, where we had in fact done just that, there must have lurked a hidden, deeper meaning. *Thou must turn right — but not hence! Only the meekest of traveller shall turn right when instructed. The wise traveller will carry on, perform a U-turn and then take the second left at this juncture.*

***

We soon descended into the valley and joined the main highway at a small mountain town by the name of Pozza di Fassa. Either side of the road was lined with banners plastered with pictures of Mickey Mouse and the slogan, *"Disney Mountain Fun!"* I wondered which of the great mountains that lay ahead was Disney Mountain, why it didn't feature on our map and what exactly Disney had to do with Mother Nature's majesty anyway? It transpired I had been wondering aloud and Drew assured me that he did not hold the answer to any of my questions.

It was only a few kilometres from there that we caught our first close-up of the Dolomites (with the 3004-metre Catinaccio d'Antermóia), that the moment we realised for sure, one hundred percent, that Italy's mountains required no animated input. We parked up at the first available opportunity — distracted driver struggling not to crash the car off the side of the road — and got out to wander, jaw-dropped toward the mountain.

Neither of us had ever seen a Dolomite, let alone one so big, and up so close. I imagined myself as a country boy (no real flight of fancy given that I grew up in rural Scotland) on his maiden stroll down the sidewalks of New York, neck craned in awe at buildings that scraped the sky. This mountain was something else, beyond the imagination or ability of man. No wonder Corbusier had described the Dolomites as the most amazing architecture in the world.

They broke from the earth's crust like giant teeth puncturing the pasture's green gums; pale-blue and ash-grey rock like ragged coral; an idyllic landscape transformed into one both mesmerising and menacing. I had seen mountains before, (the Alps, the Cairngorms), but the Dolomites were another species altogether, requiring a distinct classification.

The Dolomites take their name from the Marquis Déodat Gratet de Dolomieu. In 1788, whilst on a study trip along the road from Trento to Bolzano, the Marquis collected some rock samples for chemical analysis. The results revealed the mountains' unique chemical composition — a calcium and magnesium carbonate — that gives the Dolomites that unusual, very pale appearance. It was actually the Marquis' friend, a chemist called Nicolas Théodore de Saussure, who analysed those samples, but De Saussure was a selfless sort and the rock became known as Dolomia. Had it not been so, Drew and I might well have been staring up in awe at the Saussurites.

The ancient inhabitants of the area, the Ladins, knew the mountains by another name: *lis montes pàljes*, or the pale mountains. A Ladin legend states that dwarves who lived in the region created the Dolomites' unique colour by spinning moonbeams around the peaks into a bright, diaphanous web. Apparently, they did this to alleviate the homesickness suffered by the daughter of the King of the Moon, who was also the spouse of the King of the Mountains. Those crazy Ladins were probably smoking too much Edelweiss to bother considering the rock's chemical composition but there really was a sense that we were casting our eyes over an alien landscape, no surprise that writers and artists have long taken inspiration from the Dolomites.

The mountains' geological history goes back even further than dusty writers and loopy Ladins — around 300 million years hence to the Palaezoic era (and what an era that was!). The Dolomites are actually cliffs left over from a prehistoric sea that once filled the region, cliffs that were formed from rocks that are themselves the creation of the accrual of excreta from marine organisms that once lived in that sea. Millennia of effects from the forces of gravity, atmospheric agents, ice and running water have all made their mark, sculpting the amazing geological gems that stood before us and will stand before many more long after we are gone. 300 million years is a long time to wait for a mountain range but, in this case, it was worth every second.

***

We drove into Canazei feeling slightly stunned and a tad disappointed. Not only had we hoped for a civic reception but also civic-reception weather. The skies were still dark and heavy, rain still crashing down, a whistling, almost icy wind licking up around us. The thought of retrieving the bikes from the boot and cycling off into the murk was far from appealing — so instead we decided to carbo-load and headed in search of lunch.

We settled on the Hotel Laurin, opting to sit outside under the awning in an attempt to acclimatise, wolfing down suitably excessive plates of spaghetti Bolognese and ravioli con funghi porcini. To the backdrop of our chattering teeth, and the Ibiza anthems that blared from the P.A., the waiter made unnecessarily cruel jokes about the unseasonable cold and our uncontrollable shivering. If it is this cold down here, we wondered, just how bad will it be up on the high passes? (I appeared to have left Mr

Optimism standing by the roadside staring at the mountain.)

By the time we returned to the car, pessimism had fully permeated. Our heads really weren't in it, somehow unable to connect our presence in Canazei, the proximity of the bikes *and* the mountains. We'd come all the way from Scotland for ... what was it again? If either of us had suggested forgetting about it and driving back to the prison's warmth there would have been no counter argument waiting in the wings.

Slumped in the car, staring out at raindrops bouncing off glass, I wondered if weather watching is a common tendency amongst all British cyclists, just as the weather is said to be Britons' favourite topic of conversation. How many hours of potential cycling had Drew and I wasted between us, time spent gazing out the window, wishing the rain away, imagining the sun's rays breaking through a grey day that only optimism, and not meteorology, suggested was brightening? How much improved as cyclists would we be if those hours had instead been spent in the saddle? Might we then have developed immunity to the adverse conditions that so often dog our days? What's wrong with us? I wanted to know. Our heads certainly weren't in it, our bodies somewhere else altogether.

The rain was coming down heavier than ever but, thankfully, something inside us snapped — that was it, time to go, then or never. The weather was set for at least the remainder of the day; any further delay and we could kiss the Sella Ronda goodbye, possibly forever. We were still (relatively) young (relative to Noah) but it was conceivable that neither of us would ever visit the Dolomites again. Our first, and possibly only, chance had to be grasped.

✳✳✳

Shelter abandoned in resigned acceptance, we pedalled out through Canazei and into the windblown sheets of rain. After about a kilometre we came to a sign-posted junction where the road forked right to Passo Pordoi (our scheduled last climb of the day) and left to (our scheduled first) the Passo di Sella.

A hundred yards into the Sella climb and Drew was already in some discomfort. His heart rate had rocketed, his lungs felt fit to burst and the sweat poured off him despite the chill conditions (at least the rain had stopped, for now). Those symptoms were at least partly the effects of his virus and not all down to the severity of the climb; the road really wasn't all that steep — the gradient around

8% — and the plentiful switchbacks and wide corners provided a degree of relief through variety and a slight ease of incline.

Whilst my companion laboured, I felt surprisingly good. I didn't feel *amazing*, wasn't flying the way Pantani had raced up this very road, but was faring so much better than expected. A look at Drew's contorted grimace and it would have been insensitive to admit out loud but I was thoroughly enjoying my first Dolomite. The recurring knee injury (a bursitis) that had sent me into fits of pre-trip panic appeared to be a thing of the past. I was sitting easy, if not pretty, twiddling fourth gear, not labouring down in first as my pessimism had predicted. A mix of emotions ran through me: excitement (oh, to be riding up a Dolomite!), and also relief (oh, thank god, I've finally made it onto a mountain after all the months of dreaming, worrying and shambolic planning!).

I settled into my stride and, a bit further up the road, turned round to check on Drew's progress. It was then I heard, drifting up through the low cloud, the words, "snapped", "please" and "no". I eased up, dropped back down to Drew and shoulder-to-shoulder we tapped out what Italian riders might call a *piano* tempo — soft, nice-and-easy does it.

Drew was plainly in pain, cursing the limited amount of training miles he'd put in before we departed Scotland, cursing the virus that had left him weakened and weary. I told him not to worry, that we were only on our first climb and he would ride into fitness over the coming days, but he wasn't amenable. Mind made up, he began to complain about breathlessness, that it felt as if each intake failed to fill lungs already hindered by the after-effects of that infection. He also expressed concern that his symptoms might be an effect of the altitude. I was no doctor but he surely had a point. The highest peak in Britain is Ben Nevis, some 1343 metres above sea level. Yet we had started our ride 125 metres higher than that and were well on our way to topping out at 2240 metres. It was more unlikely that he *wouldn't* have been suffering in some way from the altitude. Either way, I smiled sympathetically and kept on pedalling.

Normally one likes to ride a climb from bottom to top without putting a foot down, that's usually part of the challenge, completing the task in one measured effort. Stopping at any point can be seen (by me, anyway) as a degree of failure. However, I had splashed out on a new camera specifically for the trip and wanted some decent pictures for posterity. The steam rising off our heads as we pulled up next to the armco barrier indicated just how cold it was and just how hard we had been working to reach that point on the mountain — evidently we had earned a rest.

Around us, overflowing the viewfinder, was the kind of scenery you could not, and should not, take for granted. Where the rain had dampened, the rock surface glistened and shimmered silver and blue like oil on water. These weren't mountains; they were assembled armies of giant, bejewelled stalagmites; they were the mountains of Italy in the same way that Versace are the clothes of Italy — utterly, unashamedly showy. Curtains of rippling rock draped downward from high within the cloud (some 3000 metres up) as if excluding us from the "real" world, separating two bit-part actors from the audience. We were in an immense arena, topped by a ceiling of grey, couldn't possibly have asked for a more extreme, visually mesmerising distraction from the ardour of the task.

Snaps duly snapped, dropped jaws retrieved from the roadside, and we pressed on. After several minutes of shivering we had warmed up again. My pedalling came easy and, all things considered, I was actually looking forward to the other three climbs — and that at the point when I had expected to be begging for mercy. Drew was less impressed, back to the self-deprecating comments, bemoaning that lack of training. I persisted with the reassurance, casually tossing nuggets of "wisdom" about his riding into form, all of which fell on deaf ears. The thought of three more minutes of cycling, let alone three more climbs, or three more weeks of climbing, came to him like a blow to the back of the head. From there I decided to keep my motivating mouth shut.

***

With eleven kilometres of Dolomiti tarmac passed beneath our tyres we reached the top of the Passo di Sella, a snaking section of steep hairpins I recognised from the photograph set as the desktop on my iMac at work. Unlike that Giro race-day pic there were no crowds of tifosi gathered on the grass verge, not a soul to cheer our arrival at the battered brown sign that marked the climb's official summit. Despite the solitude, the feeling inside was surely as good as any derived from the adoration of a crowd. Inwardly, I was cheering for myself, cheering for us both. It was relatively small but sometimes the first step of a journey proves to be the biggest — we were officially on our way, wherever that way might take us.

The mountaintop was shrouded in cloud, the rain back on,

falling heavier and colder, conditions even worse than those we'd abandoned with the car back down at Canazei. The pass was flanked on one side by a souvenir shop and on the other by a café so, despite the weather, in some ways our maiden summit was more hospitable than expected. (You don't have to climb to the top to guess that there's no souvenir shop or café on Ben Nevis.) The warm glow of success already replaced by a cutting chill, we slumped on a sheltered bench at the side of the shop and donned our thin rain jackets. That position normally functioned as a viewpoint, or so we presumed, but no view was offered to us beyond mile after mile of thick, grey soup.

A gaggle of Scandinavian walkers strolled over from the direction of the café, to mill around, smoke cigarettes and discuss the merits of wearing twelve individual layers of thermal and waterproof clothing, and having a further twelve stuffed inside their over-sized backpacks. We edged along the bench, away from the smug, smoke-filled air, toward a couple of older, Italian cyclists. Perhaps it was the cold or the lack of oxygen that prevented our communication, but our proximity went unacknowledged, two pairs of cyclists on one mountain but inhabiting entirely different worlds. The signori appeared far better prepared for the elements than we were, their legs covered, bodies snug beneath heavy jackets, hands encased in padded gloves, and still they managed to look thoroughly cold and wet. (Wearing shorts and short sleeves, Drew and I must have appeared utterly desperate in comparison.) Then, as the wind picked up and the raindrops battered off the shelter, came a moment's cross-cultural connection: both parties of cyclists mumbled their disgruntlement and glared jealously at the hideously well-prepared walkers.

Brain activity slowed by the cold and exertion, Drew and I still hadn't decided how to proceed. Before setting off we had agreed to wait and see how bad conditions were at the first summit before making a decision on whether or not to attempt the remaining three. As we reached that initial goal I had been 75% certain we would continue, but as the rain soaked through my thin jacket and on to goose-bumped skin, that certainty dropped below 50%. After another few minutes, my body was convulsing in time to Drew's hacking cough and my certainty lurked down around the 25% mark.

The Norse walkers were on to their second packet of cigarettes by the time I noticed the smell, perhaps some exotic brand they were smoking. The pungent aroma blew in on the breeze, forcing my nostrils to curl up in disgust. It was acrid, reminiscent of dung but not the normal cow smell I'd become accustomed to growing up in the country. I felt that I should recognise the ghastly guff, reprimand the offender or at least inform the polite members of our company that I wasn't the source. Only I couldn't quite place it, my one certain conception being that I hated whatever lurked behind the evil stench.

It was ghastly and getting stronger, but when I asked Drew if he could smell anything he suggested I was standing too close to myself. Sometimes it's good to be choked with the cold. Just as I began to seriously question my own cleanliness, not to mention my sanity, they appeared round the corner — one minute only there in fragrance, the next stood beside us, bold as bucolic brass. The stench incarnate, three scruffy, utterly manky billy goats tottered onto the viewpoint decking. They stared up with faux-innocent eyes, apparently singling out my repulsed expression, hideously unaware (or aware and sadistic) of the damage they were doing. In my time I have fallen in middens (dung heaps), come home from a day's mountain biking plastered in a mess of mud and sheep shit, but never have I smelled an animal viler than the billy goat. The cheese made from their milk is probably the only food on the planet I will not eat, unable to get beyond the smell — *oh, that smell!* Worse than the aroma of vomit, and those three Dolomiti goats reeked of superior-strength stuff.

A minute or so in the animals' proximity and even the fumigating Scandinavians had retreated. The living, breathing lumps of hairy goats cheese were on the rampage and intent on eating anything in sight. Big Billy trotted over and stole the half-eaten banana from my hand, gobbling it down in one, skin and all. In the absence of any other obvious scraps, one of the two smaller specimens began to nibble at my shoes. I stood up and shuffled away, partly to avoid being eaten alive, mostly because I was retching and about to vomit.

Drew, who still couldn't smell anything, and who, luckily for him, likes goats cheese, stayed put on the bench. That'll teach him. The smallest goat took this proximity as permission to nibble, jumped up onto the windowsill, tilted its stupid face ninety degrees as if asking a favour, and launched its gnashers at the sleeve of

Drew's jacket. I joined the two Italian cyclists in a fit of hysterics. Laugh? I almost puked.

The Italians' laughter petered out as Big Billy began to make a feast of their gear-cable outers, whilst deputy made a start on the tyres. The Italians quickly retreated in the direction of the scared Scandinavians, leaving one brave Scotsman to defend himself from death by nibbling, whilst his cowardly compatriot edged as far away as possible without falling off the edge of the mountain. I peered into the cloud-heavy void, wondered what lurked on the other side of the rickety wooden safety rail to which I was pinned, if it could be any worse than my current predicament. The retching had fully replaced my laughter, the smell seeming to have seeped in to pollute my very soul.

Word of this odd, odorous battle of the species spread and a fresh band of cagoule-clad tourists arrived to observe the messy menagerie. Encouraged by the audience, and delirious from the cold, Drew and I began to respectively chat to and plead with the goats. Drew joked about having to turn down their advances, delivered a sad monologue about holiday romances never working out, whilst I attempted to ascertain if even a morsel of mercy lurked within the hearts of my cloven nemeses. Soon everyone was laughing — everyone but me, still too busy pleading and retching.

The jokes and the banana skins soon ran out and there was only one thing for it: escape. We stepped back into what had become torrential rain, took one look over in the rough direction of the Passo di Gardena (the next climb of the four) and the decision about whether or not to progress was made for us — the sky so black we could barely see the other side of the road, let alone the next mountain. We were soaked and shivering; to continue round would have been reckless.

It was the only sensible conclusion. Press on and either of us could catch hypothermia, at the very least an illness (or a relapse for Drew) that would rule out the coming days of cycling. I had visions of us, one mountain later, knocking on a random farmhouse door, begging for shelter and hot minestra. To duck out and go back down the way we'd come was definitely the easy option, but it was nevertheless a painful decision to make. We felt like failures, like we'd chickened out. Oh well, at least these chickens would live to fight another day, and another mountain.

***

We dropped back down the Sella, the coldest descent I'd endured since childhood days spent mountain biking in the snow near Fochabers in the north east of Scotland. Activating the brakes was almost impossible, hands so cold I couldn't feel, let alone move my fingers. It was utterly treacherous, thirty miles per hour felt like sixty and I was only going that fast because I couldn't slow down. My teeth chattered, my arms vibrated and soon my whole upper body was shivering and shaking so much I could barely see where I was going. A downward glance revealed calves turned a nasty shade of blue, the colour spreading up and over my knees. I attempted to turn round to check on Drew but couldn't unlock my frozen torso. A foot down for extra friction, I skidded to a stop as Drew shivered and shuddered up next to me. We agreed with grimaces and grunts that it was both nasty and dangerous, a touch scary but less so than the previous day's tunnel.

About four kilometres from the foot of the climb, an older Italian cyclist, cocooned in full wet-weather gear, shot by like an avalanche late for a meeting.

"If I wasn't so cold I could go downhill that fast too, matey," I thought, before adding, "sod it, you only live once."

I shifted up a gear, pedalled hard and cared a little less about my lack of braking ability. A few corners later and I'd caught up with the tardy avalanche. He appeared to know the road well (either a local or a Zen master), seeming not to brake at all into most of the corners. I held his pace for a couple of hairy kilometres and then relinquished the challenge. It was only the first descent of our adventure and I didn't want to jeopardise the whole trip for the sake of my ego (a handy excuse out of which I would get good mileage for at least the first week).

After a descent that felt considerably longer and more arduous than the ascent, we were back to the car. Somehow resisting the urge to abandon our bikes at the roadside, we dismantled and stowed them in the boot as quickly as numb hands and icy, addled brains allowed. Then it was engine on and heater on, to pray that the air blowing noisily through the dashboard vents would hit before hypothermia.

Ten minutes of hot-air therapy and our teeth were still chattering but we'd recovered sufficient mental faculties in order to wonder what it would have been like had we continued round the Sella Ronda. At that point in time, instead of soaking in hot air from the car's engine, we would have been at the base of the Gardena, shivering and blue with three climbs (and three more chilling descents) to go. Confident that we had made the right decision, I sat back to hallucinate mugs of tea and white-pudding suppers (a Scottish fast-food delicacy).

As we further thawed and our cognitive powers dripped fully back into place, we acknowledged and discussed the sense of disappointment. Not only had we cut short the ride but doing so meant that was now a total of four climbs lost, and still only two days in to the trip. Drew also expressed his annoyance at having felt so out of shape on our escapade's initial ascent. Again I assured that he would ride in to better form and soon shake off the effects of the virus. He clearly wasn't biting, said he felt like cancelling the rest of the trip if it was going to be so bad. Unsurprisingly, he hadn't enjoyed his climb of the Sella and now baulked at the thought of all the mountains that lay ahead.

I really did believe that continued riding would improve his fitness; I had also hoped that bagging the first climb would have given him the bug, a keenness for mountain passes to replace the cold virus. Instead it appeared to have put him off altogether. There's an Italian saying, *l'appetito vien mangiando*, hunger comes with eating, and I could only hope that the more climbs we encountered, the more my friend's appetite would be whetted. I wasn't about to tell Drew, but along with the return of body heat had come a buzz of excitement. Having one giant scalp tucked under the straps of my sodden bib shorts was a hell of a lot better than none. Bring them on, I thought, just get me a Gore Tex body suit and some gloves.

That was definitely a lesson learnt: from then on we would know to expect the worst from mountain weather and never again treat it quite so lightly. We'd started our ride in bad conditions and shouldn't have been surprised by the harshness higher up. Even when rolling out in bright sunshine we'd still need to be better prepared. Mountain conditions can change dramatically from one hour to the next. You could begin a climb on what appeared to be a beautiful summer day and find rain and cold, even snow at the summit. It's said that, in terms of climate, rising 300 metres in altitude is equivalent to moving 350 miles towards the pole at sea level, so you can guarantee it will get colder the higher you climb. Also, the thinner atmospheres associated with high altitudes are less capable of holding heat — a rough guide to bear in mind is that temperatures drop around 1.5 to 3 degrees Celsius for every 300 metres gained. Those differences can be further accentuated by the overall increase in winds as you climb out of sheltered valleys and onto exposed mountainsides.

For our future rides we would stow proper rain jackets in our back pockets, even when the foot of the climb was bathed by baking sun. If it didn't rain up top we'd at least need to don our jackets to keep warm when stopped at the summit and, more importantly, to act as insulation from the cold wind on the way down. (If you've ever seen a Tour de France rider stuffing a newspaper up his jersey before beginning a mountain descent, then that's why. The paper provides a layer of insulation between a sweaty chest and the cooling air.) We would also pack gloves and a cap to keep our digital extremities and that old brain thingy warm on the way down. It's no use having hands so cold they can't work the brakes, or a head so cold it can't think how the brakes were supposed to work in the first place.

***

We drove back to Trento on our newly discovered "shortcut", i.e. the route we would have followed in the morning had I properly deciphered the map's code. The road down through Montagna and back onto the motorway seemed to descend forever, at least for tens of kilometres, illustrating just how high into the mountains we had ventured. From the comfort of the motorway we saw the many little villages, churches and lone houses that clung to the sheer mountainsides. I wondered who lived in such precarious places, what kind of men or women first decided those would be good locations to live and worship.

We remembered that Drew had left the picture of Minxy stuck to the cell wall and worried that an altercation with the prison authorities might be waiting for us down the road. What had the cleaner thought as she skirted round our cell that morning?

"So many bella women in our city and these perverts seek comfort in the grottesco!"

Would all our belongings be thrown onto the street? Could the staff and the swaggering Pope Channel fans look at us any more strangely if they tried?

Thankfully, or perhaps not, the prison's cleaning staff hadn't ventured anywhere near our sweat and dead-mosquito-stained cell.

We left Minxy to do whatever it is Trenthouse Playmates do and headed off into town. Saturday night in Trento and success: we found another restaurant, one we could afford, and a rather good one too, well worth the time spent wandering, almost aimlessly. The exterior of this new gaffe was swathed in scaffolding, so we weren't even sure of its name and forgot to bother asking, or even to look at the front of the menu, and I am therefore unable to make a recommendation. Whatever it was called, the food certainly passed the hungry cyclists' taste test.

We ordered identical dishes (so there could be no arguing about who had made the best choice), starting with *canederli*, traditional Dolomiti dumplings made from stale bread, speck ham and herbs. These came served in a rich tomato sauce and were pretty tasty, despite the whole stale-bread thing. We had both been craving burgers (sure signs of iron deficiency) and so neither of us could resist choosing mains of *burger alla Bismarck* (with no idea what the Bismarck tag indicated, my only concern being that it might be a form of steak tartare, neither of us being so iron-deficient that we craved raw meat). The waiter arrived with two fantastically juicy, medium-rare, home-made steak burgers, packed with fresh herbs, not a gram of gristle, and each of them topped with a fried egg (which, we presumed, was the "Bismarck" flourish).

We enjoyed those delicacies at a small, four-person table, separated from the adjacent dining duo by nothing more than a petite lamp. It felt rather too close for comfort, like our presence was an intrusion on our new neighbours' quiet evening, and vice versa. I tried not to glance over too often but had spotted that we were sat next to another all-male party. They looked too tubby to be cyclists and too dissatisfied with each other's company to be a romantic couple. Must be a business meal, I concurred, and from there my imagination ran wild. The small one with the coiffed grey hair had the air of a Mafia don, like a mob-movie cliché come to life: hoarse voice, jacket hung over his shoulders, more gold jewellery than most men could carry, let alone afford. He handed the other guy a little black book — either the numbers from their racket or a list of people to be taken out in the next hit. There followed considerable gesticulation and growling from The Don until, eventually, the pair mumbled agreement on something very Italian and very hush-hush.

"Some poor bastard's for the chop," I whispered to Drew. "I

sure hope they don't have a sister called Minxy and an insider at the local prison."

It wasn't until they got up to leave that I realised "The Don" was in fact "the wife" (which explained the jewellery and the hair, but none of the other features) and the "Mafiosi" had probably been arguing over the bill, rather than some poor patsy's fate.

The next couple to arrive were a mother and son, or a young man with a fetish and his "girl". They spent the entire time listening in on our conversation, him translating into Italian most of what we said. Mamma appeared mightily amused and I considered like leaning over the petite lampshade to ask for a tip when we eventually got up to leave.

The two sozzled, lightweight cyclists sauntered back across the town square, climbed the prison steps, passed the gang of lads who loitered menacingly in the doorway, and staggered on by the gaggle ensconced in front of the Pope channel — hostels, such great places to meet great people. The only non-papal option for entertainment was an evening in the laundry room so we returned to the cell to clean our bikes and peruse maps of the next day's ride. (What a Saturday night in Trento for the trainspotters on holiday!)

Whilst perusing, Drew remembered and reminded that Alpe di Pampeago, our second scheduled appointment for the following day, was a real brute. According to the folder's printed profile — which Drew duly memorised before waving around like a prosecutor clutching the trial's damning document — the Alpe's gradient averaged out at 10%, with slopes that offered nothing even close to an easy section, ranging from 9% through to a stinging 16%.

That forewarning proved too much for him. Whilst I was in the bathroom, he used a pot of strawberry jam and a plastic knife (smuggled passed the guards at breakfast) to stage a suicide scene for my amusement, lying patiently on his bunk, waiting for me to discover his wrist-slit "corpse". More than a morsel of concern tempered my mirth. He tried to convince us both that it was all for the laugh, his thoughts miles from despair, cruising high upon the slopes of the trip's next challenge, but I wasn't so sure. Much of our chat that evening had been interrupted by his pausing to gaze mournfully into the middle distance, to ruminate about what they might be doing "back home" without him. I got the distinct impression that he could hardly wait for it all to be over (even though it hadn't really started yet), so he could return to tell them all about it, and just how much he had missed them.

DAY 4:
QUEENS OF THE DOLOMITES

Passo Fedaia (Marmolada)
Start point: Caprile | Height: 2057m | Height Climbed: 1059m
Length of Climb: 14.1km | Average gradient: 7.5% | Maximum
gradient: 18%

Alpe di Pampeago
Start point: Tesero | Height: 1740m | Height climbed: 766m
Length of climb: 7.5km | Average gradient: 10.1% | Maximum
gradient: 16%

We awoke to a cooler but altogether drier day. Breakfast was
served, as usual, on a plastic prison tray: one roll, one portion of
butter, one thimble of jam, one mug of revolting coffee. Try to
take any more (or dare complain) and you'd get a beating in the
exercise yard or spend a day down the hole. The only difference
from the previous day's prima colazione was the addition of a
James Brown soundtrack. The guard behind the slop counter had
the appearance of a European MTV VJ, the type of *rad, crazy* guy
who likes to high-five, wear his jeans low, and wishes for nothing
more from life than to wake up one morning and discover that he's
turned into an American skateboarding champ. Rad dude also liked
to play his music real, crazy loud, in order to show the inmates that
he was more than his job — like the girl at Edinburgh Airport but
with fewer bird sounds. So he set about impressing us with James
Brown and all that grunting, puffing, heartfelt blues about sod all;
getting deep and meaningful and "sexy!" because — just because,
baby. I hated it, hate blues and funk and that awful combination of
the two that's supposed to turn even dull students on summer jobs
into unstoppable sex machines. I gulped my dishwater coffee,
bounced my stale bread into the bin and somehow resisted starting
a riot.

***

Despite being second climb on the day's schedule, the Alpe di Pampeago was already prominent in our thoughts. As a result of Drew's consideration and consternation the previous evening, the big red blocks from the folder's profile sheet were now imprinted onto our minds. Dancing menacingly inside our heads like derisory demons were the painful gradients represented by that red ink.

Driving north toward the Dolomites was even more daunting now that the skies were clear. Those giant peaks gathered on the horizon like the battlements of the almighty organic fortress these two "warriors" had been tasked with raiding. Once again we headed through Bolzano, this time diverting onto the correct road, passing the dreaded Pampeago and venturing on toward our day's initial appointment, the Passo Fedaia.

Before long we were in the Valle di San Pellegrino, ignoring stunning views down onto the flat plain in order to gulp in awe at the obvious severity of the road's ascent. One section had signs warning of a 15% gradient, which looked impossibly steep. The Pampeago had a 16% gradient waiting for us, the Fedaia an 18%. How much difference would those additional few percent make, how much steeper could a climb possibly get? Some roads are so precipitous that the climbing process becomes solely about making it to the top by any means, minus the grace of good technique or the glory of velocity, and I suspected we were in for just such an experience.

Despite (or perhaps due to) the fearful gradient, I'd recommend anyone heading out to that part of the world to go for a ride on the Passo di San Pellegrino. It was easy to see why the Giro d'Italia had frequently chosen to race along that road, and Drew and I regretted not having made a similar selection. The Pellegrino was a semi-coiled spring draped across the valley, spiced by the aforementioned awesome gradients, a challenge without doubt, but surely also a blast to ride. A twisting, turning, smooth sweep of tarmac, as Drew pointed out, Jeremy Clarkson would make a mess in his skin-tight Wranglers given the chance to drive a fast car on such a highway. All we wanted was to abandon the bloody car, get out on the bikes and ride. Only the schedule's restriction (and a healthy dose of fear) prevented us from doing so.

Drew attempted to distract from the gradients (those immediately proximate and those upcoming) by asking me to, "look at those shoes."

"What shoes?" I replied, bewildered.

"Mine's a pint of McEwans Export, thanks."

That "explanation" (say, what shoes, quickly in a Sean Connery Scottish accent and apparently it sounds like, what's yours) led on to him singing the jingle from an old Scottish beer advert, one I hadn't heard before, one I feared he might have dreamt up in some altitude-induced stupor.

"McEwans is the best beer, the best beer, the best beer, McEwans is the best beer, the best buy in beer … ."

He insisted the kids in his class had sung that very ditty on the bus during school trips, perhaps on their way to visit the local brewery — only in Scotland. I suggested that Drew might have imagined it all but, whatever the case, the bloody tune had stuck, wormed its way deep into my ear. The last thing I wanted was to ride up a mountain with a beer jingle pulsing through my mind but such torture often afflicts on long climbs. Some random song — the catchiest, most saccharine and inane ditty I've recently had the misfortune of hearing — will get trapped inside my head. It might be an irritating line from the chorus, sometimes just a random section from the melody, as I grind my way upward it will repeat on an endless loop. This aural interference can benefit by acting like a mantra, giving the mind something else to focus on other than the pain, but more often than not it serves only to drive me to the edge of insanity.

In *Touching the Void*, Joe Simpson's story of misadventure upon the slopes of Siula Grande, he tells of how the song *Brown Girl in the Ring* by Boney M got trapped in his head as he scrambled exhausted and half-dead to safety. Having had that song for company it's surprising he didn't just fling himself into the void to end the misery.

The beer jingle proved belligerent but was soon vying for a place in my consciousness with the unofficial anthem of our day's first climb. The Passo Fedaia skirts the side of the Marmolada, a mountain affectionately (or is it respectfully?) known as the Queen of the Dolomites. This regal moniker was the inspiration behind Drew's self-penned back-up song, entitled, *Marmolada, Marmolada, Queen of the Dolomites*, the lyrics of which were an endless repetition of the title, sung to the tune of some annoying Ibiza anthem — leaving my poor brain trapped between an ear worm and a hard place.

***

Located between the Gruppo di Sella (to the north) and the Pale di San Martino (to the south), the Marmolada's ridge forms a natural border between the two Dolomiti regions, Trentino and Veneto. The Marmolada also boasts the Dolomites' two highest peaks, Punta Rocca at 3309 metres and Punta Penia at 3343 metres, hence the regal moniker. The Marmolada is so high that it also has its own glacier, the northern slopes of which are permanently swathed in snow and ice.

Passo Fedaia is a perennial Giro d'Italia favourite. At the base of this climb in the 2002 edition of the race the late Marco Pantani climbed off his bike and sulked into the back of the team car. He cited fatigue from a recent bout of bronchitis as his reasons for withdrawal but, considering his alleged battles with depression and drug addiction, it's amazing he even made it that far.

I remembered watching those events unfold live on Eurosport, despondent to see the best climber of his generation labouring at the back, finally succumbing just as the mountains had begun to bare their teeth. The pace had been high as they hit the start of the climb and Pantani clearly knew just how much harder it was going to get — but such actions were the antithesis of his normal style. He was more commonly the man attacking off the front as the mountains bit hard, the man with the swashbuckling spirit, the one they called *Il Pirata*, the pirate.

That's the thing with the mountains, as the peloton fragments, riders become isolated, their team-mates disappearing in all directions. If you have any weaknesses then the mountains will bring them to the fore, make them glaringly obvious to all around. Pantani must have known that the Fedaia was no piece of cake; Drew and I had only partly fallen for the self-told lie that it would be our day's easy climb, that only the Pampeago was going to hurt. Our flippancy was but a thin shield to help us reach the mountain's lower slopes, whereupon it would quickly melt away, leaving us defenceless yet (we hoped) determined.

***

The first few kilometres on from the start at Caprile were reasonably steep but in no way severe. The gradient stalled at around 5%, enabling us to linger under the easy illusion. The next few kilometres rose little above 3%, and by then irreverence was almost in total control. Not for long though. At the small village of

Pian, the road escalated dramatically, up to around 8%, the pain in legs and lungs forcing a double take, my mind assured that the village name was either an anagram or a sign-writer's typo.

Then came further, unexpected respite, and with it revived irreverence. This easier section continued through the next village, Bosco Verde, lulling us deeper into that false sense of security: we had already conquered the hard part, surely nothing left but to cruise toward the summit. I even began to wonder, was the climb really worthy of its place in our itinerary?

My disrespectful doubting was short-lived. After Bosco Verde the road got back to what famous Italian mountain passes are best at, kicking abruptly upward. A persistent stream of cyclists hurtled downhill toward us, none even attempting to return our forced cheery waves and smiles, let alone our grunted hellos, no matter what language we grunted them in. As if in recompense for that lack of manners the road provided us with a yet another short downhill. We sighed relief, even as we freewheeled on and into the first of a series of tunnels — an unlit affair but short enough to avoid a repeat of the Lake-Garda Goonie fiasco. Those brief descents and the sections of lesser gradient undoubtedly provided moments of welcome respite but they also made it near impossible for us to get into, and stick with, any kind of rhythm. Each dose of deliverance was encored by a burst of pain as we pushed and pulled, struggling to find the right tempo and a suitable gear for the latest new gradient.

After a final tunnel at Malga Ciapela the road kicked again. We rounded the corner and discovered the brutal truth of the Fedaia. The long, straight road rose almost vertically, seeming to advance heavenward in perpetuity like a surreal nightmare. We hoped upon hope that this was the steepest section of the climb, could only dream of the short descents that had so recently "disturbed" our precious rhythm. According to the profile in the folder, this ruinous road had a maximum gradient of 18%. I hoped upon hope that this was it. Any steeper and we'd need ropes and harnesses. The tarmac leapt straight up from open pasture and shot into the blue sky high above; almost inconceivably, it looked way steeper than the scary sections of the San Pellegrino we had driven up earlier in the day. *18%? Don't you mean 28%?*

Blatant climbs like the Fedaia, those with vast exposed stretches of ridiculously steep road, are the ones that do the most psychological damage. Twisty, wooded ascents, where the road ahead remains hidden, allow your brain to be tricked, even when you've memorised every last detail of the profile, as Drew had. You'll be on a steep section, grovelling along, see a corner up ahead and think, "round that there's bound to be a downhill, at the very least a section of flat." Even upon rounding that corner to find more upward action you still suckle the same trustful teat, aiming for the next bend and the hope of another dreamy diversion. However, when the road is laid out in front of you like that section on the Fedaia, rising obviously ever upward, there's no way to kid yourself it's going to be anything but tough, and tough it was. We were out of our saddles, working hard just to keep the pedals turning, and if we hadn't gone into first gear it was only out of some perverse determination to save that most precious escape route in case of something steeper (*something steeper?* Is that even possible? Please, no!), to trick ourselves into believing we had something, anything in reserve for the Pampeago.

Weary faces hung over our handlebars, (barely) living gargoyles that washed with bright-red waves of exhausted embarrassment, now ashamed to acknowledge the cyclists who descended toward them. Compared to the downhillers' grace we looked like baboons trying to ballet dance.

Drew told me between gasps,

"I'm ... worried ... that ... we're ... going so ... slowly ... someone ... might ... well ... walk passed ... us ... whistling idly ... whilst ... carrying ... a sofa."

Confused faces peered out from the air-conditioned cars that rolled down the road toward us or idled by on their way to a picnic at the top. I dared not catch any eye. You really are all alone on the mountain, nowhere to hide. That's why Pantani had climbed off his bike in 2002; he knew the climb, understood that continuing would have meant his suffering in full view of the world.

Another car cruised by, heavily laden with overweight tourists who gawped as if they were driving through some cross between an asylum and a safari park. Then another slowed down to get a better view of the frothing freaks, just as a burst of aggressive determination overruled my shame. I thought, "so what if I'm struggling, like to see any of you lazy gits get out of the car and cycle up this. Most of you couldn't even manage to *walk* ten metres of the Fedaia, and I'm pedalling all the way to the top. Just you watch!"

Moving so slowly, with no shade upon the exposed straight, the heat also became a factor. I felt like I was riding through wet cement, the claggy force rapidly draining my reserves, pulling me back down the slope. Thinking the tar might actually be melting, I looked down through my legs to the back wheel and only then spotted the flat tyre. Getting a puncture during a bike ride isn't something I would normally welcome but on that occasion I felt overjoyed. There was my excuse to stop; and no wonder I'd been struggling, having ridden for half a kilometre with a deflating back tyre. Grinning like a lottery winner, I rolled to a halt, the gradient almost tipping the bike into a wheelie. So excited, so out of breath I could hardly speak to Drew as he pulled up next to me.

"Have you ... got a ... spare ... tube ... man?"

Thankfully, he did. Feeling like we were in danger of baking to death, I rapidly replaced the tube and got the tyre almost up to pressure using my mini pump.

Back on the bikes and our reward was a severe struggle just to get going again, to pick up enough forward momentum so we could get our feet clipped into the pedals. We somehow succeeded, wrestling our bikes to the top of the long straight, there to be welcomed by the final section of hairpins (over ten of them; I lacked the oxygen and vital brain sugars to make an accurate tally) and the warning signs, alerting to us to gradients of 15%. We couldn't believe it — those hairpins didn't look half as steep as the long straight that had so nearly claimed us. Where the hell was *its* warning sign?

Coming off the ramp of the first hairpin, we received our day's opening (and only) encouragement. An Italian motorist leant out of his car and bellowed, "*forza, forza!*" Somehow we cracked gargoyle masks of pain to smile in appreciation. That last section hurt, tifoso or no tifoso. Drew's theory is that the last kilometre of a climb is always the easiest: no matter how steep the gradient, or how tired your legs, impetus comes through knowing that the end achievement is so nearly within reach; easier to push that extra measure when you know the pain is just about to stop. And stop it did, eventually.

The views that surrounded us come the summit were almost as breathtaking to behold as the climb had been to ride. This Queen certainly deserved, and received, respect. We saw sheer walls of mountain formed by concurrent, ragged pillars of grey limestone, the sky peering in over the top. We saw swathes of white snow and ice, tiny tufts of green grass breaking through, battling in vain to bring some colour, evidence of life to an otherwise barren landscape. It was almost a relief that the climb had been so hard. How incongruous to have sauntered to that altitude, to be faced with such a view having idled in the passenger seat. The grovel and toil were apt, fitted with what we had found and added to the sense of achievement, the idea (as our senses indicated all too obvious) that we had arrived at a position truly extreme.

We posed for our summit-sign snaps and pedalled over to the Lago di Fedaia, a dammed lake, the furthest shores of which blended into the horizon. Standing on the edge of the calm water, we enjoyed uninterrupted views over the other side of the pass and beyond toward the Sella group. The cloud, cold and rain of the previous day were from another world — thank god — our sweat-drenched skin drying nicely in the warm sun. We sighed, satisfied and relived, like untroubled tourists ready to hop aboard the coach and head for home, our trip's toil already over and done with.

Such serenity hid the area's brutal recent history. During the Great War, Italy's front-line with the Austro-Hungarian Empire ran right through the centre of the Marmolada massif. The forces on either side constructed numerous rocky outposts that were linked by networks of trenches and tunnels. Austrian forces fashioned cities of ice, barracks built deep below the surface of the glacier, safe from the dangers of Italian shellfire but susceptible to the inevitable avalanches that claimed many lives. The fighting there was some of the most gruesome of the entire war, with appalling conditions easily as intolerable as any on the Western Front. The 1916 to 1917 winter was particularly harsh, with over ten metres of snowfall, the highest ever recorded in the Dolomites. Those horrific conditions, referred to by troops at the time as "the white death", claimed many lives. Total losses by both sides in two years of fighting on and around Marmolada amounted to over 9000 dead: one third killed in action; another third claimed by avalanches; the remainder by the cold. Most of those fallen remain entombed in the rock and ice, thousands of men who simply disappeared beneath the snow, their bodies still being found to this day by climbers on the summer slopes.

***

Canazei's Hotel Laurin (the previous day's lunch stop) again delivered us with an unwanted side dish of Ibiza party tunes, this time served along with two (very much desired) plates of lasagne. The patron, pre-occupied during our first encounter with laughing at our goosebumps, had progressed to mocking our accents, determined to believe, and somehow persuade us, that we were in fact Dutch — and that despite repeated chants of, "vengo Scozzese", which left us sounding like crazed Scottish M.C.s trying to rap along with the god-awful music.

We ate and perused a day-old copy of *The Independent*, caught up on news of the Tour de France. Lance Armstrong was en route to yet another title (yawn). Along the way he'd created a sub-plot side-distraction by personally chasing down a non-race-threatening breakaway containing the Italian Filippo Simeoni. Simeoni had made himself a target by daring to speak out on the methods of Armstrong's doctor and trainer, one Michele Ferrari. Armstrong had heard that Simeoni was in the break and jumped up the road after him, "in the interests of the peloton", as he put it. We weren't sure we agreed with Armstrong's suggested motivation. Okay, so apparently Ferrari did more than offer advice on performance-enhancing substances, but this was the same Ferrari who had openly expressed attitudes to EPO use that were at least naïve and at worst dangerous (suggesting that when taken correctly the illegal blood booster was as safe as orange juice). To say there was just a whiff of suspicion surrounding the man was like suggesting that billy goats only had a very slightly unpleasant odour.

The 1998 Festina scandal had blown my innocent eyes wide open and, as far as I could see, not much had changed in cycling since. I found it hard to conceive that anyone in the higher echelons of pro cycling was any kind of innocent angel. It did, however, annoy me that it was always the riders who were treated like the world's worst criminals whenever a positive test was announced. What about the doctors who surely supplied the substances and equipment in the first place? And were we really supposed to believe that team managers, especially those who were renowned for ruling squads in dictatorial fashion, never once spotted that their riders were doping, hadn't in any way assisted with the deception?

Fed and watered, we lobbed the newspaper into the bin and drove south-west, back to Tesero, on roads wet from a morning deluge we'd thankfully missed. We were soon at the foot of the Alpe di Pampeago (remember, the day's difficult one), pedalling uphill out of town, farting like troopers and cursing the lunchtime lasagne. (A tailwind is usually welcome but that was not the kind we favoured.) The town's church bells tolled as the two daft, gas-bloated soldiers headed off on their personal war, battling gravity like King Canute facing-off the tide. On we wheezed and parped, through the hillside suburbia, hard to believe we were headed for, if not already on, the slopes of a killer climb.

We passed a turn-off for Passo di Primadiccio, veered right and onto the wooded section of our ascent proper. As the bells faded into the background, the alarm of discomfort rang loud in our ears, already apparent that we really were onto the day's toughest challenge. Pain built upon pain, heaped itself on top of further pain until soon, much too soon, we were scrambling around in a world of pain. The climb had somehow sensed our recent underestimation of its challenge, not only wanted to set us straight but also to exact a cruel revenge along the way.

The Pampeago offered not one ounce of respite, no switchbacks, small downhill sections or flat tunnels — just steep section after steep section, into corner after corner, the road slowly snivelling its evil little way upward through the thick, dark forest. For some reason I had again felt it necessary to avoid using first and second gear, my leaden legs grinding round in third, on and on, pushing with as much strength as I could muster, a punishing process akin to a continuous cycle of weight-lifting squats. And we weren't just battling the gradient. The rough road surface also took its toll, sending rattles and vibrations up through the handlebars, testing hands, wrists and shoulders. All that was bad enough and through it our guts spun like whirlpools as they battled to cope with the exertion and that lasagne.

I glanced down at my gears, wiped away the sweat just as it was about to drip from my chin, wondered if we had even achieved the climb's hardest section. According to the folder's profile, which I didn't fully trust, at around the halfway mark we would face that 16% gradient (only 2% less than the high-point of the Fedaia, which had felt like riding up a wall). I hoped we had passed the worst, couldn't bear to think that it might be about to get even harder, that we were still only duelling with the "easy" bit. I looked around for confirmation or inspiration but found none. There were no road signs telling us how far to go or what the gradient might be, and the top of the climb remained ever elusive, obscured by the tightly packed trees. My hope that respite might lie in wait around the bend was quickly kicked into touch. This climb was Groundhog Day: we ground on and on, rounded a corner, checked out the next hundred yards of pain; then we ground on and on to the next corner to do it all over again. It never got any easier.

The first time the Giro d'Italia raced to the ski resort at the summit of Alpe di Pampeago, in 1998, Marco Pantani was second on the stage (behind Russian, Pavel Tonkov) and went on to win the race overall. We'd known before we set off that Pantani had sprinted up to Pampeago at an average of 17.5kmh. That might not sound so fast until you consider that just walking up some of the steepest parts of the climb would tax your average Joe or Joanne. Looking down at our speedometers it was hard to conceive of Il Pirata, or anyone else, tackling that road at such a speed. You shall know our velocity, and we were only scraping 10kph at some points, battling with everything we had just to reach those giddy heights. Where was Doctor Ferrari when you needed him?

There were three tunnels before the summit, the last of which was long and furnished with a further-degraded road surface. As I rattled, wheezed and farted through the muddy half-light, a little back down the tunnel Drew was following suit, laughing at the ridiculous gassy echoes as his expulsions ricocheted off the curved walls — anything to distract his mind from the pain. By that point I too was almost crying, but through discomfort and not with laughter, the thought of having to ride through a muddy tunnel seeming like the worst imaginable fate ever to befall mankind. I was working hard, physically, mentally, and all just to remain upright, to keep on creeping on.

A tourist coach followed us through the latter half of the tunnel, an event that under normal circumstances wouldn't have caused concern. However, considering I had almost cried over a bit of mud, the addition of that very large bus to the already cramped confines felt like the final straw. No longer could I weave wearily around the road, forced as I was toward the gutter by the behemoth's superior mass and force. The roar from its engines echoed like a million farts, everything vibrated, each nut and bolt of my bike, every atom in my body. With each centimetre of upward progress that cacophony built toward a grand conclusion, possibly mine. I set aside the pain of the ascent and instead prepared for impact.

Just as I exited the tunnel, the coach roared by, scraping my jutted elbow as it did so. I glanced over, half-expecting to see Drew spinning around, caught like a rag doll in one of the numerous wheels but, thankfully, he was somewhere amidst the haze of exhaust fumes further back down the road. The driver obviously thought the experience hadn't been memorable enough for the skinny white cyclist and decided upon sounding the preposterously loud horn, the fright of which caused me to wobble and very nearly fall onto the verge. I stuttered to a halt, unclipped and waited for Drew to appear from out of the orange incandescence. Together we crawled toward the small-town summit like discoverers embarrassed to realise that someone else had got there first, and in far better style.

The summit sign was there right in front of us, bolted unceremoniously to the side of a building at the start of the village — a little disappointing after all that effort. We hadn't expected a welcome party or a victory parade but had at least fancied a rocky peak or a decent vista as recompense. All we got was a row of shops and restaurants, a hotel and a small chapel that doubled as a war memorial. Pampeago was definitely the tougher of the day's two climbs but it hardly compared to Marmolada's grandeur.

***

I spent the majority of the descent stuck behind a very slow car, most likely one with mechanical problems, or with a non-Italian driver (surely not a local sticking to the speed limit?). Drew had taken an early chance and overtaken, sped off into the distance before the twisty section through the forest. I'd missed out and been forced to linger, glued to car's back bumper all the way down, never getting much above 30mph. To occupy the additional time I had tried out a cornering technique known as counter steer, which I had read about online, whereby you literally steer the bike in the opposite direction to that of the curve. For example, you apply forward pressure onto the right handlebar as you come into a right-hand turn, as if trying to steer left. The more pressure you apply, the more you can lean in and the tighter your arc around the corner can be. It sounds a bit odd, but I tried using counter steer more than the brakes to see me round the sharp bends and was pleasantly surprised when it worked a treat.

As I finally swooshed back down and into Tesero, my tailwind had blown itself out but the town bells were tolling once again, signalling the return of the intrepid warriors. Two more climbs ticked off the list, our day's mountain battle over, the war far from won.

DAY 5:
THE FOLDER OF DOOM

Passo dello Stelvio
Start point: Prato | Height: 2758m | Total height climbed: 1808m | Length of climb: 24.3km | Average gradient: 7.4% Maximum gradient: 14%

Passo del Mortirolo
Start point: Mazzo di Valtellina | Height: 1852m | Total height climbed: 1300m | Length of climb: 12.4km | Average gradient: 10.5% | Maximum gradient: 18%

Passo di Gavia
Start point: Ponte di Legno | Height: 2621m | Total height climbed: 1363m | Length of climb: 17.3km | Average gradient: 7.9% | Maximum gradient: 16%

I awoke exhausted and suffering a red-raw sore throat, slumped back onto the sweaty pillow, trying to convince myself that the discomfort was a result of gasping for oxygen upon the climbs and not the onset of Drew's virus. It was an inauspicious start but I supposed the fatigue was understandable, given my recent exertions, and that I hadn't slept well (once again) due to the heat. I was tired but thoughts of the day ahead took me to the point of collapse. Lucky I was already lying down.

Back in Edinburgh we had sketched out that day's itinerary without meaningfully considering the task involved (oh, blissful ignorance!). Priority had been placed on gathering together the climbs we *really* wanted to ride, the big names we'd tuck under our belts and boast about for years to come. Of lesser concern had been the practicalities of aiming for so many high-mountain conquests and, in this case, featuring three of them in one day. Even when discussing it the night before we had still refused to admit to the undoubted difficulty, the inescapable lunacy. To make matters worse, each of the three climbs ahead was supposedly harder than either the Fedaia or Pampeago, perhaps even harder than both combined — the on-paper statistics and online anecdotes certainly indicated as much.

Even the drive to the first climb was going to be tough, and that was taking into account the expensive short-cut we'd planned along the toll road toward Merano. Basing ourselves in Trento for the five days had seemed like a good idea (as so much had, on paper, back in Edinburgh, buffered by distance, buoyed by sugar-based snacks and endless mugs of coffee), thereby giving us one central base for all the Italian climbs. Hindsight had already made clear that we would have been far better staying near the foot of each of the days' initial escapades. (Such are the mistakes made by the novice traveller.) Never mind, at least we were in a nice hostel and making so many new friends.

My worrying was disturbed by mutters from the bunk below, something about leg fairies having sneaked into the cell at night to swap Drew's healthy legs for leaden versions.

"Think they feel bad now? Wait till you've ridden the Stelvio, Gavia *and* Mortirolo in a day."

Just to say their names in one sentence was painful enough. I wanted to be back in the blissful ignorance.

***

We hit the road after an early breakfast — one roll, one mug of dirty hot water, etc — and, despite the lack of nourishment, the fatigue and our worry for the task ahead, it was hard to feel down on such a cracking day. Sunny, hot and not a single cloud in the sky, we were enjoying the kind of weather Italians take entirely for granted, the kind that would cause mass hysteria and an economy-destroying wave of absenteeism should it ever reach the shores of blustery Britain. I sweated profusely just sitting in the car, my body still not even partially acclimatised. It would have taken several-hundred-thousand years and some kind of evolutionary process for me to fully adjust to the heat. I was a Scotsman used to his cold country, a Scotsman who on occasion even found that chilly homeland a little too warm for comfort. What chance did I have in Italy, in July?

Our recently laundered kit was also cooking, laid out in the back of the car to dry. We had washed it all in sink the night before, wrung it out in our spare towels, just like racing cyclists of old, in the days before team buses came plumbed with washing machines. As damp lycra sizzled and crinkled, I gazed at the passing countryside, drifted into consideration of what it was like to climb at the limit of my physical capabilities.

As the road began to bite I would come to hold my body in full awareness. Part by part it would reach my attention, not just my legs but every sinew of muscle, as if extreme exertion had forced me, for the first time, to acknowledge my own physical existence. Each fibre of my being would call out at some point upon the climb, individually, sometimes in unison, eventually a loud scream of pain brought on by the oxygen debt. Quads, then calves, then one knee, then both; hands upon the bars, seemingly doing nothing, would also begin to grumble. I'd change position, trying to stay supple but then my forearms would hurt, and then my shoulders. My lower back would ache. My sit bones would feel like my saddle was fashioned from a breezeblock so I'd stand on the pedals to gain some relief and then my neck would begin to twinge.

A glance down to treble-check what gear I was using and I'd be distracted by the rapid, frenzied drumbeat: my pulse frantic, my heart a piston struggling to keep up with the runaway train, so intense I could feel the effort resonating through my bones. The only possible distraction from that cacophony would be the gasps as I struggled to haul sufficient air into my lungs, to find any oxygen at all in the thin mountain air. I'd try to focus on the tempo, to keep it all under control, within my limits, to stop it from racing away — I had no jurisdiction over the mountain so I must try to be in control of myself.

Then I'd consider my asthma and wonder if those laboured breaths were a symptom or if a non-asthmatic would be feeling as awful, clutching, grabbing, gulping the air but never able to get enough. I had used my inhaler before the climb, so I must be okay, right? I'd think back to my recent asthma review and the nurse repeating her warning like a line from a ghost story, "*asthma attacks kill lots of people, all the time, every day. You must never be complacent.*" Well, I'm not lots of people and I'm not complacent, so I'll be fine.

I'd look ahead, try and distract my mind from the pain, to shut it out, zone in on achieving the summit, nothing to see but the steep road ahead, going up, and up and up. Always up. So much up. Eyes back down to the speedometer and the realisation that I'd only covered a few miles out of the ten or more to go and I'd know from having seen the profile, or from Drew's marvellous memory, that it would only get steeper the further I climbed.

"Don't let it win," I'd tell myself, "the mountain will not win. I will win."

A song would come to distract me, sometimes one I chose; usually a hideous earworm that chose me (Marmolada, the McEwans jingle, etc). I'd count the drops of sweat falling from my chin, listen to the metronomic chink-chink-chink of the pendant I wear on a chain around my neck, tapping as it swung to hit the metal zip on my jersey. Thirst might then become the overwhelming sensation and I'd reach down for my bottle, take a few greedy gulps of electrolyte energy drink and think of the Mont Ventoux and Tommy Simpson.

Just then, sudden understanding would interrupt all thoughts: I'm enjoying myself! The pain had built toward a crescendo, a climax through which I had crashed, settling in to a new rhythm, suddenly able to enjoy the experience. I'd relish the prospect of conquering the climb, for that was why I was doing it, that moment of victory so nearly realised. I had remembered the reason and it had all made sense. Yeah, it hurts but I love the hurt, it's the best kind, the pain of achievement and that pain makes me stronger. I spent a lot of money to come out to Europe and ride, and I know why: for that feeling, for something so difficult to describe, to explain to the non-masochist. I used my whole annual holiday entitlement for this trip, much to the bemusement of many ordinary (normal? Is what I'm doing abnormal? Yes, of course it is.), non-cyclist folks.

"Pedalling up all those mountains? That doesn't sound like much of a holiday to me! I'd rather lie in the sun drinking sangria."

Not to them, but to me it hurt less than roasting away a hangover on some over-crowded beach.

There'd be another pause, an expanse of noise and the realisation that I'd been off somewhere in my head, pre-occupied by diversionary thoughts. Up, out of the saddle, taking what fight there was left to what was left of the mountain: *attack it boy; don't let it attack you!* The road would tilt steeper and I'd be glad to have one, maybe two gears left; I'd drop down and try to spin a bit more. A few cars would pass by, maybe the first few I'd noticed since I lost myself in concentration: holidaymakers, day-trippers, Italian, French, German, all staring disinterested at the idiot on the bike.

Time would run more slowly as I fatigued, as if I was slipping into another dimension, a world altogether different to the one inhabited by the tourists in the cars.

There are different rules when I'm on the bike upon the climb, an intensity that doesn't exist in the humdrum of everyday life. The most amazing, insane, sometimes scarily vivid thoughts spark across my mind. These days I all too often dwell upon considerations of my late father, happy reminiscences from childhood, sometimes a bitter-sweet dream from the night, the week or the month before. Less welcome, but sadly more common, are the horrid scenes from his final days, haunting, taunting, a thousand times harder to overcome than the mountain I was about to summit. At that moment I would definitely exist somewhere else, in another dimension, no wonder the people in cars had failed to notice. By blocking off the pain, or because of the pain, I had slipped out of the normal physical universe and I would remain in that other dimension until the summit. There, at the final crest in the road, I would re-enter to realise, back to the conscious world, elated, resurrected, to enjoy an achievement seemingly built elsewhere.

***

The Italian Alps proved to be even further removed from Trento than the Dolomites (you'd think all those hours back in Edinburgh examining maps would have forewarned us but apparently not). We drove north until almost upon the Austrian border, another country altogether lurking beyond the rocky frontier — an exciting notion to a boy from an island nation. Skirting the spa town of Merano, we saw the first brown tourist-route sign for the Stelvio: jolly good of them to mark the way for us, old chap!

More numerous than the signposts were the shrines, petite dedications to the Virgin Mary, and the occasional life-size carving of Christ upon the cross, that peppered the Italian roadside. They'd be plonked at a random bush or lay-by, in a field or at the end of a driveway. One memorable example was a giant, larger-than-life crucifix nailed to the gable end of a guest house, so big it was hard to tell if the building supported the cross or vice versa.

Even more common were the motorbikes. They buzzed by in an incessant stream, heading toward the mountains like prospectors on rumour of an untapped golden seam. I wanted to lean out the window and holler through the rushing air, "what do you lot get out of the mountain experience?" Cyclists have a number of motivations: the physical and mental challenge; the fitness benefits; the feeling of being out in the wilds, knowing that isolation has been achieved under one's own steam. I guessed our motorised cousins had similar reasons, no physical challenge as such, but the opportunity to ride their bikes on some of Europe's most amazing highways, surrounded by scenery that would make concentrating on the road a challenge in itself. From my limited yet ever-expanding experience of those motorcyclists it looked like many of them had also presumed the mountain passes would be empty of other traffic, that they'd be able to ride at racing speeds, taking corner-cutting lines, as if upon closed roads at the Isle of Man TT. They'd encounter an almost equal number of pedal cyclists and only occasionally show the respect their fellow road users deserved. The remainder of their time was spent at speed, swerving around the cars and slow-moving (or not-so-slow where the Dutch were concerned) motor homes.

We were in the middle of a tunnel when the next line of bikes roared by. Drew leant out of the window and yodelled, his call drowned by the throb of BMW and Suzuki horsepower. Somewhere, on a hillside not too far away, the yodel drifted up on the breeze, snapping Goat Peter from his reverie, sending him and his smelly flock home for an early lunch of banana skins and bicycle spokes.

***

Three hours after leaving Trento, we pedalled out of the village of Prato allo Stelvio. The road meandered along the edge of the River Solda's white, rushing torrent, the scenery lush and gently sweeping. It was highly scenic and not at all reminiscent of my Stelvio preconceptions. The pictures of the pass I could recall featured a series of switchbacks streaked like a scar up a scree-covered slope. In no mood to complain, we got on with the joy of being free from the car, cruised unconcerned through the fresh valley air, relaxed about the task ahead, all 24-and-a-bit kilometres of it.

There's said to be evidence of a footpath and a trading route over the Stelvio that dates back to the early Bronze Age. Fast forward to 1808 and the Austrians decided time had come to construct a proper road and a quick connection between Lombardy and Tyrol. The engineer Carlo Donegani and his team completed the massive project in just 63 months, an incredibly short time when you consider the size of the task and their lack of modern machinery. (The Stelvio was then the Alps' highest paved pass, a title only relinquished when the French opened the 13-metre-higher Col de l'Iseran.) The new Stelvio route regenerated commerce between the two regions, saw fighting between the Austro-Hungarian and Italian forces during the First War, and later helped develop ski-tourism upon the Stelvio glacier — all that but a piddling prelude to the arrival of two skinny cyclists from Scotland.

The Giro d'Italia has brought much sporting action to this magnificent stretch of road. The most famous example dates from 1953, when the Giro made its Stelvio début and Italian legend Fausto Coppi tamed the mountain with a typical display of strength. (That year he won four stages in the race as well as the general classification.) Some of the most famous images of cycle racing in the mountains are those of Coppi that day, an attack sure to rate highly in cycling folklore for generations to come — there's even a monument to his achievements atop the mountain.

A couple of kilometres up the road we passed a house reminiscent of your typical Alpine log cabin. At first glance it appeared entirely, innocently picturesque but backtracking for a closer inspection revealed that instead of being surrounded by beautiful blooms, or painted in calming colours, the cabin was encased in a thick layer of bones and skulls. A sign on the gate warned anyone daft enough to venture beyond the boundary to, *beware the dog*. As the bones all appeared (we hoped) to come from non-human animals, I wondered if there shouldn't also be a sign warning dogs to beware the house. By the look of things, the remains of the entire region's lost canines were nailed to the timber — or were they cyclists, corpses gathered by the old man of the mountain as he scoffed at the idiocy of yet another failed Stelvio conquest?

Probably not, but it still felt like we'd cycled into the opening scenes of a daft teen horror movie, or a *Goonies* sequel. And if we had actually been in those opening scenes, that would have been the point in the plot when Drew and I decided to climb the gate, to head up the path and do a bit of snooping around. Thankfully, we were far too sensible (and far too wary) for that kind of malarkey. Besides, there was another kind of horror lying in wait for us further up the road.

Not long after the house of bones, but still within the river-valley confines, we caught up with a group of Italian roadies. All older gents, each man and his bike was immaculately presented, not a strand of silver hair out of place, goatie beards trimmed to perfection. Their kit looked as if it had only recently been removed from the packet, their tans the perfect Pantone shade (around 1206). Their steeds were of the expensive European variety: one Pinarello and two Colnagos (the Ferraris of pedal power), bikes that exhibited no apparent experience of dust, dirt or mud. These men (assuming they were mere mortals) had an ethereal air, suggesting a great calm and wisdom derived from many years in the saddle — not only did they *know* cycling and the road, they were at one with both. Here were the ancient Stelvio Shaolin monks, gliding along, effortlessly ascending the massive mountain.

Catching their group delivered us a dilemma: did we stick to their pace and chat, see where they were going, maybe tag along, or did we keep to our own (possibly excessive) pace, say hello and quickly leave them behind? The latter option opened up the worry of cracking a few miles later, having the group to which we'd earlier waved goodbye saunter passed, laughing at the young show-offs and their tactical ineptitude. We chose to ignore such doubts, to believe in our own abilities and pedalled a little faster. Judging by their godly appearance, by the way they casually acknowledged yet calmly dismissed our presence, our wise elders did indeed know a whole lot more about the mountain than we would ever learn. As we pulled away, their conversation sparked up again but the only word I clearly discerned above the crystal crash of the Solda rapids was our old friend, "piano."

The village of Trafoi came at about 1500-metres altitude — all that climbing and we'd only covered around five of the fifteen miles. We had numbers on our minds: miles ridden, height achieved, hairpin bends rounded. That latter count was still down at zero, surprising given that we'd read somewhere of the Stelvio's whopping forty-eight hairpins. The legendary Tour de France climb of Alpe d'Huez has a "mere" twenty-one hairpin bends and, if memory served correctly, that countdown had taken an age to complete. Forty-eight on the mighty Stelvio and we'd yet to encounter a single one? Presumably they lurked somewhere up ahead.

Not long out of Trafoi and the road veered right, parted ways with the river, up the steep valley side and into forest. The frothing rapids fell away below as we edged into eerie silence, the sounds of crashing water replaced by the evidence of our efforts and the mental noise from the creeping countdown: the numbered hairpins had begun. Whilst 48 had taken an age to reach, 47 took almost as long again (the bends were numbered from 48 down, or up, depending on how you looked at it). They most certainly did not come at all thick or fast, each requiring a monstrous effort to achieve. *How much longer to the next one, how much longer?* The question circled our minds like a moth around a lightbulb, reminding on an incessant loop: there are forty-eight in all; there are forty-eight in all; there are forty-eight in all ... .

When 46 finally swung into view, we were looking far from cool, certainly not ready to have another cyclist cruise by, his grace putting our grovelled progress resoundingly to shame. This mystery animal was decked in the full kit of the Lampre professional cycling squad, everything team-issue down to the socks, even perched upon a team-edition bike fitted with SRM Power cranks (a piece of kit that only serious riders use). I tried to get a look at him, to see if it really was a pro on a training "jaunt" but he was too darn fast to identify. Whoever it was, he smiled, offered a pleasant ciao and then cruised off into the distance, his movements as natural and effortless as the river cascading through the valley below.

We stopped for photos at 36, where a break in the trees offered amazing views across the valley to what I guessed was Ortles, which, at 3905 metres, is the region's highest peak. A German couple descended toward us, Herr stopping to wait for slightly more cautious Frau. The couple were on matching bikes and decked in matching kit, right down to identical altimeters — oh those crazy Germans! We proceeded to attempt a conversation in poor English and even worse German. Herr consulted his altimeter, told us how high we were and how much we had left to climb.

"1,500 metres left to go," he gleefully reported, and we didn't quite believe him.

In fact, Drew was so convinced there couldn't be that much *up* left ahead of us that he started an argument with Herr, oblivious to the fact that his opponent was not only German but also a German with an altimeter — absolutely no way he was going to be wrong.

Our foreign friend was adamant, insistent, even consulted the reading on his wife's matching meter, just to be sure. The evidence was there for all to see, in duplicate, and Drew finally accepted the bad news with grumbled grace.

Our grumbling soon turned to their laughter when we filled them in on the detail of our day's schedule, and how we intended to celebrate our completion of the Stelvio with rides up the Gavia and Mortirolo. The Germans laughed, and they laughed, and then some more, shaking their heads in disbelief, Herr having the temerity to suggest that we probably wouldn't be fit enough to ride *one* mountain, let alone *three*, especially considering:

"How much you Scots like Berti."

Drew agreed that Herr had a point but the comment left me confused, wondering who on earth this Berti person was and what he had to do with our levels of fitness. Was he referring to Berti Basset? Did he think Drew and I looked like liquorice men who might melt in the sun; or did we look like confectionery addicts, overweight and incapable? The more the Germans laughed, the more Drew conceded, the more confused I became, left with no choice but to demand an explanation. It transpired that "Berti" was in fact Herr Altimeter's mispronunciation of "party". He assumed that all Scotsmen were beer-fixated party monsters and therefore unlikely to be fit enough to ride one mountain in a month, let alone three in a day. I smiled viciously, barely resisted a Basil-Fawlty-esque war-mentioning outburst. Instead we offered our goodbyes and continued upward, in search of 35, and whatever else was set to follow.

From there on, the hairpins hit with a little more rapidity. Each bend proved welcome but the left turns especially so as they allowed us to stay on the right-hand side of the road and ride through the shallower line. On the right turns we were forced to take the steeper, left-hand, inside line in order to avoid the oncoming traffic, of which there was a lot. (If you do ever go to ride the Stelvio I'd recommend avoiding the first week of July, as that's when the mountain plays host to the International Motorcycle Meeting. Instead, aim for Stelvio Bike Day, usually occurring in late August or early September, when the road is completely closed to all motorised vehicles.) On we ground, forcing our bodies into the Stelvio's high-mountain meat mincer, the road rising at ever-inhuman increments. We were far from the top but it was already clear this climb was going to make many others, perhaps *all* others — even the twenty-one hairpins of Alpe d'Huez — seem like a cakewalk. Gilberto Simoni had been on to something with his proclamations about the Italian climbs being harder than anything found in the Tour de France. I certainly couldn't recall ever having seen anything as awful on Tour TV coverage.

As we approached the upper edge of the tree-line, gaps in the branches revealed snippets of the road ahead, around twenty-eight of those under-hyped hairpins left for our "enjoyment". From such a distance, and given the scale of the backdrop, it looked like little more than a tiny black squiggle drawn onto the clouds with a marker pen — so painfully far away and yet its pull was powerful. So we pedalled and pedalled and pedalled, but failed to bring it obviously any closer. We pedalled and pedalled and pedalled some more and I began to wonder, was that road really part of the same climb, even part of the same mountain?

As the forest fell back below us, the road opened out leaving the valley's sheer drop completely exposed — and what a drop it was. A quick glance over the barrier left no doubt as to the altitude, no altimeter required: we were bloody high up. We clung close to the opposite side of the road, vertigo distracting from the effort of the ascent.

It was around there that I first became aware of, and then started to count, the discarded energy-gel packets and energy-bar wrappers that littered the roadside. Every few feet I'd spot another, and then another, eye-catching silver-foil detritus that sparkled like sequins in the undergrowth. I wondered if we had reached the point where cyclists traditionally chose to replenish their energy levels; had a rider near the front of that year's Giro reached into his pocket at that very spot, to send a devouring domino effect backwards through the bunch? That juncture might have been highlighted in the road book, the designated point where team directors were advised to blare instruction through their radios, riders' earpieces ringing with the reminder to *eat, eat, eat!*

With my mind so comprehensively fixated on food, the bonk that followed should really have come as no surprise. The "bonk", in case you're not familiar with the terminology, is less exciting than it sounds, not the tabloid-newspaper description of a sex act, but the point in any strenuous exercise when your blood-sugar level drops to a point that leaves you unable to adequately function. The bonk usually hits in an instant, like someone has flicked a switch and turned off the power supply, leaving you utterly ravenous, light-headed and unable to concentrate, let alone power yourself up one of the world's toughest mountain passes. The only way to avoid the bonk is to eat properly prior to and during your ride, to do so *before* hunger strikes, maintaining a sufficient level of gas in the tank to get you through the journey.

I raked around in my jersey pockets, manic, shaky and incapable hands searching for the apricot-jam croissant I was certain existed, was certain I had stuffed into the back pocket of the jersey I was certainly wearing. Failing fingers came across an inner tube, my cap and a pair of arm warmers. I rested a moment and then rummaged again, once more coming up with the same inedible selection, adding my rain jacket to the list of foraged items. So hungry I was about to eat an arm-warmer, I tried again and finally struck sweet, sugary gold. There it was, the same type of twelve-in-a-bag, jam-filled croissants I could barely stand the thought of when sated, now ripped from its wrapper and devoured in a manner that suggested I hadn't seen food in months, which was pretty much how I felt. A few gulps of energy drink, the little of it left in my bottle, and the shaking subsided. Focus almost returned, I offered a small prayer to the bakery and its dedicated staff — their croissant had surely saved my skin.

Hunger temporarily sated, panic reared to take its place. My concern was over whether or not I'd make it to the summit before bonking again, or worse, that I might go one step further and "hit the wall". The bonk can be relieved by an intake of energy; hitting the wall is more serious, requiring extended rest and refuelling. From that rocky outpost of fear I made a stupid decision: to ride as fast as possible in order to reach the top as quickly as possible. That way, somehow, I might dodge the bullet sure to be fired by the bonk's big bad brother.

Off into the zone I went, scooting passed Drew, who had stopped to wait for my recovery, going way too fast, riding hard but inefficiently. Round the next corner and I was lost, deep within the recesses of my mind. As sugar levels ran dangerously low and the air further thinned, my brain-function juddered and stalled. I was an automaton, locked in self-preservation mode, looking after number one, not a care for my companion nor for a view that, moments before, had left me craning upward in awe and downwards in terror.

Somewhere within the last ten switchbacks I snapped out of the fugue, looked round for Drew, the idea that I had been riding with someone else slowly gaining credence. I eased up and that other person came into view, far in the distance, an ant in my curious gaze. All the while I was watching him, the worrywart voice in my head persisted, nagging incessant, telling me to forget about my friend: *hurry, hurry, hurry, before the bonk comes back! Forget about him, save yourself, save yourself! What if you hit the wall? Don't look back, don't look back!*

I could feel the energy ebbing, certain my fate was but a matter of timing, unrelated to the effort I expended, sand slowly draining from the hourglass. Then the cold shakes set in. *I told you to hurry!* The fear shouted its final warning and once again I succumbed, made a dash toward the summit to counter the risk of never reaching it. At hairpin 5 I changed up a gear and heaved round the pedals in a manner that suggested I had excess energy to give — head down, the alarm ringing in my ears, teeth gritted against the pain. At 4 my quads were in agony; at 3 I felt twinges of cramp; 2 and my lungs burned from the effort; by hairpin 1 I didn't care that the summit lay just ahead at the end of the long, steep, straight ramp. Managing the next pedal stroke was my only concern.

Somehow I managed to haul the pedals round full-circle, and then again another hundred-or-so times after that. By the top I could barely see the summit sign, and not just for a lack of brain activity. A gaggle of German motorcyclists had gathered round it, the pride of their "accomplishment" all too obvious and all to audible. What exactly they had achieved I wasn't sure. None of them looked how I felt: totally and utterly spent, yet inwardly exhilarated. Through a break in the sea of leather I glimpsed the white numbers: 2758. I had ridden to that altitude and was still alive. Had there been any energy left I might well have danced a celebratory jig.

On the other side of the road was a stall selling frankfurters but the smell and sight of the food failed to move me — odd considering that five miles back down the road I would have swapped a kidney for half a hot dog. Then I remembered: five miles back down the road. There I had committed, if not a crime, then at least a cycling-etiquette faux pas. In my fixation with keeping a bike-length ahead of the bonk I had ridden off and left Drew on his own. He wouldn't be happy, *I* wouldn't have been happy had he done the same to me. I recalled our Spanish holiday from the year before and the day when we'd escaped the horrors of Fuengirola to cycle up to the Pico del Veleta, (the highest paved road in Europe, no less). Drew had grown thoroughly bored of waiting for me to slog along in his wake and had steamed off ahead without so much as a by-your-leave. That "abandonment" had pissed me off and I'd sworn never to do likewise to him or anyone else I happened to be riding with. Yet, there I was, alone at the Stelvio summit, my mate riding solo, miles back down the road.

I freewheeled over to the crest of the final ramp and its gob-smacking view of the zig-zagging squiggle of road. Just a glimpse of the tiny blue dot a few hairpins down and I could already feel Drew's anger.

I was busy snapping some shots of the view when he inched icily by. He shrugged off my feeble, guilty encouragement and headed directly to the summit sign. I followed on, a short, safe distance behind, cajoled him into posing for a photo (a grimace in place of the customary smile). In distinct contrast to our funereal air came the arrival of the Stelvio Shaolin monks. They looked far less together than they had twenty miles back down the mountain but good cheer far outshone their fatigue. Welcomed by a gaggle of similarly aged ladies, they erupted with displays of joyous emotion that suggested the climb wasn't actually a regular training route, their shared sense of achievement all too obvious. I dared to wonder if Drew and I would be undertaking such exploits at their relatively advanced age.

***

As we began the descent, I attempted to settle our as yet unspoken differences, apologised for having ridden off, did my best to explain, to blame it all on the bonk. Drew insisted he wasn't offended by my abandonment but the sullen expression suggested otherwise. Thankfully, distraction came snake-shaped: the hairpins that had taken an age to achieve on the ascent now hit thick and fast. In and out of them, we leant this way and that, braking hard and often, keeping to our side of the road in order to avoid oncoming motorbikes and their insistence on sticking to racing lines.

My already stiff neck began to ache; my hands and arms hurt, turned numb and tingly by the vibrations that resonated through the bars, with the efforts of holding on and hauling on the brakes. After such a gruelling ascent all we desired was an open road to set us free, not to mention a blast of cool air to clear away the bad feeling. Further down-mountain we got just that. The road pulled back up alongside the river, its sweeping bends and straighter lines delivering speeds approaching 50mph. We began to catch and overtake cars, as well as small groups of more cautious cyclists, who watched with bemusement as we roared by. Drew lead the way, apparently venting his anger on the road, and I was only too keen to try and keep up, preferring a two-wheeled duel to any off-the-bike ill feeling.

Back at the car, a quick look at the clock and it was finally confirmed that using Trento as a base had indeed been a rookie-traveller mistake. A huge swathe of our day had been consumed by the drive from Trento, another chunk swallowed by the Stelvio, any remaining hours already escaping our clutches, beginning to dip below the horizon. It was nearing four o'clock. The drive to Mazzo, start point for the Mortirolo, second climb on the schedule, would realistically take us two hours. That was two hours on top of the time required to refuel both our bodies and the car. Then we would need at least (who was I kidding?) two hours to ride up the mountain (make it three, given the way our legs felt), leaving us, at around 9pm, to descend the entire climb in darkness. Assuming we were then daft enough to press on, we'd be faced by an hour's drive to Ponte di Legno to begin the third and final climb of the day (or night, as it would then be). That stricken-schedule-following scenario would see us returning to Trento at around four in the morning, if we made it back at all.

Thoughts of further riding that day were ended by the following words of wisdom:

"F*** the schedule, because the schedule is well and truly f***ed".

Which, to be honest, was just as well, because so were we.

***

We fully understood that the failure to ride those two climbs would be regretted. The Mortirolo is often said to be the hardest climb in the world. The 12.4km ascent has an average gradient of 10.5% and has destroyed the dreams and legs of many a Giro d'Italia contender. Describing the Mortirolo, American Giro-winner, Andy Hampsten, said,

"The Mortirolo's super, super hard, you're just nailed to the road at the beginning ... . It's so steep that the legs can't really accelerate or snap — you just can't get any real speed out of it — it's ridiculously steep." [1.]

I wasn't quite sure why we thought riding it straight after the Stelvio was a good idea. Why we'd then thought that following such a duo with a jaunt up the Gavia was yet another mind-boggler. The Gavia is infamous for the decisive roll it played in the 1988 Giro, ascended on a stage that went down in history as, "the day strong men cried". Temperatures hovered around zero degrees Celsius and blizzards swept across the high passes. Whilst Dutchman Erik Breukink won the stage, the aforementioned Andy Hampsten rode through the snow and into the warm glory of the Maglia Rosa (race leader's jersey), becoming the first, and as yet only, American to win the Italian Tour. Photos of Hampsten from that day are also part of cycling legend, the skinny Coloradoan riding over the pass looking more like the Abominable Snowman than a pro bike racer.

The plan that skulked inside the folder (or *The Folder of Doom*, as Drew re-named it post-Stelvio) displayed optimism, audacity and a shed-load of sheer naivety. Sitting on the sofa back in Edinburgh, slurping coffee, munching biscuits and idly flicking through maps and climb profiles, it had all seemed so easy. The cold hard truth of just one of those three giants had slapped us both back down to earth, a crash landing sufficient to shatter our dreams for the day and to edge us toward a trip re-group and re-think. It wasn't only the on-bike task we had underestimated, our calculations for the in-car time had also proved hideously inaccurate. We would press on with the trip, of course, but taking each day as it came, certain that with each new dawn we would be forced to lose a climb here and there from the sky-high masterplan.

***

That evening, somewhat disconsolate, we wandered around Trento in search of somewhere to eat. Both of our "usual" haunts were closed but we did eventually bumble upon a small pizzeria, graced by a six-foot-tall, effortlessly elegant waitress. (A few days away from our girlfriends and we were already falling in love with random waitresses, the word *bonk* back its tabloid meaning.) Her grumpy-yet-graceful service brought us equally good-looking and better-tasting food. Great pizza on our last night in Italy? It all made perfect sense. Well, something had to.

DAY 6:
CIAO DEVIAZIONE!

Leaving Trento (and Italy) was no tearful farewell, more a casual ciao. Ciao to the prison cell, the sweaty sheets and Minxy, left upon the damp, mosquito-stained wall for the next inmates to ogle. Ciao to all the new friends we never made, to the Pope Channel and breakfast as punishment. Ciao to Crazy-Cool who had sound-tracked our final prison breakfast with Jamiroquai, a musical move sure to destroy any thoughts of staying on. The girl at reception flashed me the sweetest smile as I returned the cell keys, the only cordiality I had encountered during five days inside. Flattery faded as I realised the coquettish gesture was but an indication of quite how pleased she was to see the back of me.

My sore throat had worsened overnight, a red-raw patch in the place where my tonsils used to be. The timing of our rest/transfer day was therefore welcomed, time for my body to fight the illness that was threatening, rather than fight for survival on a mountainside. Regular gargling with soluble aspirin relieved the discomfort but only long enough for me to chatter nervously to Drew about how my mild malaise *definitely* wouldn't develop, and that there really was *nothing* to worry about — *is there, Drew? Is there? Please tell me there's not!* His lack of response only fuelled my neurotic, hypochondriac panic.

We were soon cruising along the toll road to *libertie, egalitie, fraternitie* and a whole host of very big mountains. I'm an unashamed Francophile; the very prospect of being there gave me a buzz. What is it about France that I love so much? Could it all be down to the Tour? Did those three-week allotments of (televisual, half-hourly-highlighted) magic from the summers of my youth spark the flame of an eternal love affair? Is it the cheese, the wine, the words of Albert Camus or Jean Paul Sartre? Perhaps my enthusiasm can be blamed upon the French girl in the language programme we watched at school, my first serious infatuation.

Heat haze shimmered off the road as lorries bombed down the (in name only) slow lane, racing the ubiquitous caravans (always

Dutch and always in the fast lane). As the grey concrete whizzed beneath our wheels, I found time to sum up our Italian experience. Whatever the mountains of France held in store, surely nothing would be as alien and awe-inspiring as the Dolomites' silver-grey shards, nothing quite so precipitous as the Pampeago — please, oh please nothing as cold, wet and smelly as the Sella! We certainly hoped there would be nothing ahead more daunting than the Stelvio. For mile after relentless mile it had drained the energy and sapped the will, every metre of upward progress paid for in pain. When the road had finally broken free of the forest, it laid bare the majority of those dreaded (in our minds, infamous) hairpin bends, that tarmac scar slashed onto the barren mountainside like the result of an almighty Zorro's sword practise. The Stelvio had looked evil but in reality it was just a mountain road upon which we'd projected the iniquitous characteristic — and it might have been more enjoyable had us Scots not been quite so keen on Bertie.

An hour into the drive and the landscape, in any direction, was almost pancake-flat. Italy and its mountains had disappeared into the rear-view mirror, I feared forever. Would I one day return to the Dolomites, to the Italian Alps? I sure hoped so, already wanted to. In those high passes lay unfinished business: three quarters of the Sella Ronda, the Gavia and the Mortirolo, names from my Italian dream that would remain in the chimerical clouds until the day I returned to claim or be claimed. Despite those disappointments, leaving Italy also brought a sense of achievement: we had ridden some of the world's toughest, most beautiful climbs, and were well on our way to a whole host more.

***

On the outskirts of Milan, the autostrada's oncoming traffic had drawn to a complete standstill, a car on fire amongst the jam — thank the almighty god of the tollbooth we were going the other way. It was to prove the longest drive of our trip, (for once the dreaded schedule, in that Folder of Doom, had been correct), and tiresome enough without smoking traffic jams. As we switched the CD from Doves to The Stone Roses, the mountains loomed again. The combination of excitement at what was to come and the uplifting soundtrack proved infectious. Only getting hopelessly lost in Turin could have deflated the burgeoning mood. And that's exactly what happened next. The schedule's instructions/scientific equation left us bewildered, especially when none of its complicated calculations matched up with the lane options and road signs that actually lay ahead. We gambled on one of three exits and lost the bet. Our forfeit was to drive up and down a series of one-way streets, round and round in ever-frustrating, ever-decreasing circles, struggling not to deliberately crash the car and put an end to the collective stress.

Seconds from suicide, we pulled in at the side of the road, to catch breath and rearrange sanity, plumped once again upon heading in the assumed compass bearing of our destination. (No, you were supposed to bring the compass!) Eventually, at the end of a small one-way street (the seventy-eighth we'd driven along that day), we spotted upon the horizon a glimpse of greenery, what we hoped was one of the parks that our map had marked on the city's outskirts. Before long (make that another half-hour of hell) we stumbled upon the tangenziale and were somehow back on the autostrada to France. True to the theme so far, our trip's longest journey had turned out to be even longer than we had estimated. Just as well we hadn't scheduled any mountains for later in the day.

***

After what felt like weeks on the road, we crossed the border into France. With our transition came an almost instantaneous reduction in speed — from the land of the Ferrari to the land of the Citroen 2CV. We drove up the Col de Montgenèvre and dropped down the other side into Briançon. That pass is thought to have been used by Hannibal on his epic Trans-Alpine journey, and our traverse was as part of a similarly cumbersome caravan: a queue of cars backed up behind a convoy of articulated tanker lorries, giant beasts that crawled precariously, almost jack-knifing round each of the numerous hairpin bends.

Briançon instantly made a positive impression (after so much time spent in the car even Milton Keynes would have sufficed) and we quickly decided that opting to spend five nights in such a scenic spot couldn't possibly be a mistake, no matter the schedule's flaws.

With over 12,000 inhabitants, Briançon is the second largest town (or city, depending on who you ask) in the Haute-Alpes. The striking settlement is split in two: up on the hill the old town, dominated by a 17th Century fort; down in the valley below, the modern new town. Its position at over 1350 metres above sea level makes it the second-highest "city" in Europe, a gateway to the Serre-Chevalier region that's corralled by imposing peaks. A quick look at the map revealed a host of cycling legends. To the north and west the Lautaret, Galibier and Télegraphe; to the east the aforementioned Montgenèvre, and Sestrière; to the south Vars, Izoard and Agnel. No wonder Briançon has played host to so many Tour de France stages and, given its proximity to the Italian border, a good deal of Giro stages too. There's even a plaque upon the wall of the city gates commemorating legendary Italian cyclist Gino Bartali, winner of three race stages into the city.

If such inspiring surroundings aren't enough to attract, consider Briançon's boast that it enjoys over 300 days of sunshine per annum, that's more than most Brits see in a lifetime. Great weather is something a British cyclist does not easily take for granted, even one who had as yet failed to acclimatise to temperatures approaching forty degrees Celsius. The air felt considerably hotter than it had in Trento, as if the increased altitude had put us that bit closer to the sun's burning mass.

***

We checked in at the Hotel Edelweiss and met the owners, a couple whose names we either never learned or instantly forgot, quickly re-naming them Pat and Frank. Frank chatted in English, asked about our bikes, enthused sycophantically, as if Trek and Look were the only two bicycle brands on the planet worth bothering about. (In retrospect, I think it was patronising rather than sycophantic; Frank exaggeratedly interested and impressed as he might have been with a pair of kids showing off their first bikes.) However, on asking if we would be allowed to keep those sacred relics in our room we were given short shrift, instructed to deposit them in the garden shed next to Frank's beloved red tandem (an obviously cherished possession, but a tad less beloved than the shiny Harley Davidson he kept out front).

We worried about leaving our sweethearts in the distinctly low-security shed, the prospect of completing the trip sans steeds like an oar-less and boat-less paddle up the proverbial creek. (We weren't alone in our emotional attachment to inanimate objects. Many Tour riders have been known to keep their bikes in their hotel rooms between stages.) Frank attempted to allay our fears, insisted that taking the bikes to the bedroom was a no go, and that the shed would be locked at night. The smile vanished, the arms crossed and we felt no choice but to place our faith in the very tall, very burly and bearded Frenchman.

While our bikes settled in to their cobwebbed lodgings, we took a tour of our own, more salubrious surroundings, surveying the facilities like newly installed kings of the castle. Hotel Edelweiss surpassed our expectations, couldn't really have failed to provide a welcome break after five long nights in that Italian prison/hostel. The room itself was something else after the cell's cramped confines: clean and comfortable, proper (non-bunk) beds, a bathroom with a bath, a TV, a carpet and more than enough room to swing several-dozen cats. Minxy would have been mightily impressed.

On stepping out of the hotel, we faced a choice: walk uphill to the old town, or down to the less scenic new town. We opted for the former, as we'd spotted a few restaurants there on our drive down. The only snag with this selection was that the "hill" our hotel was halfway down (or up) was of a more severe gradient than any of the French climbs we intended to cycle — at least 20%. I shuddered to think how big the local newspaper-delivery boy's thighs might be.

Not only did our trek have to contend with the gradient, the wind also proved a factor, so strong and hot that within a few metres I was gasping. Although it felt like we were battling the hair dryer of some giant hilltop Vidal Sassoon, we were actually up against what's known in Alpine regions as a foehn wind. This phenomenon occurs when a deep layer of prevailing wind is pushed over the mountaintops. On its journey up-slope the air expands and cools, causing water vapour to precipitate out. This dry air then passes over the crest of the mountain and begins to move down slope. As it passes over the crest and down the leeward side of the mountain, the air comes under greater atmospheric pressure and heats up, creating a very strong, very warm and exceedingly dry wind. Foehn winds can rapidly raise temperatures by as much as thirty degrees and for that reason are often known as "snow-eaters" or "Rolf-killers".

With perfect comedy timing, Drew recalled having read that Briançon is a renowned health centre, its high altitude and extremely dry air seen as beneficial to the treatment of a variety of medical conditions. He pressed on, followed the anecdote with a suggestion that this exposure might help my sore throat. I was too busy drowning in sweat to offer a witty comeback, to propose that the local medics might actually be prescribing a walk up the hill as a form of euthanasia.

At the summit we found a settlement that reminded us of a smaller scale, but altogether brighter, version of Edinburgh's historic Old Town. We marched upward along the Grand Gargouille, drawn by the deliciously refreshing sound of water trickling along its small, freshwater canal. Just as with our home city's most elderly district, Briançon's is an authentically aged backdrop whose modern raison d'etre is the attraction and retention of tourists. The café prices were indicative of just such a purpose, painful on the wallet but strangely comforting: after sticking out like sore-tourist-thumbs in Trento, it was nice to be in an area aimed squarely at holidaymakers and their money.

The petite square and its eateries were bordered by a shanty town of souvenir stalls, every second one stocked with a burgeoning litter of toy marmots. A relative of the groundhog, the marmot is common to Alpine regions but hardly ever seen, usually evidenced only by its call, a sound like a helium wolf-whistle. (We still hadn't laid eyes on a real one and were beginning to wonder if the enigmatic creatures were really just the Alpine equivalent of Scotland's mythological Loch Ness monster.) Each of these more obvious toy marmots was equipped with a "cute" electronic whistle actuated by a motion sensor. With tourists continually flitting passed the stalls the litter was in constant song, the saccharine appeal of their sound lasting little more than thirty seconds. After five minutes, Drew and I were ready to begin a cull. Off switch duly located, (we found it hidden beneath a flap of the vermin's faux fur), we had successfully silenced an entire stall by the time the shopkeeper emerged from the shade to shoo us away.

***

After a period of rest (it was a rest day, after all), some napping, a bit more rest, some lazing around and a further bout of napping, we were still fatigued and in no mood to face a second fight with the foehn wind. Instead we turned tail and skipped down to the new town in search of our evening's nourishment. There we found a music festival in full swing, a gala with French folk songs, Euro pop, lots of beer and even more moules — so many moules that piles of discarded shells littered the streets.

The first band we encountered had a penchant for exceedingly bad hair and equally awful REM cover versions. The small crowd, each and every one shiny and happy, loved it, throwing beer down their necks and mussel shells over their shoulders in an unabashed show of joie de vivre. Round the corner, the crowd pulsed with a distinctly Euro excitement, the kind of cheery banality that brings a cringe to most Brit observers of the Eurovision Song Contest. People of every shape and size, every age and ability, were packed down either side of two long tables. Waitresses hurriedly delivered more beer and mussels to the sound of manic yelping, the populace high as kites, teetering on the verge of mass hysteria.

To say that Drew and I felt like strangers in a strange land would be under-egging the moule pudding. We were afraid and paranoid, our pasty cheeks flushed with embarrassment, unable to shake our obvious outsider status, convinced the locals were beginning to break from the revelry to stare (they were pointing at us too; we were sure of it but dared not look for fear of catching any eye). We vainly tried to blend in, hovered around two empty seats at the end of one of the tables, forcing smiles across our fear-streaked faces. Blocked in on all fronts by crowds of maniacal feasting, we stood transfixed, arms crossed, sweat pouring, eyes darting, dodging the heavy mussel-shell flack. What do those song lyrics mean, we wondered? Are they about us or are we being vain? Have we stumbled upon some kind of Alpine Wicker Man? There was only one thing to do: panic! We dodged a laden waitress, a duo of dancing octogenarians and darted through a gap in the crowd.

Relieved to have escaped with our lives, we death-marched into the receding foehn wind, back up the hill to the old town. Starving hungry, we slumped at the first available restaurant and plumped for the tartiflette. A quick check with the phrasebook revealed that this was a typical Alpine dish, involving layers of sautéed potatoes, lardons, onions, cream and all topped with cheese (usually Reblochon). Ours came served with plates of green salad, some cured ham and, thankfully, not a mussel in sight.

The menu had boasted two different versions of the dish and as Drew had chosen the more expensive "deluxe" version, and we'd be going Dutch on the bill, I'd had no choice but to follow suit. I quickly discovered (alerted by the awful smell) that the extra cost of this upgrade covered the substitution of the fruity Reblochon with a ripe, particularly putrid fromage de chèvre (you probably already know that means goats cheese; I didn't but I quickly learned and I will never forget). I was far from happy, stuttering pathetically around the verge of tears. It's already clear how I feel about stinking goats and their stinking cheese (*oh, Sella! Why have you cursed my existence with these infernal beasts?),* but I was also exceedingly hungry. Exhibiting more fear than I'd shown in the midst of the new-town's freaky festival, I scraped the reeking crust to one side, then over onto a neighbouring table, then out the door and down the street. Somehow, despite much retching, and much to Drew's amusement, I ate the remaining ingredients. Every mouthful brought whiffs of goat stink, the flavour infused through the rest of the dish, not to mention my skin and bones, on and into my very soul. Just like I'd done on the climbs of Italy, I dug deep and showed my mettle. Future challenges lay ahead but none would prove quite so demanding.

DAY 7:
THE RAIN MAN COMETH

Cime de la Bonette
Start point: Jausiers | Height: 2802m | Height climbed: 1589m
Length of climb: 24km | Average gradient: 6.6% | Maximum
gradient: 9%

Our first night in (comparative) luxury had involved a long
struggle to sleep before several hours of sweaty semi-slumber. We
stumbled down to breakfast feeling more tired than we had before
going to bed, wondering if the altitude of Europe's second-highest
city might already have taken its toll. Even thinking about the ride
that lay ahead was draining (despite us having decided to omit the
Col de Vars and "only" tackle the Bonette). We were also suffering
upset stomachs, entirely lacking hunger but required to fuel up for
the challenge ahead. So we sat down to force-feed on the highly
civilized continental spread, blissful silence (apart from intestinal
rumblings) in place of the prison soundtrack, a cafetière for the
coffee, dishwater reserved for the dishes.

We ruminated and stared out the window, mountains filling the
horizon in every direction. Quite an awe-inspiring and intimidating
view it was too, hard to digest given how tired we felt, harder to
conceive what it must have been like to live in Briançon centuries
before it was opened up to the world by roads and rail, electricity,
phones and television. Such obscure outposts must have been, and
felt, disconnected in every way, especially during winter, with no
news of outside events for weeks on end. For the people, the
mountain ranges and valleys would have been the world, a limited
perspective that probably lingered into the early days of the Tour
de France, its *Grande Boucle* coming to connect countryside and
capital city.

Walking back up the stairs after breakfast was an effort in itself,
adding to our worry over the coming climb. Could we, should we,
really be so tired, our legs so heavy? Had we already succumbed to

the trip's ordeal? The French Alps, the Pyrenees *and* Mont Ventoux lay ahead of us; we could ill afford to be exhibiting weakness (or cowardice) at such an early stage.

We manned up (well, almost) packed up, retrieved the bikes (thankfully, not stolen) from the shed and drove south toward Jausiers, the start of our daily allocation of up, up and a lot more up. We had decided to ease ourselves into the French climbs by tackling the 2715-metre-high Col de la Bonette and its 2802-metre-high Cime de la Bonette. That "duo" is actually just one climb, the Cime being a cheeky extension built onto the Col in order to gain the highest "through road" in Europe accolade. The Tour de France refers to this climb as Cime de la Bonette-Restefond and first raced it in 1962, when the suitably nicknamed Eagle of Toledo, Spaniard, Federico Bahamontes, was first to the top. Col or Cime, it was still a hell of a load of climbing, on a par with the almighty Stelvio and a challenge we would have preferred to be feeling fit for.

The drive to Jausiers took us up and over the Col de Vars, originally intended to be the day's warm-up ride but since struck from the schedule. First tackled by the Tour in 1922, it might not enjoy a most fearsome reputation but it was reputed to be the scene of tears from French Tour-legend, and Breton hard-man, Bernard Hinault, emotion brought on by the pain of a knee injury during the 1986 race. That was apparently the only time he ever cried on a bike, probably the only time he has ever cried full stop, the first and last time his tear ducts dared to disobey orders.

From our in-car position of comfort the Vars looked like a decent, scenic sort of affair, with plenty of hairpin corners to keep the cyclist occupied. A quick glance up from down below and you would clearly see the road above, taunting or tempting the legs. I might have noticed more but, like Drew, was too distracted, partly by the looming Bonette, mostly by queasy, uneasy guts. We were crunching down peppermint anti-nausea tablets like they were going out fashion, our stomachs barely staying put, each rock and roll of the road further bleaching already sheet-white faces.

One other thing I did notice was the Var's Napoleonic refuge, built back when the Tour de France wasn't even a twinkle in Henri Desgrange's eye. Just as various emperors and armies had once tackled and attempted to master the land (and its population), through the act of riding up we too were, in some personal way, attempting to tame the climb. We rode through its villages and pastures, we breathed its air, smelled its everyday smells, saw its myriad sights, felt its ambience. We sweated, heaved and hauled bodies and bikes on high, turning mystique into hard physical reality. Legends reduced to personal experience — in Drew's case, to numbers, lengths, gradients and percentages — to be more readily consumed, mountains broken into bite-sized chunks, chopped down with the pedals beneath our feet.

I considered what the cols might mean to the locals. More than likely they were viewed in practical terms, as roads connecting village to neighbouring village, and from there to the wider world. The tarmac in and out of town might well be a Tour icon, an infamous sporting battleground, but for 364 days of the year it really was just a road — no stories, no heroes, just a road. The legends Drew and I sought belonged to another sphere of reference altogether.

When I thought about it too much, and during our long drives I was inclined to wallow in contemplation, I worried that we might be spoiling the climbs, ruining them for ourselves, somehow diluting their magic. What if our actions were stripping away the layers, removing the sporting sheen, only to reveal dull tarmac beneath? Would we watch all future Tours' TV coverage and, as the jaws of those around us dropped in awe, say, "I've ridden that. It's just a road"? Probably not; I certainly hoped not. That wasn't the way things had gone in the case of the Stelvio, the Marmolada or Pampeago. No mere roads, those brutal climbs were now etched upon muscles and memories. I optimistically concluded that we were reinforcing the myths, adding precious layers of personal perspective to each of the sporting stories.

It wasn't long before the pyramid peak of the Bonette had grown to fill the windscreen, dazzling like the full-beam headlights of an oncoming car. Even from far away it looked like another world, a fairytale kingdom up in the clouds, hanging enigmatic like the product of a cinematic special-effects studio, another amazing mountain we were about to try and tame.

***

By the village of Jausiers, the temperature had risen so high that even getting the bikes out of the car proved exhausting. It had to be the warmest day of our trip so far, and it was still only mid-morning. We'd be near the summit by around lunchtime, the hottest part of the day — assuming we hadn't already been cooked alive. Pockets packed with bananas, jam-filled croissants, inner tubes and rain jackets (for protection from the wind come the descent), we did some stretching, poured (unappetisingly warm) water into bottles, checked tyre pressures, fumbled around for my asthma inhaler and applied the sun block. Last task was another round of anti-nausea tablets, both of us worried about a dramatic loss of ballast at the foot of the climb.

For the first few kilometres the simple act of breathing was enough to keep us occupied. The constant drone from the twin cycles of gasping in and wheezing out reverberated from our baking bodies, a respiratory racket to compete with the noise of innumerable cicadas. Welcome distraction from that combined cacophony came with the stunning scenery. Stretched shimmering to the far horizon was our first from-the-bike taste of the French Alpine landscape, great smooth swathes of verdant pasture that proved a distinct contrast to the Dolomites' sharp, grey-blue lines and aggressive, rocky shards.

Despite green waves of grass aplenty, for some reason this still felt like a land more arid than Italy, a landscape suffering beneath the sun, like Heidi with heatstroke. The valley down to our right was filled with coniferous trees and scrub that improbably eked out an existence along the banks of a bone-dry riverbed. Similar valleys we'd seen in Italy, such as that of the Stelvio's Solda, had roared with crisp, white water. Here it was dusty and dry, waiting patiently for melting snow or unseasonable rain.

As our breathing relaxed into the task, the noise from the cicadas took over. It sounded like they had congregated in certain sections, great, unseen chattering herds like giant insect generators, as if their tumult alone was all that kept the sun in the sky and the mountains upright. The cicada's song is only made by the males, as a mating call and a distraction to their main predators, produced by a pair of ribbed membranes at the base of their abdomen. The contraction of muscles attached to those causes an inward buckling, producing a pulse of sound that's as evocative of European summer holidays as the waspish buzz of the Vespa and the smell of tanning lotion.

An additional insect nuisance soon usurped the cicadas' distraction. A U.F.C. (unidentified flying creature), something like a large, brown fly, landed on my cheek, took a bite, drew blood and flew off toward Drew. There followed a yelp and the slap of a miss-timed swat hitting swatter's thigh, sounds that sent a signal around the valley to mystery insect's friends, family and neighbours. Within minutes we each had our own small swarm of U.F.C.s, landing, biting, dodging the swat, on and on, one after the other, this species' sole purpose to harass unsuspecting cyclists on their way up the mountain. Whilst neither of us was particularly amused, Drew was most aversely affected, becoming so distracted that he forgot all about his laboured breathing and veered off toward the outer limits of his sanity. Flapping hands this way and that, he brushed off one attack as another landed, shouting as if the tiny creatures could compute, as if they'd ignore the attraction of his salty sweat and politely acquiesce. The only answer was to pick up the pace, to try and drop the wee buggers — not ideal when we'd been trying to consolidate our energies for what remained of the 24-kilometre climb.

Although the mystery insects proved an irritating nuisance, their bites didn't appear to be in any way poisonous. We would have been more concerned had they been wasps or bees, neither of us ever having been stung before and in no way keen to find out on the slopes of a mountain if we were allergic. During the 2001 Tour a bee stung Jonathan Vaughters, the American rider and now manager of pro team Garmin. His face swelled until he bore a distinct resemblance to the Elephant Man, but anti-doping regulations prevented him from using a corticosteroid to reduce the inflammation, and in order to receive treatment he was forced to abandon the race.

To complete the insect theme, I estimated about an extra kilometre would be added onto my ascent by an insistence on veering wildly around the road in order to dodge the many butterflies that lay twitching on the hot tarmac. They had probably been blown there, buffeted along on thermal currents before being deposited like confetti as they reached cooler air further up the mountain. I thought it criminal to crush their multi-coloured, delicate wings under-tyre and so swerved around in avoidance, like a drunkard after a week in the pub. Swearing, swatting, twisting and turning; to the casual observer we must have looked like the archetypal midday-sun mad dogs.

It took the Col's roadside signs to bring us back to the task in hand, reminding that we were cyclists and not pest controllers, cyclists attempting to tackle the highest through road in Europe. Those blatant beacons made no secret of the total altitude to be climbed or how far we were from the summit. Forewarned is forearmed but given that I had "Rain Man" Drew riding shotgun there was little chance of missing the detail of the task at hand. Drew, who has always had a flair for memorising facts and figures, had spent much of his off-the-bike time using that gift to mentally store every last digit of the data our Folder of Doom held on each of the climbs. As a result we knew how long, how far and what was left in store; whether it was easier round the next bend or tougher; if we had already conquered the worst bit or if that joy was yet to come; just how far we had climbed above sea level and how much higher we would get. All that information and more was delivered on a loop, Drew unwittingly morphed into Dustin Hoffman's Raymond Babbitt, whilst I, by default, was a less chiselled but far taller version of Tom Cruise's Charlie.

As the tree line dropped away below, Rain Man Drew spewed forth the data, a staccato stream of numbers and positions, details that left us equally breathless. Rather than making me feel in control, the informational overload added pressure. Knowledge is power but sometimes too much can hurt, and hurt it did. Unaware or unconcerned, he kept at it, uttering numbers and mumbling warnings.

"First kilometre only 2.2% average gradient. Only 2.2, only 2.2, that's easy, that's easy. Next kilometre 5.5%, much tougher. 3.2 more, 3.2 more. Fourth kilometre 7%, much worse. 7% is much worse. Watch out, warning, better watch out! Seventh kilometre 8.5%. 8.5%. Much worse. Warning! 8.5%. 18 kilometres to go, 18 to go. 18 kilometres, that's 11.1852 miles. 11.1852 miles, that's tough, that's tough! And there's still a 9%, there's still a 9%. Better look out, better look out there's a 9% section coming. The 15th kilometre, that's 9% ... ."

As we ascended, the vegetation further thinned, revealing the road ahead and high above — always so high above — sliced across the mountain to disappear round a far-off bend. After what felt like days of effort we reached that bend, only then to go through the same rigmarole all over again: another far-off bend always waiting to be reached, another stream of data ready to be released.

"Leave me alone!" I bellowed at the tenth signpost (in place of shouting at Drew).

Whose great idea was it to put up those bloody signs? The person responsible was surely in cahoots with Drew and his attempts to slay me with statistics. They had a vendetta against me, there was no denying it. All the signs lacked was a banner at the top that read,

"Attention Rolf! Regardez la! Get a load of these numbers!"

I wanted to switch off, to zone out from the dastardly data and yet I needed to measure my effort, gauge how much to expend but still leave enough in reserve to reach the summit.

In competition with that mental hurt came pain in my lower back. This worrying discomfort was an infliction from which I had suffered mainly as a teenager, the result of having a long spine and weak core muscles. Having a mother who is also a physiotherapist had always had its benefits and she'd given me exercises, which, if practised regularly, kept the issue at bay. Problem was I hadn't done the exercises, for years. When it did come, the pain wasn't particularly intense, more of a dull ache, but sufficient to sap the energy from my torso and thighs. I wondered how long my back would hold, how long before I'd have to bale out into first gear and soft-pedal.

Despite that nuisance, I settled in and even began to enjoy the climb. It helped that the higher we rose, the more pleasant the conditions became. Green pasture opened up in every direction, with only the winding road, small streams and the occasional patch of picnicking tourists to disturb the vast emerald surface. Blasts of cold air came down the mountain, pushing the baking heat away from us and back to the valley below. The rush of cool sent shivers and ripples of sensation that left me exhilarated, breathless and carpeted with goose-bumps. By then the cicadas had faded away, Rain Man Drew and the mystery-insect invaders had run out of steam, leaving only the clink-clink of pendant bouncing off jersey zip and the slurp-slurp of our attempts to remain hydrated.

This easing of the landscape, temperature and tempo had a calming effect on our mood. No longer were we battling Europe's highest through road; this was little more than a casual bike ride in Alps. Such serenity was in complete control by the time we reached the old military barracks of Casernes de Restefond, at about five kilometres to go, an accepted sense of safety in tow with the knowledge that we had very nearly conquered the climb. Additional succour came when Drew informed me that the last section wouldn't get much above a 6% gradient and that there was even a section of 3% to look forward to. With that certainty grew the casual acceptance of our place atop Europe, confidence coming with every turn of the pedals.

In contrast to our increased comfort (should that really be, decreased discomfort?) came a growing harshness to the landscape. All that green grass was replaced by barren slopes of scree that fell sharply away from the roadside, as if the land was now struggling to keep hold of the mountaintop. Devoid of beauty, those higher reaches were all about altitude, the Bonette not there to entertain with its elegance or to impress with gregarious geological formations. It was very high up, that's what it did best, altitude the be all and end all.

As we cruised closer to the pinnacle, the shallow gradient (that 3% section of Drew's prediction) provided the impression that the road was actually descending a touch. We picked up speed, zipped along as the thin line of tarmac shot away from under our front wheels, stretched tenuously toward the very edge where mountain met sky. It felt instantly precarious, definitely dangerous, like riding along a tightrope strung high above the French countryside. We paused for a digger that was shovelling fallen rocks from the edge of the road whilst performing precarious three-point turns. The scene was so obviously at altitude I half expected the driver to be wearing a space suit, but he should definitely have been wearing a parachute, just in case. The road kicked up again for a few added minutes of pain (who were we to argue) and that was that — we had reached the summit safe in the knowledge that no other peak we encountered on our way was going to be quite so high up, nor quite so breathtaking.

Cold and inhospitable but as usual this was a summit surrounded by a gaggle of motorcyclists. Most of their handlebars ported a laminated list, their schedule of climbs, obstacles to be greedily gobbled under diesel-driven tyres. They were following the Route des Grande Alpes, first conceived at the turn of the last century by the Touring Club of France. The 680km Route begins in the northern Alps near Lake Geneva (Lac Léman) on the Franco-Swiss border and travels south to Menton on the French Riviera, taking in plenty of the most famous cols along the way — including cycling legends such as the the the Col de l'Iseran, the Col du

Galibier and, of course, the Bonette. It would have been ungracious for us to begrudge those bikers their summit swarm, given that many of the mountainous routes taken by the Tour de France only exist in their modern, asphalted form because of the Touring Club of France and their efforts to open the Alps to *all* of the people.

A shot of the summit monument (a giant lump of rock with a plaque bolted to its side) almost biker-free, and we teetered toward the edge of the road in order to fully absorb the view. There was a vista truly frightening — we were actually looking down on vast mountain ranges. They rippled all around like rows of shark's teeth, its mouth open, ready to consume any creature daft enough to swim too close. At that moment it was nigh on impossible to imagine that there was anything else on the planet but mountains — forests, rivers, beaches, towns, cities, houses and the people in them, all temporarily consigned to myth and memory. Carried away by the moment, I imagined us as mountaineers, conquerors of the world's highest peak, two men who'd (almost) left the planet behind, its detail so far below as to be unintelligible. Add in the knowledge that we'd reached such extremity under our own steam and the sensation was literally awesome.

***

Rain jackets on to keep off the cold wind, we turned and were soon gathering speed with every metre of the descent. Hurtling toward infinity, the road's open edge rushed toward us, a fall from the outer limits of a flat planet lying in wait for anyone unlucky enough to misjudge the bend. Some of those drops looked horrific, others the sure-fire route to an untimely death. I was heavily onto the brakes on the entrance to the sharpest corners, and much sooner than necessary, not just to slow me down but as a reminder that I was in control of the mountain and not vice versa. The Col, which had come upon us in (at times grinding) gradual increments, now vanished in a frightening blur, the upper section through the scree slopes gone quicker than I could say, "slow down Drew, I'm scared!". As the air warmed slightly, we flew through the pasture, following an impossibly twisty path, like some heat-seeking ordinance escaped from the old army outposts.

In those lower and less extreme surroundings we relaxed enough to enjoy the plummeting process. Whilst sinuous, the road was a touch wider and entirely open, allowing us to look far ahead

— three, four and more corners in advance — making it safe to take the fastest, racing lines, the way Tour riders descend. And that fun was no momentary flash. Given how long the ascent had taken, it made perfect sense that its opposite seemed to go on, and on, and on ... .

Drew commented later that when travelling at speed (around fifty miles an hour) he had imagined he could hear every little noise his bike emitted, as if able to sense the minute stresses and strains being placed on each nut and bolt, each link of the chain, each millimetre of carbon fibre and aluminium. He struggled to concentrate on his lines through the corners, more concerned that a wheel was about to unravel or the entire bike to disintegrate beneath him. (Luckily, Mr Trek and his bicycle corporation had done more than enough R&D to ensure such a disaster did not occur.)

When descending at high speed it's best to disconnect your brain, not literally, of course (that could prove messy, and fatal). In essence, you shouldn't really think at all, just stay loose and allow the bike to flow around the bends. The more you think, the more you fear, the stiffer you get and the worse you'll ride. The aim is not to think about crashing, just ride within your limits and visualise a positive, silky smooth descent.

At such speed, cycling feels like flying and we really were riding by the seat of our (synthetic) chamois pants. My front brakes began to squeal with the heat — I could have fried an egg on the rim's breaking surface had I not forgotten to take a dozen free-range with me up the mountain. (One thing to note, whilst we often hung our helmets on the handlebars for the hot and slow ascents, they always returned to our heads for the descents. At speeds like that, and on roads like those, I would have been too scared not to wear mine.)

As we plummeted, the road returned to obscurity, blind corners making the racing lines distinctly inadvisable. Leaning heavily over, applying that newly discovered counter steer, we stuck to our side of the road, forced our bikes through the tightest bends. We cruised on into the warm air of the lower valley and instantly began to sweat, cooking inside our rain capes like boil-in-the-bag fish. I unzipped, half expecting a wash of cool air but instead endured a blast of dry heat. Jackets flapping, we raced through the deserted town, no one around to witness our heroic return, the locals still hiding from the sun.

Back at the car, we collapsed into two plastic chairs that had been abandoned in the shade outside Jausier's only bar — an oasis that was firmly closed for whatever constitutes the French equivalent of siesta. By then we both felt *really* sick, as compared to the earlier bog-standard sick. We'd been so busy concentrating on the ascent, the cicadas, the mystery insects, the gradient, the on and on and up and up, the descent, the death-defying corners, the sizzling rims and creaking wheels, that we'd somehow mislaid the malady.

After a short rest and some water, the biggest waves of my nausea had settled but Drew's were still crashing in and over; he was feeling worse than he had after breakfast and we'd long-since munched the last of the peppermint tablets. We observed the ants that swarmed over a nearby boulder — *wait a sec', I just found myself a bleedin' metaphor!* — the tiny insects' frenzied activity upon the huge mass of rock comparable to our scramble up the mountain. Well, almost. Difference was, the ants were seeking a source of food, theirs a matter of survival; our escapades fed nothing more than curiosity and egotistical desire. No matter how much it had felt that way at the time — the pain screaming against a stubborn refusal to stop — we had no actual need to achieve the summit, nothing at all to prevent our turning around and freewheeling back down the mountain.

As I relaxed with the ants, Drew returned to the car, to flick through the Folder of Doom and its overly ambitious, semi-kaput schedule. Pained expression writ large, he laboriously turned the pages, as if *reading about* was the equivalent to *riding up* each climb, twice over with a buckled wheel and a pedal missing. He tortured himself with the steepest gradients, the longest climbs and the worst drives, before throwing the folder aside with a sigh. A few moments would pass, during which he'd huff, puff and fire an accusatory glare in my direction, only to snatch the folder back up and go through it all again.

Worryingly — for me that is — he was now referring to *the* folder as *your* folder, suggesting that not only the black ring-binder and its paper contents, but the very motivation behind our travel and travails belonged solely to me. The trip had shifted in his perception, was now sliding dangerously away from being considered an adventure and headed toward something that resembled a severe form of corporal punishment. What had wholeheartedly been *our* mountainous dream was turning into the stuff of *his* nightmares, and it was all my fault.

As for how to arrest said decline, I had no idea. I did know Drew well enough to be aware that when his mind was made up on something it usually remained resolute; and when he perceived that he had suffered some slight or wrongdoing he couldn't, *wouldn't* allow himself to forget, would dwell upon the matter until the valve on his pressure cooker eventually blew. For him to be thinking of the trip as a me-against-him situation was not good. Not good at all.

One Friday a couple of years back I had made the most tentative arrangement to meet up with him for drinks following a works dinner. To say it had been a supremely shaky plan was to put it mildly. He hadn't even been certain he wanted to go out in the first place, and I had been pretty much set on going home straight after the dinner — so, in essence, there probably weren't even going be any drinks to meet up for. I'd thought nothing more of "the arrangement" until my mobile rang in the middle of dessert.

"Why haven't you called me?" Drew demanded to know. "I've been ready and waiting for hours but you haven't called. I'm passed the point of even wanting to go out now but by the sounds of things you're all having a great time there without me. You've ruined my night, my weekend, my life! Thanks for nothing!" Or words to that effect.

He'd hung up the phone and then quickly tossed his irrational upset into the pressure cooker. There it had stayed to simmer and stew in its own juices until, within a matter of days, he was acting like I'd forgotten to invite him to my wedding, killed his granny and, worst of all, sold his bike for a tenner on eBay. Weeks passed without us talking, a stand-off that lasted until I capitulated, called him up to grovel apologetic. I promised never again to do whatever it was I was supposed to have done, the thing I probably hadn't done in the first place (of course I hadn't done anything wrong; I'm faultless, beyond reproach, right?).

"I'm so, so, so, eternally sorry. Please forgive me!" Or words to that effect.

If that was how he had reacted to a missed night out then how bad would things be should he convince himself that *our* trip was actually *his* punishment and that I was the one administering the abuse? Very bad, was my educated guess.

So, for the sake of his, mine, and the trip's survival, I would have to try and distract from any negativity and to generally keep his spirits up. It would be hard to cajole someone along on a cycling holiday they didn't want to be on, harder still to enthuse them toward the top of a 3,000-metre mountain. It was a struggle enough to keep my own spirits aloft, to talk my own subconscious round each time it strayed toward black thoughts, to wondering what the hell all this hurt was in the name of and why the hell we weren't lying on a beach drinking cold beer and ogling hot girls.

If only I could return Drew to that night in the pub, to that Reekie reverie when the (in his mind, harsh) reality we were now living was still but a giddy dream. Not only had he lost (or was rapidly losing) sight of where we were — in France, on the trip of a lifetime — he was also forgetting that the schedule wasn't a legally binding document. It was nothing more imposing than the shaky plan we'd drawn up in Edinburgh, back in that rosy, alcohol-inspired, caffeine-fuelled time when we'd boasted of riding every major climb in Europe. We'd been like kids in a candy shop, "I'll have that, and that, need one of those, need that, two of those big ones, ooh and that one too," greedily grabbing names off the map and stuffing them into our gobs without adequately considering how hard they would be to consume individually, let alone in conjunction.

Drew was now ticking those mighty names from our wish list as if it was a countdown to his own demise, but it didn't have to be that way. We might have bitten off more than we could comfortably chew but there was no reason why our break away should descend into a runaway nightmare. During our impromptu post-Stelvio review we'd already agreed that the schedule was flexible, that it could and would be changed to suit the available time and energy of each new day; it was up to us to shape it into something manageable and worthwhile — more importantly, into something enjoyable.

By the time Drew's nausea turned to dry baulking we realised there was probably more to his symptoms than plain fatigue. We'd stayed overnight in Europe's second-highest city, had just ridden its highest through road — surely some of what we felt could be attributed to the effects of altitude? I sent a text to my mountaineer mate, Glenn, pretty certain he'd be able to advise us on the symptoms of altitude sickness. Not that I knew what we'd do if he confirmed the diagnosis.

***

We were resting back at the hotel when I received the text with Glenn's reply. Our symptoms did match those of altitude sickness: headaches; nausea; vomiting; dizziness; malaise; insomnia; loss of appetite. He suggested that our altitude at Briançon was at the low threshold for heights that could cause the condition, but that riding up to near-on 3,000 metres would only have exacerbated matters. He suggested resting until we had become acclimatised; only then get back on the bikes. I read the text to Drew and then slumped back down on the bed. Rest was easy, rest we could do.

It was possible that we had indeed been suffering mild cases of altitude sickness, Drew's a tad less mild than mine. The general advice was to ascend by increments to higher altitudes (too late for that), avoid overexertion (also too late), eat light meals (our appetites had only just returned, so why should we be further punished?) and avoid alcohol (come on, you're getting ridiculous now). Doctor Rae-Hansen knew of only one real cure and ordered his patients to take a stroll downhill (lower altitude, you see) for crêpes filled with cheese, sour cream, mushrooms, sautéed potatoes and ham, for it all to be washed down with a glass or three of (purely medicinal) vin rouge.

The previous evening's gala thankfully over, the place felt comfortingly quiet. The mussel-shell slag heaps had long since been swept away, no need to avoid eye contact with the dancing maniacs, no bad-haired Michel Stipe lurking round the next corner to scare us witless. Relieved to be almost alone, and at least another hundred feet closer to sea level, we slumped outside a restaurant and waited patiently for a waitress to arrive. The heat of the day had almost completely blown away — there one minute, gone the next — as if someone had flicked the off switch. A dusky wind kicked around our heels, blowing out the old day, sweeping the land clean and refreshing us into the bargain.

DAY 8:
MINE'S A LANSLEBURGER

Mont Cenis
Start point: Lanslebourg | Height: 2081m | Height climbed:
682m | Length of climb: 9.84km | Average gradient: 6.9%
Maximum gradient: 10.6%

As a result of the previous day's malady we decided to move
our next rest day forward, but to replace complete inactivity with a
leisurely jaunt up the slopes of Mont Cenis. This would, hopefully,
allow us to overcome the alleged altitude sickness but still keep our
legs ticking over. Following the post-Stelvio collapse of the
schedule, and Drew's post-Bonette onset of dread, each day would
be taken as it came. We had reached an understanding that all the
remaining climbs on the original long-list weren't even likely to be
attempted, let alone achieved. Some of the days with multiple
scheduled climbs would be whittled down to leave just the biggest,
most famous name or names. Others, that created complete
logistical and physical nightmares, would be scrubbed entirely, we
hoped with minimum of shame and disappointment. The aim was
to find a balance between enjoyment, exertion and impossibility,
and to remove the heavy weight of expectation that hung over
Drew's head like the polished blade of Madame Guillotine.

Exhaustion brought on by the stroll from the breakfast room to
the bedroom highlighted the sense in our decision to push the
mighty Col d'Izoard back a day in favour of Mont Cenis and its
lesser challenge. The queasiness had abated but we'd suffered
another night of fitful sleep (not that any interruption could be
attributed to the wine, of course), and I was also holding on to the
sore throat developed in Italy, although it did seem to be on the
wane (a recovery surely attributable to the previous evening's
grape-based tonic). As for Mont Cenis, neither of us could quite
recall why it had made it on to the schedule. It wasn't exactly a
legendary Tour climb, certainly wasn't one we had known much

about before, or even after we had planned the trip. Drew remembered having read that the views from the top were really beautiful, which was all nice enough but still didn't explain the selection. However it got there, on paper it wasn't a particularly arduous ordeal and so wouldn't go completely against the carefree spirit of our rest day. Mont Cenis in the morning would leave us time to get back to Briançon, have a post-ride wander, buy some souvenirs (bite the bullet and buy a toy marmot), maybe even go the whole hog and write some postcards: *wish you were here, but in all honesty, it's probably better that you're not.*

***

We headed out on the convoluted drive (yeah, another one) that would take us up and over the Col de Montgenèvre, down into Italy and then back into France via the Tunnel de Fréjus. The morning light was crystal-clear and the air, not quite up to temperature, tasted fresh, as if cleansing the lungs with every breath. I got to wondering if that was the reason we liked to cycle — not for the physical challenge or the adrenaline rush but for more pastoral motivations. Did we ride to connect with amazing landscapes, in order that we could so directly and exactly feel the world around us? The hills were already alive (not a cue for singing nuns), with a myriad of other outdoorsy types: ramblers, runners, climbers and cyclists, all applying sun block, buying bread for their picnics, getting ready for their own encounters with Mother Nature and all her glory.

We dropped down the pass, toward the border with Italy, to a checkpoint that was swarming with guards. Whilst signalled at to slow down, we weren't actually stopped, as many others had been, thanks to our hire car having Italian plates (because of which we'd decided to assume dual "Bri-talian" nationality). The contents of numerous car boots had been scattered to the winds in a frantic search for some kind of contraband. It was, we surmised, most likely one of the authorities' regular wars on marmot smuggling. We'd read that eastern-European gangs made a lucrative trade in smuggling the superior French marmots into the rest of Europe, selling them on the black market without paying so much as a cent in live-animal duty. (The French marmot is highly coveted for its extremely loud whistle, up to five times louder than the call of an ordinary Italian or Austrian marmot.) As the border guards probably knew, and as the smugglers didn't care, the real concern was that before long there wouldn't be any French marmots left in France. (And if you believe any of that nonsense then you'll believe that I totally *adore* goats cheese.)

Further on we came to a splintering bunch of older male cyclists, crawling uphill and scattered along the road in ones and twos. As we approached, Drew informed me that,

"Those guys will never make it as pros. They're too old, you see? They've left it too late."

"What insight!" I exclaimed. "You have the mind of a cycling genius. You can spot talent a mile off. You're the new Cyrille Guimard, or something like that."

"You're right," he continued, acknowledging my sarcasm and coming back with some more of his own. "I'd make a great coach. Only an expert like me can spot the small details that tell if a rider has what it takes. And it's not just a cycling mind, I have an eye for it too."

One of the frailest men I have ever seen riding a bicycle, was furthest off the back of the bunch, almost travelling in reverse, perhaps hoping to slip away unnoticed and home to his bed.

"Just give up now, mate," Drew offered his advice to the befuddled grand-père through the open window. "You'll never make the Tour, you're wasting your time — more importantly, you're wasting *my* time."

A little further up the road we came to another, slightly younger, slightly more vital gent.

"Lose the beard and you might just make it," Drew's impudent advice bounced haughtily into the hirsute Frenchman's ear, and quickly out the other side. "Remember, aerodynamics are key!"

Those gents might not have been sporting gods but they certainly were sardonic superstars, turned out in an amazing array of retro kit — not replicas, most likely stuff bought way back when the gang (and Eddy Merckx) were still racing. A few of them sported huge seventies sunglasses that dwarfed their faces like twin satellite dishes, relics from the days when Oakley Factory Pilots were but a twinkle in Jim Jannard's eye. At the head of affairs were another couple whose garb looked even older, apparently wearing woollen jerseys, woollen shorts and, could that really be a woollen Campagnolo chainset?

Equally old-school were their bikes: steel frames that appeared distinctly deficient in comparison to the modern, chunky carbon fibre and alloy we've become used to. The spindly tubes looked impossibly fragile but the evidence of their longevity was obvious for all to see. The shock of seeing those "relics" brought home just how much bicycle design has evolved since I first started cycling. Things didn't really change until mountain biking came along. The first off-road steeds were the playthings of Californian pioneers who, after initial attempts at modifying cruisers, took matters into their own hands and built bikes to suit the specific needs of their novel sport. By the late 1980s, those pioneering spirits had sparked a wildfire of innovation. It seemed like every few months that another piece of radically new kit hit the market; new frames, suspension, gearing systems, brakes and pedals, nothing was left unchanged. The west-coast flames spread far and wide and eventually crossed disciplines, enthusing the skinny tyres of the road-bike market — why should the muddy types get all the new kit and, more importantly, why should the companies who sell the kit to the muddy types make all the money?

It's either an after-effect of all that accelerated advancement or evidence of the increased influence of manufacturers' marketing departments, but every year the road bike you own becomes "obsolete", as lighter, stronger, faster, allegedly better-working kit is rolled out in a glare of publicity at bike shows from London to Las Vegas. The veterans we passed on the road to Mont Cenis were proof positive that there's more to cycling than constant consumption and that the latest in technology isn't always strictly necessary. Just get out there and ride, woollen shorts, beard and all.

***

We reached the Tunnel du Fréjus, shocked to discover that a drive through (and back) was going to cost us €36.50. Trying not to look like tight-fisted Scots (it proved a struggle, even in a car with Italian number plates), we asked the girl in the booth what exactly we were going to get for the excessive cost? Would there be topless dancers perched on our bonnet all the way through? Would Jean Michel Jarre be popping up with a laser light show at the midway point? At the very least we expected complimentary snacks and beverages. Instead of any of that we got one hell of a long, ghostly orange, freaky mother-f***er of a tunnel.

At the entrance was a sign with instructions in four languages, the English part of which read, "*declare yourself!*"

What were we to say? "We are tight-fisted Scottish cyclists

unhappy at the cost of using your tunnel. We might be suffering from altitude sickness or we might just be unfit and a little cowardly. And, by the way, we haven't smuggled any marmots."

There was one escape refuge for every few-hundred metres the entire length of the tunnel. I wondered what chance there would be of surviving a big fire, even supposing you made it into such a refuge, and what the hell was in there that could possibly help? Did they have smaller, vertical tunnels with ladders leading up to safety on the mountaintop? An asbestos will-making kit, or a meat thermometer so you could tell when you were done? With thoughts like that, the further in we ventured the more intensely discomfiting the tunnel became; it was panic-making, knowing that you couldn't turn around (U-turns are expressly forbidden), that there were miles and miles of tunnel in front and behind, miles and miles of impenetrable rock on all other sides.

It took 13 years to build the first Fréjus tunnel and, despite the unsettling nature of the journey provided, one has to admit that it really is an amazing feat of engineering. Why climb all that way over a mountain when you can bore your way through it? (That sounds like the title for a new Channel 5 series.) And what a long way it was, 13 kilometres that felt like an awful lot more. Thankfully, just as Drew was about to fall asleep at the wheel, hypnotised by the long string of orange lights and the uneasy quiet, we were reborn, once again in France (border re-crossed at the tunnel's midway point).

***

We parked up in Lanslebourg (a name, for some reason, we couldn't help but say in an exaggerated, drawling American accent) for the start of the Col du Mont Cenis. The length of drives to the climbs (that one having been exceedingly long and even longer than predicted, just like all the bloody drives) had provided us with further perspective as to the enormity of the challenge presented by the Tour de France. Most stages are at least 150 kilometres long and some of the mountain stages are well over 200 kilometres. It would be arduous enough to drive those distances day after day; to cover them on a bicycle must surely count as an inhuman undertaking. The longest ever Tour de France stage was during the 1920 event, a 482-kilometre monster from Les Sables d'Olonne to Bayonne — a lunatic task that betrays the sadistic spirit at the heart of the Tour's beginnings.

By that point we were both hungry and, on being unable to find anywhere that served Lansleburgers (get it? Oh, never mind), we ducked in to a small bakery in search of a rolle du saucisson. At €2.60 our pastry snack proved a bit pricier than the British Greggs variety but a whole lot tastier. The woman behind the counter was equally delectable: exquisitely, gorgeously French, and so very un-Greggs. (Note to self: make sure to delete that comment before allowing Gaby to read this diary.)

The Col du Mont Cenis made its Tour de France début in 1949, with Pierre Joseph Tacca first man to the top, and has been raced another four times since. From the outset of our ride, Drew appeared to be under the illusion that we were at the head of the Tour's latest ascent (or was he trying to get it all over and done with as quickly as possible, keen to get back to resting?). In no mood to ease us in, he ratcheted up to an obscenely high tempo, driving the speed through the roof in order to blow away all but his strongest adversaries — I struggled just to ride along in his slipstream. We averaged well over 20kph for the first three kilometres and then, *thankfully*, the elastic snapped. The incline steepened, the heat turned more oppressive, and we were suddenly going much, *much* slower. Drew peeled off from the front, his duty done, sadly no superstar in the wheel to follow through and take up the charge.

Apparently Cenis was a pass we had Napoleon to thank for, and it appeared that the road hadn't been tended to since the bogeyman and his armies last strode the continent. The surface was very poor, the lower sections almost akin to a typical Edinburgh road (I'm exaggerating, they weren't quite *that* bad). I was disappointed; it's not what one demands when one has taken the effort to leave Britain with one's bicycle and do a spot of mountain bagging — *wot wot?* It wasn't just the road surface that reminded of home, either. The pine-forested middle section of the climb was peppered with an abundance of purple thistles; at once we could have been in Scotland, albeit Scotland in a heat wave.

Thanks to a mix of recovering from Drew's frantic start and conserving oxygen as part of a rest-day mentality, we talked less than we had on the previous climbs. Our brooding silence was possibly also symptomatic of the stress of being stuck in one another's company for so long without a break.

"So, what have you been up to lately? Oh, yeah, same as me... ."

To be honest, I was glad of the silence, far too busy perspiring to talk. The sweat poured from my shaved head, an incessant salty waterfall that crashed over and into my eyes. My mitts were soon sodden, soaked sponges unable to cope with the constant brow mopping. Grateful for the long branches that draped shade across the road, we eased our pace as we passed through the cooler air within, greedily gulping it down as if it were pints of iced water. For a couple of kilometres that was all I could think of: raising my tempo to reach the shade, easing my tempo in order to linger in the shade — repeat until fade or faint. I zoned in on the rhythm as a meditating Buddhist might focus upon the breath and before too long as I gone. In body I was still upon the bike and upon the mountain, but in mind I was somewhere else altogether.

It was a good while before I snapped back into consciousness (disturbed by a car coming down the mountain or by the salty sting of sweat) only to realise that I had no idea where I was. I knew I was on a cycling trip (the bicycle beneath me and the hot sun above were dead giveaways) and a while later I concluded that I was probably in France. As to which climb I was riding up ... frankly, I had no idea. I racked my brain, recited the name of every climb I could think of, including those I was sure hadn't made it on to our schedule, not even our long, long list, but nothing seemed to fit. After a good deal of cognitive crawling, all I could muster was that this mountain had a lake at the summit. A lake, a lake, a lake ... ? What's French for lake? Lac. Lac, lac, lac ... ? A minute or so later Lac du Mont Cenis sprang to mind, and only then (okay, so it took another couple of minutes) did I get it. Had my brain been starved of oxygen or was I subconsciously missing Rain Man Drew's running commentary? One thing was for sure, there was no way he would have forgotten what climb we were riding.

With the realisation of my location came another flash of inspiration: on remembering that it was supposed to be a rest day, I sat back in the saddle and dropped into second gear. A leisurely look around and I smiled, inwardly, and outwardly to Drew, hoping in vain to elicit a mirror reaction. I relaxed my shoulders, took a few deep breaths and a few deeper slugs of electrolyte drink. Life really wasn't so bad after all; life really was pretty bloody good.

From there my addled mind set to work on an adaptation of a Blondie song, a bastardised ear worm that lodged itself inside my head, no way I would ever forget its lyrics or the climb, even if I actively attempted to do so.

Cenis Cenis, oh with your lake so blue,
Cenis Cenis, I've got a crush on you,
Cenis Cenis, I'm so in love with you, whoa.
Oh when we climb it always feels so nice,
And when we descend it seems like paradise.
Cenis Cenis I'm so in love with you, whoa.

As my brain fried, the road lunged upward and away from the forest, catapulting us onto open pasture. We rolled into a blaze of direct sunlight and — as quickly as that — it was all over. The summit had taken us completely by surprise; even Rain Man Drew was confused.

"Is this it? The climb is 9.84 kilometres in length. Have we covered 9.84 kilometres? The top of the climb is 2081 metres above sea level. 2081 metres, are we at 2081 metres? Should we keep going? Keep going, keep going, just in case."

To make matters worse, there was no summit sign, no souvenir shop, not even a gaggle of over-excited motorcyclists, just a hazy view down onto the big blue lake. Mont Cenis had not been breathtaking or life changing. Instead it had proved to be little more than a rather hot, medium-length, medium-difficulty climb and, thanks to the tunnel, a very expensive round trip. Six climbs under the belt and our expectations had considerably heightened. Despite our protestations to the contrary, we wanted climbs that would exhaust and astonish. Nothing less would suffice, even on a rest day.

***

For dinner we forsook the usual contracted bumble around town, marched determinedly uphill and promptly plonked for a restaurant called Le Gavroche. There we had our first taste of snails — when in Rome, er, Briançon, and all that. Our allocation came to the table arranged in the recesses of a circular earthenware dish, as if held in a ring of tiny eggcups. We were each armed with a metal device that looked like eyelash curlers, but was in fact a clamp in which to hold the hot shells, and a thin two-pronged fork with which to gouge around inside the former home and final resting place of Monsieur Escargot. Out he (or she, how do you sex a snail?) came and into our gobs he/she went. They were superbly garlicky and of a similar texture to their molluscan relative, the mussel. The last of mine to be dragged from shell to mouth offered a gritty crunch and I assumed that this particular snail had spent its final days of life lounging around on the beach.

We followed those delicacies with the plat du jour — turkey kebabs prepared in the Provençal style, served with a pomme purée and some crisp, roasted vegetables. We wolfed it all down Jacques-Anquetil-style and very nearly ordered the same again for dessert. Instead we chose crêpes, deciding not just to push the boat out but also to hole it below the water line and then throw its oars away. Decadence, you say? Of course not, we were pre-loading with carbs in advance of the coming climbs, and besides, we needed something extra to soak up the last of the wine.

Events took a turn for the even worse on the walk back down the hill, when Drew popped into a shop to buy some cigarettes, taking the whole Anquetil thing a step too far. (What next, Drew? Will you be off in search of a glamorous blonde to bring back to the hotel?) His excuse for this poisonous purchase was a notion to take a ciggie up the Galibier and light it just as he was cresting the summit. (Of course it had nothing at all to do with a particularly bad habit of smoking whenever he'd imbibed a drink or three.) The look on the faces of the other frazzled cyclists as they spotted a rider sprinting (sprinting? Who was he kidding?) to the top whilst puffing on a cigarette would surely be priceless. Or so Drew attempted to assure. And with that he ripped open the packet.

"Itsh purely practish, for the Galibier, you undershtand?" He slurred and I was too tired and convivial to do anything other than concur (and walk a few steps upwind of the reek).

Puffing on a cig at the top of the Galibier! Oh how we chuckled at the very thought, chuckled for the sake of chuckling, chuckled because we were a little bit drunk and happily on holiday in France.

That joviality was interrupted by the simultaneous bleeping from our mobile phones. We'd each received a text from our girlfriends back home. The pair, sisters, had fallen out with one another (alcohol's pessimism whispered suggestion in my ear: the sisters' row is a bad omen sent to spoil the trip). We shared the differing sides of their story, agreed to try and keep out of the argument. I put my phone back into my pocket, changed the topic of conversation and we somehow ended up discussing string theory, quantum physics, the immense size of universe and all the galaxies that surround the little blob of rock and water we call planet Earth.

"In the grand scheme of things, all those mountains that we think of as being really, really big are really just really, really small."

"That's heavy, man. Really, really heavy."

"Hang on."

"What?"

"Go back a bit."

"How far back?"

"To the mountaintop cigarette bit."

"And?"

"That mountain you mentioned?"

"What about it?"

"Did you say, Galibier?"

"Yeah, I did."

DRAMATIC PAUSE.

Drew and Rolf together: "Oh, shit!"

"The Galibier is really, *really* big!"

DAY 9:
A POSTCARD FROM THE EDGE

Col du Lautaret
Start point: Briançon | Height: 2058m | Height climbed: 853m
Length of climb: 27.75km | Average gradient: 3.1% | Maximum
gradient: 5.2%

Col du Galibier
Start point: Col du Lautaret | Height: 2642m | Height climbed:
585m | Length of climb: 8.52km | Average gradient: 6.9%
Maximum gradient: 12.1%

We didn't need a map in order to locate the Col du Lautaret.
Right outside our hotel there was a very big, arrow-shaped sign
pointing toward the Boulevard du Lautaret. All we had to do was
head in that direction and keep going, straight out of town, up onto
the Col itself. Easy. No map, no car journeys, no toll roads or
tunnels to contend with. For once in the trip our planning had
come up trumps, a feat to be savoured but never repeated.

I still marvelled at the idea that someone could grow up on a
street named after, and in the shadow of, one of cycling's best-
known mountain climbs. How would you *not* get into cycling living
on such a street? It would be the equivalent of someone with no
interest in football living on the street beside Old Trafford, or a
non-petrol-head living in the pit lane at Le Mans (could prove a bit
noisy for a Sunday morning lie-in).

We had read in several places that the Lautaret is little more
than a blip on the side of the Galibier, but it proved to be the
hardest blip either of us had ever ridden. It's over 24-kilometres
long, and from the start we could pretty much see the road ahead
in its entirety, laid along the valley's cleft, inching upward to a
summit resolutely and distressingly distant. That sounds bad but, to
be honest, from Briançon it didn't look like much of a climb at all,
more like a long, flat straight with a mountain at the end of it.

Looks can be deceiving and, rest assured, the Lautaret felt pretty perpendicular.

All things considered, it should have been an easy climb, a nice warm-up for the Galibier, but the foehn wind had other ideas, and our blip ended up feeling more like the Stelvio in slow-mo. The Lautaret might only have an average gradient of 3.1% but with a 50kph headwind hurtling down the valley toward us it felt much closer to 10%. When out and about around windy Edinburgh, Drew and I had always said that we would rather ride up a hill on a still day than along a flat and into a headwind. Until that moment, we had yet to formulate an opinion on riding up a mountain into a headwind. We quickly did so and the outcome was far from favourable.

Initially, we had little time to contemplate the wind. Drew took up from where he left off on the lower slopes of Mont Cenis, deciding that the climb (and perhaps by extension the trip) should be over and done with as soon as possible, preferably before it had begun. He took to the front as we departed Briançon, out the saddle, stamping on the pedals until he was back in that full-swing crazy tempo — going so hard that once again I struggled even to stay on his wheel. From where he found that extra strength I had no idea, but I sure wished he would share some with me. I clung to the edge of his shadow, wondering if there'd been something special in the previous evening's cigarettes. (By the way, in the sober light of day, the thought of sparking up a cig' whilst pedalling toward the Galibier summit no longer held Drew in its thrall, comedy value or no comedy value.)

A few kilometres in, legs just about warmed up, lungs still raw and rasping, I swung out of the slipstream and sprinted to the front, pumping the pedals in order to maintain Drew's panicky pace. One kilometre later and I was just about to crack when I heard Drew shouting into the wind. A backward glance revealed an angry face, its twisted lips yelling up the mountain, instructing the "idiot" to immediately slow down. Without any hesitation the idiot did as instructed. We pulled level and Drew revealed the obvious: two miles in and already he hated the Lautaret.

"What's the point battling into the wind like this?" He asked over the roar of rushing air. "This isn't climbing, it's outdoor wind-tunnel testing."

On occasion (perhaps each and every occasion) it can feel as if the mountain road is there for no other reason than to elicit the cyclist's self-doubt. Some mountain roads are better at this dispiriting process than others. The Lautaret was an obvious old hand. Drew began by questioning why he was pushing himself so hard, and that quickly led on to why he was bothering to push at all. To him, less than a quarter of the way up, this col was nothing more than a hideously long, equally dull, utterly pointless slog into a headwind — an opinion he felt compelled to share. I also had my doubts but the counter response came louder. The experience involved battling up a climb of which I could clearly recall images from Tours gone by. This was painful but priceless, ridiculously hard but also impossibly romantic.

While the wind maintained its velocity, Drew's doubting began to drift and we soon settled in to a reasonable tempo. On the whole we kept our heads down and our pedals turning, trying to cover ground without arriving at the foot of the Galibier fully cooked. Around the halfway point we passed the ruins of the Auberge du Glacier, an old, crumbling inn that was almost visibly slipping off the edge of the road and into the realm of memory. I wondered how many Tour cyclists had swished or slogged (either climbing or descending) passed its cracked and crumbling door frame, if any had stopped for refreshment back when the inn was in a more salubrious state.

There was only one tunnel to negotiate, coming just before the summit, enjoyably short and open-sided. (Two others further down-slope had been fenced off, their contents sealed in by a damp, eerie darkness — yet another horror-movie set in the making.) And that's pretty much all there was to report, little of note upon the climb itself; the road really was just taking us somewhere else, hopefully somewhere more memorable and less uncomfortable.

There is more to the Lautaret but it's all from a non-cycling perspective (so hardly worth bothering about). The Col is part of a pass that's been in use for centuries. The Roman road from Milan to Vienne crossed in the same location and its name comes from the small temple, or altaretum, that the Romans erected in order to placate the mountain god. One of only five "gateways" into the Ecrins National Park, the surrounding area is a huge expanse of meadow, renowned for a magnificent variety of Alpine flowers.[2] Many of the surrounding slopes are glacial, a reminder of the icy-activity that formed the peaks and valleys thousands of years before. Climbs are usually more agreeable from the summit and the Lautaret was no exception. When we did eventually stop to look, the views made up for the monotony of the ascent. The valley swished and swirled its way back down to Briançon, curving gracefully like immense ocean waves, water to wash away memories of the hellish, hair-dryer climb.

**

After the relatively dull, long, straight slog up the valley, the Col du Galibier (follow the signposts and turn right at the top of the Lautaret) did its utmost to differ, no holds barred in its attempts to impress. The narrow, single-track road looked like a crazy curl of grey hair that had flipped free in the wind and landed in random fashion around the head of the old grand peak. And as much as it impressed, the Galibier was a col intent on instilling fear, perhaps as revenge for the disrespect we'd displayed to its less impressive sister. Without a safety barrier in sight, the tarmac edge dropped off and into freefall, not even a grass verge to distract from that petrifying prospect.

With the first pedal strokes came a sense of being in the presence of greatness. This was a road we assumed to know well, a legend of whose name we required no reminder. Unlike Cenis, I was not about to get halfway up the Galibier and pause to wrestle with a mental blank. All the climbs we'd chosen were A-list names, but the Galibier was a sure-fire contender for *hors-catégorie* superstar status.

This particular legend dates back to 1911, when the Tour first tackled the Alps (having tried out on the Pyrenees the previous year). Émile Georget was first to what was then the race's highest-ever summit, and one of only three riders who managed the ascent without walking. The roll call of riders first over the Galibier in subsequent Tours contains most of the sport's greatest-ever climbers: Fausto Coppi; Federico Bahamontes; Charly Gaul; Julio Jiménez; Eddy Merckx; Luis Ocaña; Lucien Van Impe; Luis Herrera; Marco Pantani.

It was through the exploits of the latter that this road had become lodged in my sporting consciousness (and Drew's too). Above all else, we knew this as the mountain upon which Pantani had put in the attack that won the stage and put him into the yellow jersey during the 1998 Tour de France. The Galibier was the highest point of that year's race, a fitting place for the world's best climber to achieve cycling infamy, but July 27th of that year wasn't *one* monumental climb, it was an entire day of drama.

The bunch of main contenders, including the race leader, Jan Ullrich, had already tackled the 2067-metre Col de la Croix de Fer (a climb we'd see later but only from afar), where it was barely above 10 degrees Celsius and the rain had already started. By the foot of the Galibier, the temperature had dropped even further and the rain was falling in torrents. Pantani appeared unaffected by the conditions (or was keen to get the stage over and done with, in the same way Drew was beginning to treat our trip) and didn't wait long to make his move. 11 kilometres from the summit, as soon as the road looked suitably, imposingly steep, he was off on a break that most commentators, and his main rivals, dismissed as lunacy doomed to fail. It seemed unlikely that anybody could go from that far out and survive to ride alone to a stage win, let alone make a successful attack on Jan Ullrich's yellow jersey. There were still 45 kilometres to go to the stage finish at Les Deux Alpes but Pantani flew into his trademark climbing style: down in the drops, high pedal revs, repeatedly getting up and out the saddle to maintain the tempo, never a look back over shoulder.

In contrast to Pantani's fanciful flight was that of British rider Tom Simpson during the ill-fated 1967 Tour. The poor bloke was so stricken with stomach problems that he had to stop at the foot of the Galibier and empty his bowels before making a lone effort to chase down the leaders. For Simpson the day must have been a waking nightmare, no less enjoyable for the team mechanic who had to wash the shit off the bike at the end of the stage.[3.]

The aforementioned Paul Kimmage was another Tour rider who failed to find any personal or professional pleasure upon the Galibier. Telling of his unsuccessful attempts to stay with the race as it hit the steeper slopes he wrote:

"Tears fill my eyes. I decide to try again. I begin to ride faster, deciding not to give up. But the effort lasts just one kilometre. My legs are just empty. A rider passes me on the right at twice my speed. I look across to see who it is. It's a bearded tourist, riding up the mountain with pannier bags on his bike. A bloody Fred. ... the damage is done, and I am now completely demoralised. Spectators are now pushing me ... . The broom wagon is just 500 metres back ... . It is drawing me in like a giant magnet."[4.]

In 1996, a Tour stage had to be shortened, removing the climb of the Galibier due to deep snow blocking the road. In distinct contrast, we suffered below a sun so fiery I had to wear my cap for protection. During the previous two days' outings, sans casquette and helmet, my scalp had well and truly frazzled. I had only realised this affliction after waking in the night, my head searing and sore, too raw even to rest upon the pillow. A tentative hand had inched upward to investigate and, much to my disgust and a degree of foul fascination, come back down with a tranche of roasted skin.

Painted onto the road surface, some fresh, many faded, were the names of various cycling greats. We distracted ourselves from the discomfort by mentally scoring off those who had been sanctioned for, or suspected of, a doping violation. Name after name was wiped from the road, tarred over and dismissed by the brushes of our cynicism and disappointment. Cycling fans had ridden, walked and driven all the way up the mountain, armed with paint, pride and admiration. There they had daubed their tributes — at least half of which were to dopers and cheats. The unheralded fans would then have waited hours for the race to arrive — first the publicity caravan, then the official motorcade and finally the riders — favourites would have been singled out and cheered on, the dedicated spectators unaware of the full truth behind the talent they so admired.

Those thoughts left us drained through disappointment. We were slogging up the back of the Galibier beast on nothing more than energy drink and my (genuinely vital) asthma inhaler. Like every cyclist, we compared ourselves to the pros: how fast they must have ridden up here in comparison to our agonising crawl! We wondered in amazement, feeling more than a tad inferior, but an odd kind of consolation came with the knowledge that at least we were truly doing it under our own steam — no team support, no doctors, no illegal products, not even a hint of suspicion. How much we wanted to believe the latest proclamation, how we genuinely hoped the sport was finally cleaning up its act, belatedly learning the lessons; but how many times before had we believed the hype and how many times had we since been disappointed? It felt like too many to count.

I used to keep all the cycling magazines I'd bought in neat piles beneath my bed. One day I pulled that archive out for a look. A flick through the editions from the 2000s revealed cover star after cover star who'd either faced a sporting sanction or was continuing to ride under a cloud of (ultimately justified) suspicion. Inside the magazines were articles that revealed the "secrets" of those riders' winning training regimes: the hours they put in on the time-trial bike; the weight loss regime; the new pedalling technique; the new mental focus. If only they'd been honest and revealed the significant others: the pharmaceutical companies; the blood bags; the extractions and transfusions; the hormones; the syringes and shady doctors. Reading those articles with hindsight was like watching a re-run of The Wizard of Oz with full knowledge of what lurked behind the curtain.

When such thoughts came to prominence, ordinary bike riders, like Drew and me, had to become our own heroes. If only we had taken some paint and a brush up the Galibier, we could have daubed our own names upon the rough road:

Allez Rolf! Allez Drew!

Apart from that brief, breathless discussion on doping, we didn't talk much. In fact we barely grunted at one another, wasting precious little breath on *bonjours* to the lucky bastards freewheeling past us on their way down the mountain. I considered that Drew might still be in a huff about the Lautaret's long drag but our silence was more likely down to a severe lack of energy. (He later confirmed this, saying he'd been putting in so much effort that it felt like his eyes were about to pop from their sockets.) Looking up — when I could spare the energy to lift my head — I gasped in awe and whispered breathlessly,

"Is that the road *up there?*"

My gaze was dragged back down from the hideous heights by the giant stone monolith that forms the memorial to the Tour's own great monolith, its original organiser, Henri Desgrange. That mountain-in-its-own-right looked like a fitting memorial for a man with such a reputation, and its location was no mere coincidence: the Galibier had been Desgrange's favourite col. He once declared that in comparison the others were like, "*colourless, common or garden gnat's piss.*"

As if that didn't clearly enough state his opinion, he also wrote his Act of Adoration:

"*Oh Sappey, Oh Laffrey, Oh Col Bayard, Oh Tourmalet! I will not shirk from my duty in proclaiming that beside the Galibier you are nothing but pale babies; in front of this giant we can do nothing but take off our hats and bow.*"

We passed by with little ceremony; strange behaviour considering it was his decision to take a bicycle race through the mountains that founded the basis for our trip. I suppose our heroes were those who had completed the Tour's trial, not the man who set up the sadistic event in the first place. Yet without Desgrange and his strange ideas who knows where cycling would be. Who knows where Drew and I would be — probably lying on a beach drinking cold beer. Oh Desgrange, you cruel, cruel bastard!

A short stretch beyond the memorial and we were truly grovelling, on the verge of collapse — somewhere on-high Desgrange smiled in satisfaction. I wobbled toward the verge and that sheer drop piled gut-churning fear onto the exhaustion. Moving back toward the centre of the road and changing down into first gear brought temporary relief. Once again I had purposefully "saved" my lowest gear, a well-meant but pointless policy that only served to make the climb harder as a whole. Keeping first in reserve offered mental succour, knowledge that I still had somewhere left to go should the gradient become really, *really* steep (as opposed to just steep or really steep). Physically that policy was less beneficial. On all of the steepest sections, even those that came early in the climb, I should have made immediate use of my lowest gear. That way I could have pedalled a little more smoothly for a little longer, rather than having endured that constant, laborious, low-rev battle with the cranks.

Ego also had a part to play in my gear selection, betraying that keenness to show the world (as if the world was watching) that I could ride the mountains using similar gear ratios to those the pros used. *Surely even the heavily muscled sprinters wouldn't resort to first gear quite so early on in a climb?* Possibly not, but the time had come to accept that I wasn't a pro (at best I was a barely competent amateur), not even close to being close to the elite level, and I never would be. First gear was there to be used. What was the point in lugging that 27-tooth sprocket through the Alps if I wasn't going to let the chain roll onto it once in a while?

I kicked ego toward the edge of the road, then on and over that precipitous drop. (*Aargh ... splat!*) In future I'd turn a smaller gear as early and often as required. Triples and compacts, they're for wimps, right? Now and again it sure would have been nice to wimp out.

Before setting out that morning, Drew's marvellous memory

had indicated that the Galibier summit would be reached at exactly 22 miles ridden. When mile 22 came and went, the summit not apparently proximate, I began to wonder if the human compendium had lost his touch. We pushed into the pain and exchanged confused, exhausted grimaces that proved a hideous contrast to our memories of that fluid Pantani panache. In comparison to our hero we looked like another sport altogether, another species entirely. However, just as there's always someone who's faster than you, there's also very often a poor sod who's a little bit slower, sometimes even a lot slower. We thought we were grovelling until we saw him, an older gent who, despite a distinct lack of forward motion, was somehow upright on his bicycle — the thought that he might be performing a track stand was only dismissed when we heard the bleeping alarm call of his heart-rate monitor. The frantic digital chirrup suggested that a bomb was about to go off, the distressed and dodgy ticker set to explode from the poor guy's chest. We rode quickly by (well, when I say *quickly* I really mean *less slowly* than he was riding), cast a cursory bonjour over shoulder, braced ourselves for a bang and the subsequent impact of human and bicycle shrapnel.

Just like the man with the heart-rate monitor (who, much to everyone's relief, failed to detonate), the road had wound itself up into a tightly coiled spring, its last couple of kilometres concertinaed into tight, switchback bends. We were probably a little below our lowest ebb but the road, in the truest traditions of Tour mountains, was unwilling to cede any ground. As if it hadn't already been brutal enough, we were about to face-off against the Galibier's steepest gradients and a final ramp said to be over 12% but feeling more akin to 22. Looking upward, it appeared this last section of road was pitched vertically toward the sky, its stretch of tarmac all that separated us from the deep blue heavens above. Just a few more pushes on the pedals — seconds that stretched impossibly — and, about bloody time, the road levelled out for the summit.

***

Finally achieved, the top of the Galibier took the form of a large patch of gravely ground with a signpost plonked in the middle — a signpost that was, you guessed it, colonised by motorcyclists. They sauntered over from all directions, happily snapping one another's picture: chunky, leather-clad biker; lonesome little sign;

big blue backdrop. For most of them the challenge of walking the few metres from parked motorbike to signpost was probably a daunting physical challenge in itself. (Boy, had riding to the top left me feeling self-righteous!) They crowded round, laughing and joking, slapping backs and shaking hands, exuding an energy the like of which Drew and I could only dream (after a re-fuel, a lengthy period of rest and a hefty dose of amphetamine), and the more jovial the bikers, the more bitter we became. Rightly or wrongly (okay, so I know it was wrong but it didn't feel that way at the time) Drew and I assumed a divine right to the sign, a privilege we alone had earned on the arduous ascent. We grew steadily more annoyed and eventually became vocally so: two skinny cyclists about to square up to the Alpine branch of the Hell's Angels. The tension was only diffused when we set about organising a queue for the summit-sign snaps (how wonderfully British), and then forcing our way toward the front of it (so terribly un-British).

Poses struck and captured for posterity, the red mist lifted, and we belatedly noticed the view. Ahead of us stretched a vibrant sea of green grass like the rippled baize of a corrugated snooker table. Protruding through the perfect surface was row after row of jagged brown, blue and grey rock. Yet again we found ourselves looking down upon an array of massive mountains, at once inspired, mesmerised and frightened: the landscape was stunning but the descent looked truly fearful, its steepness exaggerated by our lofty position. Over the far side we could see all the way down and on toward the Col du Télégraphe, from where Pantani and the peloton had begun their ascent during the 1998 Tour. Back over the way we'd come, and far in the distance, lay the tiny line of the Lautaret. How pathetic it appeared from our new perspective (like the tail of a mouse) and how pathetic our moaning and groaning about the ascent.

***

The ride off the Galibier was almost as horrible as the ride up, a mountain intent on destroying us one way or the other. The wind whipped and snapped violently, doing its level best to cast us off and into the void; the cows that had roamed in off the pasture were there the catch those pesky cyclists who (through excellent bike-handling skills or sheer good fortune) managed to thwart the tempest and stick to the tarmac. They stared inanely, as cows are want to do, whilst we hurtled insanely toward them. When we weren't dodging livestock, we were keeping an eye out for the ascending cars, drivers intent on keeping as far as they could from the precipice, even if that meant crushing cyclists against the mountainside. I was just glad the road was dry; in the wet it would have been beyond treacherous. I couldn't imagine how anyone could ride it at breakneck speed without purposefully trying to break their neck, and every other bone, in the process. As we careered, I recalled the footage of Pantani's death-defying descent, Il Pirata at the mercy of the wind and rain, riding no-hands whilst trying to don a rain cape. No hands? I was looking round for another couple to help me steady the bars.

There are a whole host of Tour riders whose descent off the Galibier was neither as skilful or successful as Pantani's. A crash there put the rainbow-jersey-clad Tom Simpson out of the 1966 edition. Worse still, the Galibier was scene of the Tour's first racing fatality. In 1935, the Spanish climber Francisco Cepeda took a nasty tumble, badly fractured his skull and died from his injuries three days later.

When we eventually got there — by road and not unintended free-fall — the descent off the Lautaret was altogether more enjoyable. The wind was now of the obliging, tail variety, and pushed us along at an astounding rate of knots. If there had been a picture in my mind's eye of how the descent of a Tour mountain might be, then there it was, with me in the middle of the frame. It looked, felt and sounded like my recollections of that early Channel 4 coverage. The wind rattled my rain jacket, forcing a crack and flap that competed with the swoosh of tyres on tarmac and the click and whir of my chain. Cars struggled to overtake as I spun out top gear, pedals revolving in a blur. Freewheeling at fifty miles an hour, I tucked into an aero position, like a downhill skier, glided into sweeping bends that required no breaking, just a decision on how far over the white lines I could afford to go with the oncoming traffic. There, in flight upon the mountain, was the lad from the Scottish countryside who had fantasised about riding with the Tour de France. My body tingled with the suggestion of youth recaptured; I had dug up a distant, dusty dream and was living it large upon the Lautaret.

It felt like I had split in two, the boy Rolf and the man he had become, riding side by side and grinning from ear to ear, ecstatic in agreement.

"Bet you never thought you'd get to do this?" Rolf the man yelled into the wind.

"You're right, I didn't," the boy yelled back, his half-broken voice quavering with excitement. "Is it a dream or is this really happening?"

"It's really happening, boy. You'd better believe it. Race you to the next bend!"

***

Back in Briançon, showered and into civvies, we death-marched up the hill for some food. Trudging into the warm wind, whistling our morale-boosting tune, we looked like particularly thin stick men, exhausted and slowly expiring. We were headed for cheeseburgers, both back to that iron-deficient, carnivorous craving: nothing would stop us from sinking our jaws into juicy red meat, not even the hill and that infernal foehn.

We sat, ate and observed the array of idiots who ambled through the small town square. We'd witnessed a great deal of dimwits (many dimmer than either of us), more than one in every village we'd passed through. Briançon was on another scale, boasted a veritable brainless bounty, perhaps playing host to a village-idiot convention. They were omnipresent, there at every turn, hollering and mumbling, shaking their fists at shadows on the city walls, at the ice-cream stalls, at us and other unsuspecting tourists. I wondered how long we'd have to stay there to end up in a similar state. Another couple of days, perhaps? A week, tops? I put it down to a combination of the fierce sun and the vicious mountains. These were addled veterans from wholly unsuccessful campaigns of man-on-col combat. They smiled sarcastically, knowingly, as if only they held the key, the very answer to life's great conundrum — and perhaps they did, a secret discerned in the saddle, under the sun at high altitude, their last moment of clarity before a long and winding descent to madness.

Another common feature of Briançon were the expensive dogs. British pooches tend to be ordinary members of the family: floppy, scruffy Spaniels and loveable Labs. From what I could see, the French man and woman's best friend was also their most expensive accessory. Luxuriously stupid, in-bred pedigree pooches — like big, sleek, scatterbrained Dobermans and tiny, nervous poodles shaved to within a pom-pom of their lives — were promenaded around town in the same way a boy-racer might show off his car by means of laborious laps.

As we observed the comings and goings, I ruminated on our experience so far. The trip had almost reached its midway point but I was still struggling to conclusively judge the collective mood — or, more accurately, I had thus far avoided properly passing judgement, afraid of what I might discern. Italy had been a mixed bag, the pride of conquering the Stelvio and its kin partially counteracted by the disappointment of the big-name climbs we'd forsaken. France was proving to be sunnier but equally tough. We had both suffered on the day of the Bonette, be it from altitude sickness or simple fatigue, and for Drew the malaise had taken the sheen off our conquest of Europe's highest through road. The Galibier had more than lived up to its reputation as the Tour's king col but again, for Drew, the day had been partly diminished, this time by the Lautaret's tempestuous torture. Despite the difficulties and our logistical failings I was proud of what we'd already achieved. How many cyclists can say they have ridden the Stelvio, the Marmolada, the Bonette or the Galibier? We'd ridden them all and the very thought of that achievement cast a smile across my sunburnt face.

Drew wasn't sunburnt but neither was he smiling, no matter how much I cajoled. I'd put his initial, Italian grumblings down to the virus, hoped that as he improved physically his emotions would follow suit. So far it hadn't worked out that way. Each new climb had only served to remind him that there was another climb to come, and then another, and another after that. The thought of even one mountain was almost too much. He looked at the schedule and the mighty names avalanched off the page to swamp his struggling psyche; the excitement I'd hoped for turned to dread.

I truly began to worry for his state of mind (and our trip's future prospects) when he proudly recited the content of his latest postcard home: it detailed a plan to throw his bike into the first available skip upon return to Edinburgh. He also indicated a growing dislike for Briançon, stating in no uncertain terms that he'd had more than enough of the place. To an extent we both had itchy feet, were open to the idea of pastures new, but Drew's only excited anticipation came when talking of home and the renunciation of his once-beloved bicycle.

The mountain experience was undoubtedly tough, even tougher than we'd already anticipated. The climbs were genuinely gruelling;

on occasion the normal pleasure one derived from cycling felt like forcing your body through a meat mincer. I wondered if that was how the Tour became for its competitors, especially so for the "lesser" riders, the *domestiques*, aka cycling's cannon fodder. Was there any joy to be found in day after day of grinding your body into the ground for the benefit of a team leader's sporting ambitions, perhaps thanklessly hauling yourself over mountain after mountain? Was that how Drew viewed his own situation, that he was sacrificing himself for the sake of my crazy dream?

Perhaps the issue could be traced back to his original expectations. He might have assumed that every climb would be like a race-day ascent of Alpe d'Huez (we'd had the pleasure of that experience a few of years before, for our first true taste of Tour mountains): exciting, amazing, breathtaking, inspiring, the roadside overflowing with half-a-million cheering fans. The only cheering we'd encounter on this trip would come from the voices in our heads. Shame then that Drew's internal monologue was little more than an endless stream of negativity and inquisition. Upon the Lautaret I too had asked, why am I doing this? All it had taken to settle the doubts and spur me on was a look up the valley. Drew had been questioning his motives ever since the first pedal stroke on the Sella pass, and still hadn't reached a satisfactory conclusion. How I wanted to click my heels Dorothy-style and rewind us to the excited anticipation of that night in the pub, to all those times he had pissed and moaned about the monotony of Edinburgh's (relatively) flat roads.

I had my own motivations for being where I was and for what was to come, many of which I had (not so safely) assumed Drew shared. I also had my own problems to deal with, the unwanted and over-heavy baggage I'd been struggling to lug around since my father's death a year and a bit before. For me the trip represented an attempt to snatch a victory from the jaws of death's defeat: I intended to face the challenge, to grasp the time I had, to appreciate the wonder and magic of life — that which my father had understood and so doggedly, yet vainly, clung on to. Cancer had taken him but it could not, *would not* claim me.

Despite that adamant attitude, as I pedalled uphill, the pain, darkness and fury were never far away. Grief was guaranteed to bubble up and out at least once or twice before the summit, to hover and haunt like the most tenacious, shadowy, wheel-sucking rival. No matter how hard I pushed on the pedals, how much I wrestled body and bike against the gradient I'd not yet managed to shake it off. In many cases my increased effort only served to intensify and darken its presence, to sharpen the tacks of misery it scattered on the road beneath my tyres. The further I weakened, the less I was able to resist, and the more strength it gained.

Dealing with my own issues in conjunction with the climbs' Herculean task already required excessive effort; egging Drew on and over the top really did feel like an unnecessary task too far. I couldn't, wouldn't do it. He needed to find his own way through, or should I say, *over*. The flight back home that he was so keen to catch lay on the other side of some very, very big mountains. He would have to recalibrate, seek motivation anew, to remember why he was there, and do so before it was too late. We had the Col d'Izoard waiting immediately ahead of us.

***

That evening, we dined on pizza down in the new town. The restaurant was a small, rustic place with white, plastic garden furniture set up in the courtyard. It all looked a bit shabby, the waitress flustered like she'd popped in to say hello and got roped into working a shift. The pizza, however, was excellent, better than any we had sampled back over the Alps in Italy.

The evening's "entertainment" arrived just as we were tucking in to our pizzas, announced by the blaring of air horns and the screech of tyres.

"What's this", we thought, "the return of the freaky festival?"

It might not have been a festival but it was certainly freaky. Up pulled (or should I say, skidded) a campervan that had been badly disguised as a fire engine. Out from within popped a group of young men, led by another man (we presumed there was a man in there) dressed in a fluffy, all-in-one white rabbit costume. The rabbit had a noose around his neck, either the sign of a last-minute pardon or suicidal tendencies (the mask's fixed expression made it hard to judge which way his emotions were swinging).

Most of the rest of the group looked relatively normal (dressed in t-shirts and low-slung, baggy jeans), the only other notable character being the chap with the foot-high, gelled-solid wisp of hair that sprouted from the top of his otherwise bald and shiny pate. To that showpiece he had added (perhaps for the sake of symmetry) a foot-long, equally gelled and solid-looking goatee beard.

One of my worst habits, but something I have got a handle on in recent years, is judging people on first impressions. I like to think that my initial inkling is usually right but in the past it has, on occasion, been otherwise. My first impression of those guys was wholly negative and, if I'm being honest, most likely wholly correct. Were they French students on a wacky night out, on some kind of stunt for their equivalent of Rag Week? Perhaps a bunch of Belgian snowboarders had slipped over the mountains in their replica fire engine, unawares that the sweet-pack snow disappears in the summer months? Or had we actually been confronted with some kind of stag party? The rabbit costume and the noose? Did those, in some distinctly Gallic way, symbolise the fate of a man on the cusp of entering into wedded bliss?

The ten-strong group took to their seats and I expected a mass order of beers and shots, a deal of ugly waitress-ogling and groping. We readied ourselves to scrape spare mozzarella from our pizzas, to stuff it into our ears in order to block out the sound of their raucous song. We readied, steadied and waited, only for the snowboarders/stag party to sit nicely, hands safely on their laps and practically whisper their order for a round of — wait for it — ice-cream sundaes. Then, to add insult to the injury of my inaccurate preconceptions, the stag took a call on his mobile from Ms Fiancée, and the group hushed respectfully in order that the lovebirds could converse.

He told her where he was, that he wasn't drunk and that, yes, he did love her. Then, if my French-language and eavesdropping skills are to be trusted, he meekly sought her permission to have a beer. He hung up the phone in time to receive a *bon chance* from an older man who was leaving the restaurant. In my opinion it was far too late for good luck, Bunny Boy already under the thumb and still not yet married.

When I was young, growing up in the north-east of Scotland, the peace of our village would occasionally be shattered by the blaring of air horns, the primal shouts of men and the tribal banging of stick against home-made drum. The sound would begin as a distant rhythm and build in volume and intensity as the source crept ever closer to my house. I would run out to the garden, hide in the bush closest to the road and wait, eager to see what was coming, but equally afraid of what I would find. A nondescript car, perhaps a Datsun Cherry, would round the corner, towing behind it a trailer dangerously overloaded with men. All of the group bar one would be shouting, blowing horns and beating drums; the other one would be naked and covered from head to toe in thick, black oil (and god knows what else). Whilst his "friends" celebrated as if living through the happiest moment of their lives, the poor oily guy would be slumped and shivering, looking like he was about to be ritually sacrificed.

The group would pass my house, round the corner and head off across the village, the sound of their call fading but the stark impression intensifying in my curious, childishly susceptible mind. My father would calm me down, attempt to explain that the "blackening" I had just witnessed was part of a pre-wedding tradition and not some heinous crime that had to be reported forthwith. I accepted (but didn't truly understand) his explanation, and vowed never to get married.

Many years later, I lived in a flat in the middle of an Edinburgh neighbourhood locals refer to as, "the pubic triangle", the streets of which are packed with seedy bars and less salubrious strip joints. This triangle is Mecca to stag parties from across Britain, although, for some reason, in my experience most hailed from Newcastle. I would nip out for a bike ride on a Saturday morning only to run into a marauding, already inebriated band of Geordies, dragging the near-lifeless corpse of the stag behind them, their addled minds struggling to decide which dive to dive into next. As panic ripped through me I would pedal hell for leather, to escape the cloud of alcohol fumes and the stench of vomit, all the while pining for a quiet garden with a bush in which I could hide until those nasty men and their nasty ritual had gone away.

I guess if you are going to have a stag party you might as well do it properly — no ice-cream sundaes, no fluffy rabbit costumes and certainly no calls home to the fiancée.

DAY 10:
THE GOOSE IS COOKED

Col d'Izoard

Start point: Guillestre | Height: 2361m | Height climbed: 1095m | Length of climb: 15.9km | Average gradient: 6.9% Maximum gradient: 14%

Breakfast was preceded by hysterics (how nice to be back to laughing), when I recalled (how we got to talking about it I have no idea) my school friends, Jamie and Glenn, and their obsession with the movie *Top Gun*. A large part of their early teenage years had been wasted pretending the cheap mountain bikes they rode were in fact F14 fighter jets. They adopted the personae of their heroes, (I think Jamie was Maverick and Glenn either Goose or Wolfman), and whizzed around the village, breathlessly reciting the lines they had memorised during an intense study of the VHS.

A particular favourite went something like this:

Maverick: "*I feel the need ... .*"

Maverick & Goose together: " *... the need for speed!*"

Another line, which was usually encored with a rear-tyre-wasting skid, was:

Maverick: "*I'll hit the brakes and he'll fly right by!*"

However, what really struck my childhood chums wasn't a sudden desire to become a movie hero or a real-life fighter ace — they weren't even turned on by the prospect of a liaison with Kelly McGillis (yeah, right) — what hit them hardest was the death, midway through the movie, of Maverick's flying partner, Goose. In fact, that tragic passing spawned their favourite catchphrase, one they repeated ad nauseum, the line that gave Drew and I breakfast hysterics, and I don't think it's even a real line from the script.

Maverick & Goose together: "*Goose is dead! Goose is dead!*"

They would holler that imagined line with their squeaky, semi-broken voices as they bombed around the otherwise quiet countryside on Raleigh's finest bargain bikes. You could hear the emotion in their voices, see it writ large across their faces, as if both boys had only recently witnessed the gruesome passing of a close personal friend. I guess the demise of Goose was so beautifully, indeed heroically portrayed on screen (no sarcasm intended, honest) that my two pals just couldn't help but show the scars.

INT. HOSPITAL ROOM - NIGHT

Extreme CLOSE ON Maverick's face. He is emotionless. His eyes are flat and absolutely without expression. There is complete silence in the room. Then we hear the quiet, calm, probing voice of Viper.

VIPER: *How do you feel?*
MAVERICK: *All right.*
VIPER: *Goose is dead.*
MAVERICK: *I know. I was there.*

Not one sign of emotion from Maverick. Not one tone of expression. We see Viper now, and his face is strained from a very long day.

VIPER: *If you fly jets long enough, something like this happens to you. No one escapes it. It touches us all.*[5.]

So you see? It touches us all and despite the fact that we weren't there — although Jamie and Glenn clearly thought they were — we must accept the painful truth of the matter: Goose is dead.

Through tears (of hysterical joy — clearly, we were tired and emotional) Drew and I decided to ride the day's col wearing black armbands (fashioned from black insulating tape), a symbolic act both in memory of Goose and as a mark of respect for my friends' misspent youth. We would also make it our duty to regularly remind one another of the tragic loss, and to spread the word by shouting from the saddle and out the car window:

"Tout le monde! Oie, Il mort! Goose is dead!"

***

A post-breakfast lull was interrupted by the twitch of excitement, unmistakable anticipation of the climb ahead. Once again I hadn't slept well, a restless slumber from which I had been repeatedly roused by my heart rate, hammering along at around 120bpm. In my dreams I must have been pedalling some awful ascent, a delusional dry run of the coming day's main event. Whatever the real reason for my palpitations, we were only a few hours away from the Izoard and I couldn't wait.

***

The Tour first rode over the Izoard in 1922, Belgian Phillipe Thys taking the honours. One of the highest passes used regularly by the race, it has also featured numerous times in the Giro's itinerary. Aside from the heroics acted out upon its slopes, the Col is famous for its eerie *Casse Déserte* (Broken Desert, in English). This barren area, disturbed by jagged rock formations and sandy pillars, forms the backdrop to many of cycling's most iconic mountain images and startlingly illustrates the extremes to which the sport takes its participants.

By the time we reached the climb's start at Guillestre the most concerning extreme was one of temperature. (The Col can be ridden directly from Briançon but we'd chosen the opposite side as that's the ascent most often used by the Tour.) I supposed it was only apt that we should suffer Saharan heat whilst riding up a mountain infamous for its desert. Fitting, but not at all to Drew's liking. His vague mutterings soon turned to vocal attempts at insurrection. Stark warnings about what the swelter could do to such poor, pale persons "snowballed" until they'd become predictions of our imminent demise. He had a point — and I was sweating too much to deny it — but what other option was there? We had already considered re-timing the rides so that our peak efforts (no pun intended) wouldn't coincide with the hottest part of the day, but it was hellishly hot from around 11am until around 6pm. There was little we could do to avoid the heat, short of donning night-vision goggles and going out after dark. (No, *you* were supposed to pack the night-vision goggles!) Scant consolation came with the knowledge that, just like with our choice of gearing, we were experiencing the climbs in similar conditions to those the pros endured whilst racing. By that argument I wasn't much impressed, Drew less so.

We each had two large bottles of (now very warm) electrolyte energy drink. That was about one and a half litres each. Tour riders consume on average around half a litre of fluid every hour, around four litres per stage, but it hasn't always been that way. Riders used to labour under the impression that the more they drank the more they would sweat, and that sweating drained the body of energy. They therefore deliberately constrained their intake of fluids.

Seems like utter madness today but that was the accepted

127

wisdom of the time. Tour regulations even limited the amount of water a rider could take on during a stage. The modern rider has a fresh bidon waiting at the end of their two-way radio, sitting in the cool box, ready to be delivered by the following car or a trusty teammate. In the bad old days it was extremely common for the domestiques to hop off their bikes mid-race, jump into the nearest café or bar, grab a bottle of whatever they could get their hands on, be it alcoholic or not, and sprint back to the bunch to dish out "refreshments". Just the thought of imbibing alcohol whilst cycling under the sun made me feel ill.

Some riders, like German Tour-winner, Jan Ullrich, prefer the heat. He often rode badly in the cold and rain (as evidenced by his day of disaster in the Alps during the 1998 Tour). His physiology has been described as like a diesel engine, slowly powering up to top speed and staying there in the heat, but tending to chug and struggle to get going in the cold. One rider who hated the heat was Luxembourg's legendary climber, Charly Gaul. In the 1956 Giro d'Italia conditions through the Dolomites were extremely cold and so snowy that riders dropped like flies, abandoning rather than ride on. Gaul excelled in just such weather and rode so strongly that he gained sufficient time to win the race overall. (One explanation for Gaul's preference for the cold is his alleged use of amphetamines to boost performance. The suggestion is he took so much of the drug that his body struggled to regulate temperature, a side-effect that was exasperated by extreme heat.)

Despite the conditions, we weren't in any obvious trouble, no instant desire for illegal substances or freak snowstorms. Initially, the Izoard merely meandered — that's how it felt — all very nice and relatively easy. Such charity was welcome but surprising given that we had expected some kind of instantaneous and continual onslaught (at least I had; a subdued Rain Man Drew gave little away). The gradient was so lax that I had the temerity to roll ridiculous adjectives around on my tongue, words like *pleasant*, *gentle* and *meek*, as if thinking of how best to describe a newborn puppy. The wind, that cursed element from the previous day, was equally benevolent, coming, if at all, from behind, gently coaxing us onwards and upwards through the valley.

"Not so bad this after all," I mused, casting suspicious glances up the road.

We soon came upon a small village called Arvieux, a wee, rustic, cowboy kind of place, wholly enlivened by the gangs of cyclists who'd convened around a water fountain in the square. As one pedalled off another appeared, either zipping down the mountain or struggling upward, seeking to refuel and, more importantly, to boast about the ascent they had just completed or were attempting to complete. Suitably stocked with fluids, and unwilling to entertain others' tales of the one that didn't get away, we pedalled on.

At the village outskirts we passed a group of riders who were holding a tempo even easier than our own. They were younger than us, late teens or early twenties, their backs bent, heads lowered with the effort, every one apparently up for the challenge — every one except the guy hanging a few bike lengths off the back, wobbling and swaying around on the road. I assumed he was lacking in fitness and not suffering from an old-school, alcohol-based "hydration" problem but, whatever the case, the poor lad looked like he was in for a long day. We swerved round the wobbler, paused long enough to say hello to his comrades and decided their pace was insufficient, even for us. As we pulled ahead, the group rippled with laughter, to trigger our inherent, ever-present insecurity: was their mirth at the expense of our lack of savvy, our poor pacing or our dodgy Scottish/Dutch accents? Time, and the road ahead, would tell.

If we were going too fast then we really didn't think so, the pair of us pretty much convinced there wasn't much of anything ahead that required a deal of energy to be held in reserve. The meagre tailwind and other assorted distractions had successfully lulled us into that false sense of security, "it's not too bad after all", becoming the consensus opinion. But beware: the minute you take a Tour mountain for granted is the very point at which it will bare teeth, jump up and snarl angrily at your wheels — which is exactly how the Izoard reacted to our disrespect. As Arvieux faded from view, the road kicked viciously, the tailwind dropped and we immediately felt vulnerable, unarmed against the mountain.

The road slithered on and into the parched forest, writhing this way and that, seeking out the steepest slopes in order to make our lives as hard as possible. Despite the proliferation of trees there was no discernible shade to be found (and believe me, we looked for it), the merciless sun directly overhead. Each bend rounded revealed a shimmering wall of heat haze and a spell of 8, 9 or 10% gradient — more than steep enough for me to be down in first gear

(I'd been there since just after Arvieux, keen to follow through on my Galibier pledge, not about to repeat the mistake of "saving" my smallest gear; I would have gone lower had there been anywhere left to go).

Thoughts flickered back and forth between the road ahead and memories of Arvieux's fountain. *Why didn't we stop? Why aren't we there, right now, drinking in the shade and the cool, cool water?* Every so often, through gaps in the tree line, we'd catch distracting glimpses of the thin, twisted peaks and sandy structures at which we were aimed — the desert for which that fountain had become our oasis mirage. Dotted amongst the trees were an array of equally tempting scenes: shaded picnic tables with families, couples and groups of friends, all relaxed as can be and enjoying a normal, sensible summer-day activity: stuffing themselves with baguettes, with ham and cheese, with cold drinks and fruit. They paused long enough to work out where the awful noise was coming from, to discern what species of wheezing beast stalked them through the forest. They caught sight of us, red-faced, perspiring and expiring, hunched over our bikes like slaves struggling with the oars of some ancient galley. Unafraid and unimpressed, those sane people continued to chew and sip, to stare as we soldiered on, not a crumb of encouragement cast in our direction.

In 1948, Italian cycling legend Gino Bartali bonked badly after attacking from the bunch on the Izoard. As he battled on through the sleet and snow of a day diametric to ours, a spectator handed him three bananas. Bartali was revived and later proclaimed that the gifted fruit had saved his Tour de France. A decade earlier, a more youthful and better-fed Bartali hadn't required bananas to win the day, riding so hard up the Izoard that he dropped down into Briançon alone, five minutes ahead of the next man, and into the yellow jersey. Such exploits led General Antonelli, the Italian Sports Minister of the time, to hail Bartali as a living god.

To our sparse, shade-seeking spectators we were hardly godlike. I wanted to know, but had insufficient energy to enquire, had the picnickers seen so many cyclists that they'd grown tired of shouting encouragement? Had they ever cared at all? For the non-cyclist was it all just a bit passé, one-hundred percent unimpressive to see two men cycling up the Izoard — the drive up which had proved so sapping they'd been forced to stop halfway for a rest and some refreshments? More importantly, didn't they realise just how jealous we were of their cool, cool shade and their cool, cool drinks?

I was beginning to feel like one of the characters from Sylvain Chomet's enchanting animation, *Belleville Rendezvous*, escaped from the cinema screen and come to life upon the road. As the Tour passes through the mountains of Chomet's film, the poor riders appear to the viewer as overworked and undernourished horses, wheezing and panting, ready to fall by the wayside and be swept up by Madame Souza's *voiture balai* (broom wagon). The look of those characters reminded me of Fausto Coppi, five-time Giro and two-time Tour winner, compatriot and great rival of the aforementioned Bartali, as if they'd been modelled on his angular, lanky physique. Coppi must have ridden up the Col d'Izoard on many occasions but I'm pretty certain he never once struggled or panted pathetically. He won the Tour in 1949, his first year of trying, after putting in a well-timed attack on that false flat back down at Arvieux. Only Bartali could follow, and the two worked together, putting minutes into their main rivals. At the finish in Briançon, Coppi allowed Bartali to take the stage win, a birthday present to the older man.

I tried to focus on imaginings of those two great champions, conjuring their defeat of the mountain in a grainy black and white grace, but all the time I was struggling to tear my thoughts from the picnic baskets (suffering from what doctors refer to as, Yogi Bear Syndrome). I imagined my tongue licking condensation from the glass of ice-cold bottles, could almost hear the pop and fizz as the top came off, feel the icy explosion as carbonated liquid fizzed over my tongue and down my throat.

My bidon wasn't empty but sip after sip of warm electrolyte drink had done little to sate my thirst. As I struggled with the drooth, Drew complained about his heart rate.

"It's through the roof." Was his unscientific, manual measurement.

Thankfully, Rain Man Drew didn't own a digital heart-rate monitor. I would definitely have been driven insane had his incessant distance, altitude and gradient checks been accompanied by the bleeping update.

The lungs were where my main problem lay: each intake of breath seeming to do nothing but desiccate. I needed more than Bartali's bananas; I needed asthma medication and an oxygen mask. Better still, I needed an extra lung, a cold drink and a lie down in the shade.

Our bodies weren't the only casualties of the heat; the road had succumbed too. Our tyres tacked to patches of molten tar, a palpable sense that the mountain would rather consume us than allow for another pedal-powered human to reach its peak. We were the victims of a conspiracy, the gradient, the weather and the road all combining to ensure defeat. The Izoard would glue us in place, hold us still whilst the sun cooked, until the ashes of our bikes and bodies could be scattered by the winds, adding sand to the Casse Déserte.

Where the road hadn't melted we'd often see yet more fans' graffiti left over from recent races. There were a few "*Go Lance*" and a countering couple of "*Vai Pantani*", but the most common on this climb was "*Udo & Jan*". There was a half-mile stretch where the couple's tribute had been painted in almost unbroken succession, as if that part of the road had been created in their honour, or that Udo & Jan was the brand name of the manufacturer. The Udo & Jan in question were of course the Germans, Udo Bölts and Jan Ullrich. I'd never before thought of those two as a couple, Jan was the team leader, the undoubted star of cycling, Udo was just his trusty domestique who did the work but rarely took the limelight. However, to this paint-happy fan or fans Bölts & Ullrich were obviously inseparable, made to go together like horse and carriage or love and marriage. And from there I began to imagine Udo and Jan as a proper, married couple, as if they were the glamour pairing of the peloton, like a German, cycling version of Posh and Becks — oh, those thoughts, those ridiculous thoughts and the ridiculous heat were killing me! (And killing Drew too because I felt compelled to share.)

In an attempt to distract from my delirium and worries about our imminent expiration, Drew began to recite the lyrics of the folk song, *Flower O' Scotland*. For some unknown reason, that unofficial Caledonian national anthem had popped up and then stuck inside his head, playing over and over on a hellish (if patriotic) loop. My attention was focussed on the less melodic sound of creaking that came from my battered and worn left pedal cleat. That noise, normally as welcome as the screech of fingernails on blackboard, was strangely comforting, aural evidence that I remained in motion and was therefore still alive. I settled in to the frequency of the creak, the rhythm of the consequent sound and action: the cleat's creak, the lungs' wheeze, the push on the pedals. Creak-wheeze-push. I was the bagpipe backing to Drew's anthem. Creak-wheeze-push. Creak-wheeze-push. Just as with the metallic clink of swinging pendant striking jersey zip, it was another mind-clearing mantra to which I succumbed. Creak-wheeze-push. Creak-wheeze-push. Everything else dissolved from the scene. Gone were the sticky tar and the baking sun. Creak-wheeze-push. Creak-wheeze-push. Gone were my thirst and the sting of salty sweat. Creak-wheeze-push. Creak-wheeze-push. Gone was Drew, his bike, *my* bike, even the mountain up which we struggled. Creak-wheeze-push. Creak-wheeze-push. No pain in legs or lungs, no me, no mountain. Just the creak-wheeze-push. Creak-wheeze-push.

Somewhere around there I experienced what I can only describe as an epiphany. There was no vision, no figure of Christ or the Virgin Mary, just a moment where everything made perfect, joyous sense. An ice-cool breeze blew out of nowhere, rushed up the hill and clean through me. A subsequent shiver shot up my spine, rattled from the inside out, shaking me up before shooting its way on and into my brain. Although my pace hadn't quickened, it suddenly felt like I was flying, the bike but a featherweight beneath me, legs uncommonly supple and smooth. My gargoyle-on-the-toilet expression cracked with a giant smile, the man who had so recently hovered upon the edge of despair now buzzing with a blast of positive energy. In that brief moment I knew *why*: why I was riding the Izoard that day, why my life had followed a path I had no recollection of choosing. Like a drugged-up hippie staring at a Goan sunset, I was overwhelmed by understanding, unshakeably certain of my own existence, deliriously glad to be alive. I was also aware of just how privileged I was to be there, on that bike, on that road at that very moment. I could have been stuck behind a desk, staring out the window at the dogs and students who frequented the park adjacent to my office; instead I was free as a bird, soaring (albeit very slowly) toward the summit of a majestic mountain, challenging myself and responding accordingly.

Thoughts turned to my late father, to his life, his achievements and the love he had shown for all his family. Of course I missed him, did so incredibly and always would, but there on the Izoard I felt that he was riding shotgun, proving a more faithful wingman than Heras, Hamilton and Hincapie all rolled into one. He was with me, inside me, all around me, sharing the moment and proudly patting my back. Thoughts shifted to my girlfriend, to my love for her, a desire to have children of our own, so one day my son or daughter might ride the mountain with me, shoulder to shoulder, sharing in the love and wonder, the ardour and ecstasy. *This*, I thought, looking down at the spinning pedals, up at the road ahead, *this* is my church, out on a bike instead of sitting in a pew. This is where I feel close to whatever god might be. Churches are buildings designed to draw one's focus heavenward, architecture intended to inspire, and wasn't that what those great mountains had been doing? They drew our eyes, our bodies and minds upward. They lifted us from the daily grind, from the fog of our troubles and worries. Physically we climbed so that our spirits might soar.

With meticulous timing, my perfect peace was disturbed by a clutch of motorcycles speeding effortlessly upward. They zipped by close as they could without scraping the skin off our elbows, screamed away, round the corner and out of sight. Drew, distracted mid-verse, bellowed sarcastically into their dust:

"Well done lads, dig in!"

A final series of switchbacks and we exited the forest, crawling forth to the Casse Déserte like extras from *Ice Cold In Alex*. All around us lay what is perhaps the most iconic landscape of any cycling ascent. (Of course the aerial images of Alpe d'Huez and its twisting hairpins are instantly recognisable, but how many people could place a close-up of the pasture that borders the road?) The Izoard's appearance is certainly unique, if only we'd had the time to take it all in. Drew was adamant, the effort far from over, a glance here and there all he'd allow, our full concentration pressed into completing the task at hand.

We passed a memorial to Coppi, and another to Louison Bobet (the first three-in-a-row Tour winner), just enough time and energy to doff our caps, and were quickly onto a short but rather sharp descent. The road was now reminiscent of the Galibier — very narrow, with no verge and a sheer drop on one side — no safety barrier to prevent your plummet. And that plummet appeared to go on forever, deep into the distant dust, even more frightening than the Galibier (in comparison, the Galibier was about as scary as a ham sandwich). Not only that but the "safe", non-plummet side had a metre-deep drop into a drainage ditch, the road built up and sitting away from the mountain. The effect was extremely disconcerting, especially so as we gathered speed. I veered toward the middle of the road, would have remained there had a car not been coming in the opposite direction. Aiming to miss it and either drop, I closed my eyes, held my breath and somehow squeezed through the gap.

I dared to think what it would be like on that precarious road when the entire Tour de France entourage trundled through: a skinny mountain pass packed with lone riders and small groups, the autobus (that gaggle of slower riders who stick together over the climbs, seeking safety in numbers), motorbikes, team cars laden with spares, ambulances, the press, TV cameras and the dreaded broom wagon — all that as an encore to the publicity caravan, with cars disguised as giant plastic cheeses and bottles of perfume, smiley, beautiful people hanging out the back handing out souvenirs and product samples to the baying crowds. They'd all be vying for road space with the thousands of spectators, some of whom would have camped out overnight to get a ringside spot at the world's greatest free-of-charge spectator sport.

Having that short descent might sound like a good thing, a little rest before the final push, but it didn't quite work that way. Just long enough to totally break my rhythm, it left me out of sorts and out of gear. I hit the subsequent rise fumbling with my gear levers, legs confused and stiffening. As a result, the drag to the final summit, which couldn't have been much more than a kilometre, felt ten times as long. Jersey unzipped again, a few more sharp switchbacks and by the end I was coaching and coaxing myself along:

"Just 100 metres more. Please body, please, I beg you, don't fail me now! You could have failed way back down the climb but you didn't, so don't give up now. Not now, not so close. Please don't. That would be too cruel. You can do it, I know you can. So come on. Hang in there!"

We lolled toward the stone tower in the barren summit car park for another photo of another achievement, although this one, like the previous day's Galibier, felt truly monumental.

***

Photoshop the sky above the Casse Déserte to a russet hue and you could be fooled into thinking you're looking at images beamed back to Earth from Mars by Nasa's latest probe. This ethereal, alien world has almost no greenery, few outward signs of life. Ragged, jagged shards, pillars and peaks of rock appear to push up through mile after mile of sand and scree, as if projected from the very centre of the planet. Zoom out from the detail and those distensions blend into giant waves of sandy rock, which sweep this way and that like some fossilised tide. Through the middle of it all sneaks a pathetic little road, impossibly tough to ride, afforded no protection from the endless drop and the merciless sun.

After several stunned and mostly silent minutes, we dragged ourselves from the view and into the summit's cycling museum. It's a small, one-room affair with a limited display, the highlight of which is undoubtedly the collection of black and white photographs of stars gone by. These classic shots capture cycling heroes at work upon the mountain passes, including the Izoard, and many others we had recently ridden. Bobet, Coppi, Bartali, Merckx, Hinault et al, are fixed in full flight, attacking mountain roads like crazed warriors on the charge toward enemy lines. Their faces, mainly masks of pain, leave no doubt that the high mountains have always been tough, no matter the era, no matter the rider.

We had just stepped out of the museum when the group of chuckling youngsters we'd passed at Arvieux appeared over the crest of the climb. They were looking suitably dishevelled but minus their earlier amusement and that wobbly hanger on. It wasn't for a while later that we passed the poor lad, still bravely battling bike and mountain. We offered him our encouragement, a "chapeau" or two, and he responded by looking resolutely beat.

Off we sped, back down the Col, ready to remind everyone we passed along the way not of our achievement, but of the day's sadder news:

"Tout le monde! Oie, il mort! Goose is dead!"

DAY 11:
MAD DOGS, SCOTSMEN & THE MIDDAY SUN

Col de l'Iseran
Start point: Bonneval-Sur-Arc | Height: 2764m | Height climbed: 977m | Length of climb: 13.43km | Average gradient: 7.3% | Maximum gradient: 10.5%

La Plagne
Start point: Aime | Height: 2080m | Height climbed: 1400m Length of climb: 21.4km | Average gradient: 6.6% | Maximum gradient: 10.4%

We were checking out of the hotel when Pat struck up a conversation, the first time she'd uttered more than a few, cursory words since our arrival; she was smiling, which was another first — like the receptionist at Trento prison, probably just happy to see the back of us. She enquired as to where we were headed, very nearly choked on her grin upon hearing that we were ditching Briançon for Bourg-Saint-Maurice. She spat the name of that, allegedly awful place, so disgusted that she was forced to abbreviate: "*B.S.M.!*" She informed us that it was not only "new" but also, "very, very ugly" — so unlike her dear, old, beloved and beautiful Briançon. Well, we thought, she would say that, wouldn't she?

***

To get to B.S.M. we drove up and over the Lautaret, the Galibier, and down over the Col du Télégraphe. Whilst ascending the Lautaret, we passed an old lady, (in her sixties, I would guess), riding a rickety old mountain bike. Her effort and example embarrassed the young moaners who'd royally pissed and moaned about a bit of a headwind. She was giving it some, powering into the wind, just the faintest touch of a smile across her wizened face. And she wasn't alone in her effusive efforts. Half the population appeared to be out on their bikes that Sunday morning, adding credibility to my cycling-as-church analogy. The Sunday run can provide one with an equally valuable spiritual boost. It teaches you to work hard, to cooperate with others in the congregation (the bunch), to value god's green land, and fills the believer with an uplifting sense of achievement. Amen to that.

Driving back over the Galibier was even more frightening than cycling down it. The French drivers coming toward us seemed to think it was their right to drive over and onto our side of the road. That much was obvious. Quite where they thought we were going to go, I had no idea. Did they really think we would Evil Knievel into the void just to make way for them? Well yes, yes they did think that. That's why they drove toward us taking racing lines, cutting us up, leaving Drew no option but to repeatedly hit the brakes and hope for the best.

We somehow survived the Galibier — both sides — to be rewarded with a soulless drive through Albertville, out along a grimly industrialised valley and eventually on to B.S.M.. Our first impression of the place suggested that Pat had been on to something. It was a nothing kind of place, devoid of Briançon's copious charm and character; worse given that it was Sunday, with no shops open and the streets pretty much deserted. Even the Super U was closed. In the UK the shops never shut, ever. Asda, Tesco, Sainsbury's, even some of the corner shops near my Edinburgh flat are open 24, sometimes 25 hours a day. (What is it with these European companies giving all their staff one day off a week? The trade unions must be crushed, crushed I tell you!) We assumed B.S.M. shared the same fate as all ski resorts in the summer: it was there to serve a purpose and when that purpose was removed, even on a seasonal basis, it slipped toward temporary irrelevance.

We arrived at the Hôtel L'Autantic, finally finding it hidden down a country lane, scenically located adjacent to a building site. The hotel itself, we were pleased to note, wasn't under construction, although it has to be said, the staff still required some work — if our first impressions of B.S.M. had been below par, then they were about to sink to the very depths. Out from the reception's shadows strolled the hotel manager, (from henceforth she shall be known as, "the headmistress"), a tall, thin, blonde woman, perhaps in her late forties, any beauty she might have possessed masked by an expression that could crack walnuts at fifty paces. As I introduced us in mangled French she winced, refused even to acknowledge that hers wasn't our mother tongue, and that we might well have had a long journey to reach her hotel. In place of any kind of welcome we were slapped with a stern reprimand, taken down a peg or two for daring to have asked to check in at such an ungodly hour. There are rules, she insisted with a click of her heels, and the rules must be obeyed! At all times! Those rules — how could you not have known? Impertinent little boys! — quite clearly stated that one could not check in to the boarding school until after 3pm. If we did not conform to the rules then the only choice would be for us to spend a week in detention on bread and water rations.

"Do I make myself clear?"

"Yes, miss."

Made to feel like errant schoolboys for the second time in two weeks, we skulked out of the hotel and headed back into town. Once we had eaten, what else was there to do? We drove around and looked at the closed shops, we toured the empty Super U car park, even took time out to wash the car. We cursed and swore and wondered how a woman so rude could make a living in the hospitality industry. More importantly, didn't she recognise two very serious and very talented cyclists when she saw them? Clearly not.

An hour left to kill, and we realised there had been something to do all along: dry our kit. It was packed into two carrier bags in the back of the car, still wet from its wash in the sink earlier that morning, so we drove a short distance from town, stopped in a car park and laid it all out to dry on a picnic table.

The time finally passed, our kit finally frazzled and we returned to the boarding school, only to discover that the staff were intent on wearing us down and keeping us on our toes by playing the old, good cop, bad cop, routine. The headmistress had scuttled off to grind children's bones into dust (probably) and good cop — a friendly, attractive, young brunette who was the antithesis of her colleague — checked us in and showed us to our room. It was nice enough but somewhat spoiled by sporting only one, particularly small double bed. Drew and I really weren't keen on sharing a bed for two long nights, especially not after two long days of sweaty cycling. We were already exhibiting signs of the stress derived from having spent so much time in one another's pockets, sharing a bed would only have thrown us over the edge.

"What is she thinking?" I asked Drew. "She's shown us to this room knowing full-well there's only one bed. Does she also think we're a honeymooning couple? Did Trento phone ahead to tell her we were coming?"

Drew nodded in reply, resigned to our uncomfortable fate. It had become a moot point: instead of assuming we were famous pro cyclists on a secret training camp, people assumed we were a German/Austrian/Italian/Dutch/Chinese/anything-but-Scottish honeymooning couple, united by marriage and a love of cycling. Luckily, my crap French and a copy of the fax I had sent when making my reservation, (the Folder of Doom contained copies of all correspondence. How orderly and organised. And you say you're straight?), won us a twin room and left good cop under the impression that the honeymooning couple were in the midst of a lovers' tiff.

***

It was knocking on 4pm by the time we were into (crinkly-dry) lycra and out on the bikes. The day had ticked by, the headmistress' unflinching observation of the rules and our lax laundry habits having robbed us of around three hours of riding time. With it had gone our chance to ride the Col de l'Iseran. The fluid schedule had succumbed to the heat, was beginning melt and drip from the black plastic folder.

Upon reaching Aime for the start of the climb to La Plagne, Drew and I were similarly molten, the sun beyond baking, even hotter than it had felt upon the Izoard — to be honest, it was hotter than anything I'd ever experienced. So no prizes for guessing why there was nobody else around, why it felt like we had cycled into a ghost town. Even the ghosts had better sense, were off haunting somewhere more suitably shaded. The only living thing we saw (human or otherwise) was the young girl who darted along the street, ducked into a shed, then quickly ran back out again carrying several large bottles of mineral water. Everyone else, even the mad dogs were out of the sun and taking it easy.

It's no coincidence that this was the point in proceedings when Drew started to complain. No ambiguity to his grumbling, put quite simply, he didn't want to go up the mountain, thought it extremely dangerous even to consider doing so:

"It's far too hot. We will die, definitely this time. Okay, so we didn't die upon the Izoard, but that was just a fluke, a stroke of good fortune. This is set to be the day we do the foolish thing we always thought we'd never do, the day our families will look back upon in regretful grief, wishing they could somehow have stopped us. We will die!" And he slammed his fist onto the handlebars to reinforce the point.

"We won't die," I calmly countered, no reasoning or evidence offered in support of my claim.

"We will, definitely! I'm sure of it. The heat kills people all the time, that's a fact. And not just ordinary people, it kills super-fit cyclists like us too!" He screeched, imagination already skipping ahead, across the plains of Provence and up the slopes of the Ventoux.

"*Super-fit* cyclists? *Really?*" I brushed aside his (somewhat flattering) concerns with a snort and an airy wave, pedalled off up the road, hoping he would follow.

Thankfully, he did.

The ski resort at La Plagne was developed as a means of bringing winter tourists and their money into an agricultural region that was in economic decline. Work began in 1961 but it was two years before the winding road up from the valley was properly surfaced with tarmac — to prevent skiers' cars getting bogged down in the mud.

The Tour de France came a while later, first pedalling its way up to the resort in 1984, when my childhood hero, Laurent Fignon, won the stage. He triumphed again in 1987, the year of Irishman Stephen Roche's dramatic Giro, Tour and Worlds treble. The road is a dead-end, so when Tour stages visit La Plagne, they do so with the intention of finishing at the summit (although the town Aime, at the base of the climb, has hosted four stage starts). The race has, as is the case with other ski resorts, such as Alpe d'Huez, provided La Plagne with valuable publicity and a lucrative boost to its summer tourist income.

The Tour doesn't visit places like La Plagne by sheer chance. Félix Lévitan, who took over as race director in 1962, was first to arrange for stages to start and finish at, not only ski resorts, but also seaside towns, in order to boost their public profiles, and in turn to earn the organisers a Franc or deux. Indeed, there isn't a town in France — nor across Europe, witness London's hosting of the Grand Départ — that wouldn't open its arms to a stage of the

Tour. (It's also thanks to Lévitan that the Tour celebrates its best climber with the red-on-white polka dot jersey.)

For the first couple of kilometres I stayed on the front, doing my blatant best to ignore Drew's dissent. I understood his caution, that his concerns were genuine, but up to that point we had endured an exceedingly dull day. Our chance to ride the Iseran was already lost, to ruin things completely by ditching La Plagne would have been the crappy icing on a pretty shitty cake. The heat is most certainly not my friend; I'm a Scot with Scandinavian ancestry who's more used to rain and cold. The average summer temperature for the village I grew up in is 14 degrees Celsius. Just a few degrees above that and I sweat, profusely. Leave the central heating on for too long and I'm at real risk of heat stroke. I prefer riding in the rain but raining it was not and we were there, in the French Alps, in the baking heat, to do one thing and one thing only: cycle up a mountain. So cycle up the bloody mountain we would, even if it killed us.

Drew's grumbling and my forced flippancy was all a stark contrast to the time we'd ridden up the slopes of Pico del Veleta in Spain (Europe's highest paved road — oh, have I already boasted about, I mean, mentioned, it?). That was also a disconcertingly hot day but I'd been the one wearing the Team Pessimism kit, wobbling on the bike, absolutely certain that I was minutes from temperature-related expiration. Back then, if Drew had offered even the merest hint of agreement I would have been in the air-conditioned hire car with my feet up on the dashboard quicker than he could have said, "why don't we". But he hadn't agreed; instead he had pressed on, ignoring my concerns, thinking only of his own desire to ride. The bike-lengths between us became tens of metres, on until my friend was little more than a tiny dot on the heat-hazed horizon. As he danced on the pedals, I had wrestled and rolled around the road, battling against the never-ending climb, tongue lolling from my mouth like a shrivelled stick, brain boiling, skin screaming from beneath the factor thirty.

Now we were in the Alps, at a lower altitude, if not a lower temperature, and I was playing the determined half of the duo. I had paid so much money, had taken so much time out for the trip; it was the literal and metaphoric high-point of my year and I wasn't about to kiss yet another climb goodbye because of the weather, no matter how extreme it might be. I'd already been trying to turn negative into positive by thinking of all those missed appointments as my reason to return to Italy and France, but there were only so many names I could allow onto that list. There isn't always a tomorrow, recent personal events had demonstrated that all to clearly, and it was in no way certain there'd be a future in which Drew and I came back to Europe to bag all the big fish that had already got away. So, onward and upward I felt compelled to forge, keeping the tempo as high as possible, thus depriving Drew of the puff with which to complain.

Despite the thought that my best mate might never speak to me again, (assuming we survived to talk another day), I was bloody mindedly determined to enjoy the climb, and the climb appeared keen to aid my enjoyment. The switchback corners started about a third of the way up, delivering variety and a break from the long and monotonous straights. Like Alpe d'Huez, La Plagne has 21 signposted and numbered switchbacks and, like those on the Izoard, they were streaked with lines of molten tar.

By 18, the novelty had worn off and I was sweating so much that Drew's earlier protestations whispered haunting in my ear, the echoes of an earlier prophecy naively ignored. By 17, each of us was lost in his own personal purgatory, concentrating so much on the basics (remaining upright on the bike and, more importantly, remaining alive) that the blast of a passing car's horn and the occupants' shouts of *allez* almost finished us with fright. The scare snapped me back to the moment, and what a frightful moment it was. Every ounce of energy I'd held in reserve barely a kilometre before (and had used not only to pedal but to counter Drew's complaints) had all but ebbed away. This wasn't like the shaky cold of the dreaded bonk — I had eaten before the climb and had been religiously gulping my energy drink — I just felt listless, as if an unseen hand had opened me up, reached inside and turned the power dial to zero. From reckless to repentant, I coasted alongside Drew and reinforced the change by offering a flippant comment on our decision to commit suicide on the road to La Plagne.

Somehow we stumbled on, through a small village, where my greedy eye spied, of all things, a water fountain. Praising the heavens, rabid smile streaked across my foaming gob, I dropped back and, with a hoarse whisper, asked Drew to stop so we could refresh. I was sure he would eagerly do just that, that he might thank my eagle eyes for spotting the oasis, but no, that's not exactly how it went. Instead of filling his bottle or diving head-first into the icy pool, he ignored me and kept on pedalling up the road.

"What's with him?" I wondered aloud, wasting valuable breath.

Was ignorance his retribution? Did he not get that in punishing me for the dismissal of his earlier concern he was also punishing himself? Wasn't he also ridiculously hot and thirsty?

"Isn't the heat driving you mad?" I hissed. "I mean, it was earlier. Fifteen f***ing minutes ago you were practically begging me to run for the nearest shade, and now you're not in the least bit moved by the sight of a cool and sparkling spring?"

He said nothing, didn't even turn to look back.

"What's with you?" I shouted, or at least tried to, desiccated tongue lolling between salt-crusted lips.

Half a kilometre later, I was still struggling to reach his wheel when he dropped back to (non-sarcastically) tell me that his bottles were almost empty and that he would kill for some water. He went on to add, "if only we would pass a water fountain."

I almost imploded with incredulity.

"What are you talking about?" I demanded. "Are you winding me up?"

"What are *you* talking about?" He countered.

"A water fountain? Why the hell didn't you stop?"

"Stop? Where?"

"At the bloody water fountain, of course!"

"What bloody water fountain?"

That ridiculous shouting match would have carried on for hours had either of us the energy to sustain it. As it was we had already eaten into the reserve reserves of our reserves, and the conversation, if you could call it that, degenerated into monosyllables, grunts and vague, airy gestures, the gist of which was that he hadn't heard my earlier alert, too deep into his own oblivion to notice either the fountain or my feeble attempts at distraction. Worse than any of that, when he did finally get the breath to ask, he in turn demanded to know why on earth I hadn't stopped to fill *my* bottles or plunge *my* head into the cool, crisp, sparkling-blue pool.

"Well?" He demanded, "why didn't you?"

Silence.

"Did you need mummy Drew to hold your hand?"

I pretended not to have heard, satisfied that we were both

suffering from the conditions and a lack of water. We had climbed around ten miles in searing heat and had each drunk a litre and a half, nothing left in either of our bottles. (I say, *around* ten miles, as I had turned my computer off the trip-distance function. Its countdown to the end of suffering hadn't appeared to be counting down and had instead been driving me insane.) My salt-pan mouth filled with a horrible taste; I wanted nothing more from life than to brush my teeth, dreamily imagined being back at the hotel, in the bathroom. I could feel the cool water in my mouth, taste the minty fresh paste. The train of thought careered along the hallucinatory tracks until I was sloshing around in a swimming pool full of ice-cold Perrier. (I'd been leaning over the edge when my toothbrush had fallen in and, despite not being able to swim, I'd dived after it.)

What raised me from the depths of that watery illusion? A troubling question: what disease is the opposite of rabies? If rabies sufferers are hydro*phobic*, then were Drew and I hydro*phonic*? Seeking an answer from on high, I looked up and in the glare of the sun's rays saw the shape of a large bird, which looked frighteningly like a vulture, hovering above. I waved a hand to dismiss it, rubbed my lips with the back of my mitt, felt a burst of pain and the taste of blood as a layer of parched skin came away. What next, I thought, what additional prop or sensation can La Plagne throw our way to emphasise the intensity and the heat? How about a bunch of Bedouin and their camels camped at the next corner?

The climb probably wasn't too hard in itself but add in the searing heat and La Plagne verged on being the hardest ascent of our trip so far. I was doing my best to ignore thoughts of how much road there was left to cover — lost in a mindless cloud, occasionally catching glimpses of the climb, scenes recognised from TV footage and race photos — when I realised that once again I had drifted off the back of Drew's wheel. He had settled in to the heat and resumed tempo-setting duties, forcing a pace I hadn't been willing or able to hold. With every subsequent pedal stroke the gap increased.

My mullered musing then turned to the famous TV footage of Stephen Roche and his race up the climb during the 1987 Tour. His main rival for the yellow jersey that year, Spaniard, Pedro Delgado, had ridden away at Aime, but the intelligent Irishman hadn't panicked. Roche calculated exactly how much of a lead he could allow Delgado to gain before he would have to react — not only was he a tactically-minded racer, he also knew when to ride hard, and how to suffer. As the Spaniard's lead grew, heading towards two minutes, Roche made his counter move. He rode so hard in the last five kilometres that he crossed the line at La Plagne only four seconds down on Delgado, much to everyone's disbelief. Some of the most famous images of an off-the-bike Tour rider are those of Roche collapsed on the ground that day, an oxygen mask clamped to his face. Upon reviving, Roche was asked if he was okay and replied with French words but suitably Irish substance:

"*Oui, mais pas de femme tout de suite.*" (Yes, but I am not ready for a woman straight away.)

As famous as those images are the sounds of Phil Liggett's commentary from the TV coverage of the stage. As Delgado came into view and crossed the finish line, the count was on to see just how much time he had taken out of Roche. It was expected that he would have gained easily a minute, perhaps even two, so when Roche appeared almost on the wheel of his rival, an astonished Liggett nearly burst a blood vessel:

"*Again Pedro Delgado has slipped Stephen Roche on the climb. Remember, at one point he had a minute-and-a-half — and just who is that rider coming up behind? Because that looks like Roche. That looks like Stephen Roche! It's Stephen Roche who's come over the line! He almost caught Pedro Delgado, I don't believe it!*"

(Check it out for yourself on YouTube. If it doesn't send a shiver down your spine then that's either because you're a Delgado family member or because you're dead inside.)

Liggett's commentary was running over and over in my head as Drew pulled further away, and so I decided there was only one thing for it: to act like a five-year-old, pretend that I was Stephen Roche trying to save his Tour, and that Drew was the dastardly Delgado trying to wrest glory from my grip. I pulled myself together, sat up a little straighter and pushed ever so slightly harder on the pedals. With full concentration I kept eyes locked firmly on Drew's back wheel, as if my vision alone was holding it in place. Satisfied the gap wasn't growing, and almost convinced that I had the necessary reserves, plus a little excess to make it to the top, I pushed on the pedals some more. The ting of pendant striking zip increased as the cranks turned more quickly. As I moved on, the air grew a little cooler, delivering the extra spurt of energy I'd sought. I shifted up a gear, stood on the pedals, pulled and pushed at the bike until I was barely a metre off the back of Drew's wheel. Inside my head the mutated echo of Liggett's commentary reverberated:

"... *and just who is that rider coming up behind? Because that looks like Rae-Hansen. That looks like Rolf Rae-Hansen!*"

Drew responded to my triumphant return in a manner that suggested he too was playing the five-year-old's game. He hammed up the Delgado role, and instead of maintaining the pace, pressed harder on the pedals to pull away once more. No time to feel sorry for myself, no energy to shout him back, I accepted the challenge and jumped up the road, giving everything I had to get level and then inch my front wheel ahead of his.

Just as I was starting to enjoy our little spot of mano-a-mano, the stomach cramps kicked in. Those were swiftly followed by the distinct sensation that my bowels were about to perform an emergency evacuation. I had experienced such pain before but each time had been sat safely on a toilet seat and not a bicycle saddle. I couldn't think what to do; should I dart into the trees or keep going? The discomfort built and thoughts of jumping into the forest were only dispelled as we rounded a corner and emerged above the top edge of the tree line. The fright at having nowhere to hide caused me to pass wind — and, thankfully, that was all I passed.

"Please don't let this happen," I begged the god of the upset stomach as the cramps built toward an encore. "Don't you know that should the worst happen I'd have to pedal back to B.S.M. in a steaming cloud of my own stinking disgrace, that I'd then have to try and sneak my soiled state in passed the headmistress? Worse than all that, I'd have to wash my shorts in the bathroom sink!"

I was sure I recalled having seen footage of Jan Ullrich during the Tour, riding along as team-mates followed on behind spraying water from their bidons to wash away stinking diarrhoea debris.

"It cannot happen, neither Drew or I have any water left to spray! I would have to turn tail, sprint back down to the water fountain and throw myself in, arse first!"

That was pretty much how the last kilometre passed, lost to my panic, a state of stress endured until another couple of severe and, much to my relief, dry gusts signalled the end of discomfort. We arrived in La Plagne centre and Drew carried on going, riding ever onwards and upwards as if chasing the sun itself.

"Where are you going?" I shouted after him.

"To the top," he shouted back.

"We're already at the top!" I hollered hopelessly.

He was looking for the summit sign or some kind of grand civic reception to commemorate the two suicidal cyclists who had gambled with the heat and won. All he found were a couple of giant hotels, a memorial to RAF pilots who parachuted in supplies during the war, and the road back down to where he'd just come from. Just like Aime, La Plagne appeared to be something of a ghost town, no one around to welcome us, or to bear witness should I have had that nasty accident.

Over by the shopping centre we found a small billboard with a map of the resort's facilities and its name printed above, that the closest we'd get to a summit sign. A couple of photos later and a stream of buses appeared round the corner, stopping to deposit about a thousand passengers between them — apparently the town's entire population had been on a day trip and all returned at once. Or was this the civic reception of which we had fantasised? No, no it was not. Like iron filings drawn by a magnet, the swarm of citizens made a b-line for the shopping centre, every last one of them disappearing inside. What's going on? We wondered. Does the town have a back door? Is there a giant slide down into the valley, all the people going in the front and dropping out the back?

With the crowd cleared we were better able to take in the view — our broiled brains could think of little else to do. It is said that from La Plagne you can see the slopes of Mont Blanc but my geographical knowledge was insufficient to single out Europe's highest peak from the giants that towered in every direction. (It really was astounding; I even had to slam on the brakes at one point during the descent in order to better absorb it all.) The Alpine valleys looked exquisite in the late-afternoon sun. A painter or photographer would have been as excited about the light, the quality and clarity of the colours and the bright-blue sky as us idiot cyclists were about the road.

A glance back up at the resort's name and I laughed as a disbelieving grin streaked across my face. Rolf, you're right here, at the top of one of *the* Tour de France climbs. You're at La Plagne!

Through my good humour came just the faintest chink of anticipation. Tomorrow would bring the Glandon *and* the Madeleine — two in one day, no excuses, no hiding in the shade.

No time to think about them either, not yet. Stomach instantly healed and already grumbling for dinner, we turned and freewheeled down the mountain. Let the climbs come when they come, was my pragmatic, overly simplistic advice. Anticipation is useless unless preceded by thorough preparation, and for that it was far too late.

***

Back at the hotel, we attempted to sneak passed the headmistress but she was clearly on full alert, a beady eye out for evidence of our disgusting ways. She could barely stand the thought of us messing up her beautiful hotel, but the thought of our bikes made her sick, sick, *sick*, you hear me! Springing ninja-like from behind the reception desk, she grabbed hold of our handlebars, turned swiftly on her heels, dragging us back out the door and on toward the dusty outbuilding our bikes would call home for the next two nights.

Despite the ticking off, the mood in our camp had improved. Drew appeared to be back in the game, spirits lifted by the schoolboy racing games and his comeback from doom upon the road to La Plagne. Whilst waiting for him to shower, I sneaked across the hall to visit the cycling psychotherapist who had been travelling alongside us. He greeted me with a confused smile.

"Can I help?" He peered over the top of his pince nez.

"It's me, Rolf."

"Oh yes, Rolf. Do come in."

I stepped in to his bedroom/consulting room, took up the offered seat.

"I'm surprised I haven't seen you before now," he smiled in a detached manner.

"To be honest, Doc, I forgot you were here."

"Tell you the truth, so did I," and he smiled again, this time a little less certain which one of us had the doctorate.

"So," I began.

"So?"

"So, I just thought I'd pop in and update you on the mood in the mountain camp."

"Yes, the mood, excellent." He leant over to the bedside table, retrieved pen and notepad, scribbled something down. "So how is the mood in the mountain camp?"

"It's better tonight than it has been for a while. Yesterday wasn't too bad either, but on the Lautaret, the day before that, it was pretty low. Well, Drew was low."

"Why do you think he was low, was it because he hadn't pedalled up high enough?" He chuckled at his own, awful joke.

"You're supposed to be a doctor, not a comedian."

"Sorry, do continue."

"Yeah, I was saying, Drew didn't like the Lautaret. There was this awful headwind all the way up, about twenty miles of climbing into a howling wind, and he wasn't happy with it. Not one bit."

"Who would be? Sounds like riding through a wind tunnel."

"That's what he said."

"Interesting," he scribbled something else on the pad.

"I'm just worried, 'cause Drew kept questioning why he was there, what the point was to it all."

"And what was the point?"

"Of the Lautaret or the trip?"

"The trip."

"To ride the mountains we had always talked, always dreamt of riding."

"And you had both always dreamt of riding up the Lautaret into a headwind?"

"No, but it lead to The Galibier and we had both dreamt of that. *I* definitely had, and I'm pretty sure he had too. Pantani attacked on that mountain in 1998 and went from there to win the Tour. He was a hero to us both. He was Drew's cycling inspiration."

"Don't worry, Rolf, everything will be okay. Drew just gets a little homesick, and all the driving is getting to him. These crazy foreign roads and all the crazy foreign drivers can be a real stress, you know? Things will be fine."

"I hope you're right."

"Of course I'm right. So, tell me, what are you up to tomorrow?"

"The Glandon and the Madeleine."

"Both? In the same day?"

"Yeah. Why?"

"Oh, no reason, just curious. Well, anyway, hope you enjoy it."

"Me too."

"Well, that's £300 you owe me for the session, just call it €500."

"Do you take imaginary travellers cheques?"

***

Showers done and we were off into B.S.M., a second attempt at finding evidence of life. Lo and behold, we located some, at an Italian restaurant across from the town hall. Surrounded by swarms of tiny flies, we tucked into generous portions of lasagne, dining under the oppressive eye of the proprietor's giant, slavering dog. The brutish mutt appeared to be some kind of wolf/horse hybrid, far removed from the petite, in-bred finery that tiptoed the streets of Briançon. Tongue lolling from its foaming gob, the poor animal looked as dehydrated as I had felt on the climb to La Plagne. It wandered between the tables, looking utterly confused, suggesting that rabies thrived on the European mainland.

An electric billboard across from the restaurant flashed wildly, red digital text shooting across its display as if there was simply too much going on in B.S.M. for it to keep up. One of the events it was bursting to tell us about was a randonée, open to all cyclists, held in aid of handicapped children. Less nobly, the billboard also attempted to push a local comedy festival, which, if anything like Briançon's music festival, would be better billed as comedy/horror. The only evidence we had so far seen of the French sense of humour had been the waiter's joke we suffered in Briançon:

"Are you English?" He asked.

"No, we're Scottish," we replied.

"Oh well, nobody's perfect," he smirked.

"Excuse me?" We asked, because we genuinely hadn't heard what he said.

"It's just a joke an Englishman taught me," he mumbled defensively.

"What is?" We asked. "We didn't hear you."

He duly repeated himself, this time without the passing-moped interruption.

"Are you English?"

"No, we're Scottish," we replied again, highly confused.

"Oh well, nobody's perfect."

"Do you want the slap now or along with the tip?"

And off he had shirked, no doubt to spit in our soup.

DAY 12:
THE WORST OF TIMES, THE BEST OF TIMES

Col de la Madeleine
Start point: La Chambre | Height: 2000m | Height climbed: 1522m | Length of climb: 19.5km | Average gradient: 8% Maximum gradient: 9.5%

Col du Glandon
Start point: La Chambre | Height: 1924m | Height climbed: 1472m | Length of climb: 21.3km | Average gradient: 6.9% Maximum gradient: 11%

Drew was awoken at 6am by the not-so-distant strains of the hotel cockerel. Every hotel should have one, and ours did, along with its own building-site backing band. (Add in the headmistress' unique brand of hospitality and Hôtel L'Autantic was something of a find.) Being a pathetically light sleeper, I had been wearing earplugs and so missed our feathered-friend's alarm call. My good fortune only added to Drew's annoyance.

We sneaked out of the room for breakfast, pleased that the headmistress was nowhere to be seen. Instead we had good cop, the gorgeous, friendly brunette. She welcomed us with a cheery smile and politely showed us to our table, not dragging us by the ear as bad cop most certainly would have. It's amazing how one member of staff in a hotel can change your opinion of the whole establishment (think Fawlty Towers with only Polly on reception and no Basil).

We decided upon eggs from the breakfast buffet, along with everything else we could lay our greedy paws on. As Drew had been woken by the cockerel, we thought it a fitting feast, however, the only problem with our selection was that said eggs were raw and we'd be required to boil them ourselves. What? You think that sounds easy? Listen, I'm a modern man, I can cook and my repertoire goes way beyond boiled eggs, but do you think I could work the hotel's egg-boiling machine? No chance. Could Drew work the egg-boiling machine? No chance. We misread or misinterpreted the instructions and a good half-dozen eggs failed to cook, their shells cracking open to sluice raw gloop onto our plates. Failing at such a simple task so early in the day really didn't do much for the collective confidence.

I had read somewhere that in days gone by the feeding stations at races included raw eggs. Hungry riders would briefly halt at the feast, wolf down bread, fruit and other delights, lop the top off a couple of eggs, gulp the contents and head on their way. All very historically interesting but at that early hour of the morning we hadn't quite the stomachs or the hunger for egg gulping, even though our five-minute-boiled eggs were barely lukewarm and fully drinkable.

The dining room was empty but for us and a Dutch couple, the only interruption to the egg débâcle being our attempt to decide if they were friends, father and daughter, or man and wife. The man was a balding, nerdy-looking type, we reckoned in his early fifties, his female companion much, much more attractive and a good deal younger — couldn't have been any older than early twenties. Were they a couple? Were they just friends? Were they man and goods rented/purchased? The cynical debate was really heating up when, as if to end our misery, Old Dutch wandered over and explained. After asking if we were English (and then taking offence when we told him we were actually Scottish), he informed us, entirely apropos of nothing, that his *wife* had been bitten.

"Bitten?" I asked, wondering to myself if there might be a shortage of men in Netherlands.

"Yesh," he continued in that slightly slurred, almost American-twanged English the Dutch so often adopt, "she wash bitten."

"Where?" Drew asked, his twisted mind in hope of receiving some juicy detail.

"Outshide?"

"Right, but where on the body?"

"The foot. My wife, she wash bitten on the foot."

"Right."

Drew and I looked at one another, confused as to why we had been furnished with this information. Was Old Dutch just bragging, not that she had been bitten, but that she was his wife? Had he bitten her on the foot and was he proud of himself for doing so, so proud he just couldn't wait to share the fact with other men: *you'll never gesh what I got up to with the mishus lasht night!*

"I don't know," Drew vocalised our confused thoughts, "why don't you ask him?"

"Okay, I will."

And so I did.

"Did *you* bite her on the foot?"

"No," Old Dutch smiled, "of coursh *I* did not bite her."

"So who did?"

"No, not *who*. It wash not a pershon that bit her."

"Well *what* did?"

"A beasht."

"A beast?"

More confused glances, Drew and I on the verge of hysterics — so this is the comedy festival the billboard had advertised.

"Yesh a beasht."

"What kind of beast?"

"A hairy thing, big and noishy."

"A dog?" Perhaps the Italian restaurant's rabid behemoth?

"No, not a dog, shmaller."

"A rat?" I suggested, turning to Drew to ask, "do you get noisy rats?"

"A rat in big boots would be noisy, especially if it got into your attic," he suggested.

"No, not a rat. Shmaller, like a washp."

"Like a wasp but not a wasp?"

"Yesh."

"Do we win a prize if we guess correctly?"

Old Dutch half smiled, already weary with his own story, "no."

"A bee?"

"No, not a bee, bigger and shtripy."

"A zebra?" Our conversation was so far beyond ridiculous it made the egg fiasco seem like the epoch of our intelligence.

Old Dutch was getting annoyed, as annoyed as we were confused. His attractive young wife peered over, smiling, wishing her other half hadn't bothered asking the gay couple for advice, if indeed that was what he was doing.

"It wash an inshect, like a washp but bigger than normal bee, and shtripy."

"That is a bee," we cheered in unison, "a bumble bee!"

"Yes, thatsh it, a what-you-shay?"

"A bumble bee!"

"Yesh, a bumble bee! My wife wash bitten on the foot by a bumble bee!"

"Hooray!" We cheered in unison, our exuberance only quelled by young wife's distressed glances.

"So what do we win?" Drew asked eagerly.

"Nothing. My wife hash been bitten."

"Yes, we know, by a bumble bee."

"Yesh."

"And?"

"And her foot ish shwollen, sho shwollen she cannot get her foot into the pedal cleat."

Young wife duly held up a grotesquely swollen, melon-sized foot that reminded me of Minxy the Trenthouse Playmate and her potato hands.

"The pedal cleat? You're cyclists?" I asked, needlessly, of course they were cyclists, they were Dutch, Dutch people with pedal cleats.

"Yesh, and we shaw that you two are shyclishtsh alsho. I could tell from your legsh."

"Really?" I glanced down at my skinny, sunburnt pins.

"Yes and sho we wondered if you could help?"

"Yes, as a matter of fact we can help," Drew practically sprayed the man with raw egg in his sudden eagerness to assist. "My friend here is a doctor."

I looked around to see which pharmaceutical pal Drew had secretly stowed away. Then I realised he was referring to me.

"A doctor?" I asked, confused, concerned that I couldn't remember any of my seven years at medical school.

"A doctor!" Old Dutch was ecstatic, "well thatsh great! A doctor of what?"

"Oh you know," I mumbled, looking fruitlessly to Drew for assistance, worrying he would say gynaecology, that Old Dutch would tell me that he suspected his wife might be pregnant and could I take a look. "General Practice."

"General practish? Really, sho you can help?"

"I guess so."

What the hell am I doing? Why am I going along with this nonsense. What is Drew playing at? Does he think this is funny? Judging by his inane grin, yes, yes he does think this is funny.

"Of course he can help, he's a doctor," Drew's enthusiasm for my imagined profession knew no bounds.

"Did you hear that, darling," Old Dutch shouted to his young wife of large foot. "Heesh a doctor!"

She peered round the side of her bulbous appendage and smiled in a manner that confirmed I would be in no way able to disappoint through botched medical assistance.

I scampered off to our room, pretending I had gone to fetch my doctor's bag, but really seeking to gain some time to think. My first thought was to escape out the window and hide in the coop with the cockerel. My second thought led to the first-aid kit and the antihistamines I had brought in case of hay fever. I grabbed the box and darted back through to my surgery — sorry, the dining room — all the time praying that nobody had choked on raw egg, the Scottish doctor required to perform an emergency tracheotomy.

When I returned, Big Foot was beaming with enthusiastic anticipation of her imminent cure. As she beamed, my shaky hand offered the small packet of pills and I adopted my best bedside manner.

"You just need to take one of these daily, try and stay off your foot and the swelling should soon reduce."

"Thank you, thank you," she beamed. "One tablet? I shall take it now."

"Best way, strike while the foot is hot."

"And how much do we owe you, Doctor?"

"Nothing, really, unless ... you couldn't possibly boil us a couple of eggs?"

***

Bikes retrieved from the shed, a derisory snort or three from the headmistress, and we set off toward the village of La Chambre, starting point for both of the day's climbs. Apart from guilt at our earlier deception (and my ongoing confusion as to why Drew had felt the deception necessary) we weren't in too bad a shape: legs a tad stiff but nothing some stretching couldn't alleviate.

La Chambre arrived much quicker than expected but welcomed us with an attempt to outdo La Plagne's horrific heat. Bikes assembled, lycra donned and I was already soaked through with sweat. I didn't need to be cajoled into applying the sunblock, could

157

literally feel my skin cooking without it.

We had decided, for no specific reason, to ride the Madeleine first. There was little on paper to separate the climbs in terms of their difficulty, both took in around 1500 metres of ascent, and whereas the Madeleine had a slightly higher average gradient, the Glandon had the steepest sections and was slightly longer. The decision might as well have been a coin toss, however, if forced (perhaps under threat of detention from the headmistress) I would have picked the Madeleine as my preference. In my mind it stood out, amongst all the climbs on our list, for the most trivial reason: it had the nicest name. I loved the sound of *Madeleine*; connotations of (in no particular order) tasty little cakes, religious mystery, foreign beauty and romance. I anthropomorphised the mountain, turned her into a pretty French darling with a mean streak big and bad enough to kick even the strongest man (or woman) aside. *Madeleine* is more than just a mountain, *she* is a mythology, a siren tempting you onto her slopes, from where you will either rise or fall according to ability and determination. (I may have been suffering heat-related delirium, was definitely reading too much into it, but you have to admit that Madeleine sounds more poetic than Les Deux Alpes or Stelvio.) I was so taken with her that the thought of shimmying up a pole to steal a sign with the Col's name on it was more than a passing whim. Only the realisation that I'd never get the bounty back through the airport metal detector stopped me.

I couldn't help but feel jealousy toward the people of La Chambre. Once again it amazed and excited me that people lived what appeared to be ordinary, placid and apparently plush existences right at the foot of such a renowned climb. Imagine giving someone directions to your house: "just turn left after the sign for the Col de la Madeleine — assuming some smitten cyclist has gone and pinched the sign." I began to wonder, almost to worry, if I had grown up there would I have taken the Col, maybe *all* the cols for granted? I certainly hoped not, wanted to believe that something innately special or almost spiritual had drawn me to the mountains.

Not for the first time, the town bells were pealing as we set off. I saw us as two lone riders departing town for an epic adventure, like the central characters in a spaghetti western, riding into the heat and dust, ready to confront an evil outlaw. I wondered what villages such as La Chambre were like when the Tour de France first passed through their streets, how they viewed that huge occasion, when the procession from Paris came to town. Did the church bells ring out then, and indeed do they now when the modern-day Tour and all its accoutrements make their flying visit en route to Glandon or Madeleine? I wondered if the good citizens of La Chambre cared that pale white cyclists from across the sea made pilgrimages to the mountains that bookend their little bit of France.

The Tour de France first tackled the Madeleine in 1969, the year the current incarnation of the road opened, Spaniard, Andrés Gandarias the first man over the top. (Eddy Merckx dominated that year's race, winning the general classification by almost 18 minutes, and taking the points and mountains classifications along the way — the first and only rider ever to have achieved that triple.) Images of the climb were imprinted upon my mind from the 1998 Tour: it was the day after Pantani had engineered that yellow-snatching destruction of the field on the Col du Galibier. Jan Ullrich was devastated at having lost his race lead in such a humbling manner. The press, particularly the Germans, were certain his race was over, convinced he'd abandon the next morning. Instead, the young German came out all guns blazing, put in a display of aggressive riding that demonstrated strength and maturity beyond his years. He attacked near the foot of the climb, just as Pantani was taking a drink, and duly accelerated away. Only Pantani, the very man Ullrich had been trying to drop, could match the blistering pace; the others too tired from the previous day's torture to do any more.

The water fountain a few kilometres up the climb was a most-welcome find. I was ridiculously hot and thirsty, had already emptied a full bottle. Seriously struggling, I'd turned to dreaming of Scotland, my fantasies full of cycling around in the cold and rain — oh what it would be to shiver! When the moment came to pull my head out from under the stream I felt like crying, couldn't bear the thought of leaving it behind. My entire being felt devoid of energy, my head completely lacked the will. I had laboured in first gear just to reach the fountain, couldn't conceive that the top of the climb would be achieved under my own (probably literal) steam.

When I had watched riders retire from races, climbing into the broom wagon or a team car, their sad eyes avoiding the television camera's intrusion, a part of me had always cynically suggested that surely they could have found the energy — not race-winning amounts, but just enough to continue. There I was, getting a small taste of what it must feel like for those suffering what the French would call *un jour sans*, a day without, when the energy seems to have disappeared but the race continues regardless, merciless.

I knew my fitness levels weren't sufficiently bad for me to be so close to quitting when quite so close to the base of a climb. There had to be another reason, and the only factor I could think to blame was the heat — so bloody hot I couldn't think about anything else. I'd been clinging to the hope that my adjustment to the conditions was imminent, that my body was adapting by increments to its new environment, but the reverse appeared to be the case. Instead of the much-hoped-for acclimatisation I felt fit to finally succumb. With the sun beating down and the glare shimmering all around, even *looking* a few bike lengths up the road brought me to the verge of collapse. (What? You want me to *ride* those bike lengths? Really? Are you insane?) Ten degrees cooler and I would have been up a gear or two and cruising; instead I was swaying around the road, pouring salty sweat into the already rusting headset top-cap bolt. This Madeleine I had dreamt of had almost instantly exceeded her reputation, had drawn me in and was about to exact a toll for my curiosity. To top it all off was the knowledge that an ascent of the Glandon lay in wait as reward should I somehow complete the Madeleine. The very concept of a second climb sent shudders right through me, as if thinking about a Herculean task some other poor, mad person was about to attempt. It couldn't be me, because I was already beyond useless and fading fast.

I was battling with every available ounce of willpower but truly going nowhere; even butterflies were overtaking me. Drew, on the other hand, was feeling (at least relatively) great and refusing to hold anything in reserve for the Glandon. He was also refusing to wait for me, cruised off up the climb and was soon a distant blue dot upon my far horizon — surely a revenge of sorts for my dismissive attitude on La Plagne the previous day. I at once hated and admired my friend, jealousy at his strength countered only by wonder. I felt utterly pathetic as he danced delicately on the pedals, pulling the tarmac down and beneath his tyres. The sun that had become my bête noire was his best friend. Sleeves rolled up and smiling, to him the Madeleine was nothing more than an opportunity to top up the tan whilst taking in a bit of a hill. And with each glimpse of his prowess, the circling vultures of negativity closed in.

A couple of particularly steep corners later and I was audibly cursing Drew, as if his contrasting condition and velocity were all at my expense. He was purposely taunting me, riding me into the ground as revenge for my actions upon the Stelvio, for having ignored his concerns on the Izoard and La Plagne, for having forced him to come on this trip with its evil Folder of Doom. Was he really so stupid, really so spiteful? I would have spat in disgust had my saliva not already dried up and disappeared.

Brief distraction came in the shape of adverts for Gruyère cheese, small but striking billboards that dotted the roadside pasture. For a while they absorbed a little of my excess ill will, seething, nasty vibes I would otherwise have fired up-mountain toward Drew. Before long they were annoying me so much that my disgust came out aloud.

"Look, cheese marketers, why don't you just give up? I'm not interested in cheese right now. Cold drinks would be good. A cool breeze would be better. Some rain and I'd hack off an arm and gift it to you out of gratitude. But with dairy products you are wasting your time. You are wasting my time. More importantly, thoughts of your cheese are driving me insane. Beaufort — *Le Prince des Gruyères* — why don't you just f*** right off!"

It felt as if my head was about to boil, brain bubbling over with heat and bad feeling, cooked beneath the cotton cap. I tried in vain to be positive, attempted to turn my frown upside down by conjuring happy thoughts, but the effort served only to open the floodgates and the deluge that followed very nearly drowned the struggling man.

Grief's black negativity descended, draping its cloak of depression over my shoulders, darkening the corners despite the blazing sun. Over the many months since my father's death I had made a barely passable attempt at coping with my grief, which involved little more than keeping a rattling lid on the connected memories and emotions. When battling a mountain you need to be able to switch off, to fight the physical pain and avoid any emotional angst, but the more I tried to empty my mind the worse the thoughts and images became, the more frequent, the greater their intensity. Upon trying to force-form distracting visions of success, words and phrases of happiness, I instead brought forth recollections of my father during the last days of his illness. I couldn't stand them, wanted them out of my head, and not just for the pain they brought. They hideously misrepresented my father's life as a whole; entertaining them in any way was an injustice to him, like a tacit agreement that the disease had won, had taken him, wiped out all the good and left a stinking, oily black streak in its place. I knew — everyone his life had touched knew — that he was more, so much more than the stark picture painted during that horrendous denouement. Under normal circumstances I wouldn't have allowed myself to dwell on such thoughts, would have done something, *anything* else to distract. There on the Madeleine — in the heat, in that mood — I was powerless to prevent, had nowhere else to go. Flash after flash made its attack: my father gaunt and drawn, crippled and wasting away; a skeleton with skin, the light of his soul barely flickering within. He had battled tooth and nail, fought with every last ounce of his energy just to stay alive, to stay with us.

I wanted the cheese back, anything but those evil memories, but it was as if now that the thought process had begun there would be no stopping until it had reached an awful conclusion. My mind, frustrated to the extreme, hurt beyond any pain my legs had ever endured. It was toward Drew, that little blue dot high up on the next rise, that I aimed my shouts, all of which went unheard.

"Do you have any idea of what I am going through? Do you have even the vaguest inkling how I'm feeling right now, how I've been feeling for months on end?"

And I knew he didn't, and I knew it wasn't his fault.

"You're way ahead up the road, probably feeling sorry for yourself because you're homesick. At least when you go home your family will be there for waiting for you. I never talk to you about my father, about what happened, and you think that's because I'm over it. Do you really think it doesn't affect me any more? Well it does, every single, f***ing day. I don't talk about him because even the thoughts are too painful. I feel that if I speak the words then the darkness will open up and pull me in."

Crawling, almost at a standstill, I considered banging my head off the hot tarmac until the tsunami of thoughts and images had subsided. I was hunched over the handlebars, head drooped, shoulders rounded, everything I had ever known about cycling technique erased from my memory. And the images continued to come, growing more steadily sad. From Dad sitting in a chair looking gaunt and tired mid-chemo, they flicked to him in the specialist's office the day we were told that his cancer had spread. I could so clearly see the expression on his face, as if it were being replayed on a plasma screen bolted to my handlebars. That look of calm dignity, the stoic glance he sent across the room will never leave me; it has been tattooed upon my soul, sets me an example for life, just as it breaks my heart.

Then I was back to seeing his skeletal frame draped upon the deathbed. I could hear the crackling, rattling sounds of his breathing, those poor, drowning lungs refusing to give up the fight. I could smell the god-awful stink of death that permeated the house during those days. I wanted to be sick, to vomit myself inside out and clear away the poison. I wanted to stop and fling my bike into the valley below, to scream blue murder at whatever bastard — be it pure chance or god — had decided my sweet father should endure that sickening death by cancer. My brain, body and soul cried out for a release. Within minutes they'd reached bursting point; I battled to tear myself away from it all, to think of something, *anything* else.

In hindsight, it's kind of perverse that my thoughts turned to Lance Armstrong, but at the time such a switch was almost unavoidable — not for the cancer connection, but because the stretch of road along which I crawled was daubed with repetitions of his name, copious messages of support and a whole load more that were far from favourable:

Go Lance!
Lance = Truth
Lance = EPO
US EPOstal

I pictured Armstrong cycling up the mountain, cruising as if on a motorbike (or in a body supercharged with the substances his detractors suggested). As he caught my pathetic position, he eased up to ask if I was all right.

"No." I said, because I wasn't all right, and because I had little puff left to offer anything else.

He asked what was wrong; was it the climb, the heat?

I said the heat felt like a kick in the guts; I was like Charly Gaul on a double dose of amphetamine. I couldn't stand it.

"Was that it?" He asked, half-smirking at my ineptitude.

"No, that's not it. I wish it was but it's not."

I explained how my mind had been swamped by a tide of negativity that manifested as images of my father dying from cancer. The heat had aimed its boot at my stomach but it was the grief that had knocked me to the tarmac and set about stamping on my head.

My imaginary Armstrong appeared genuinely sympathetic, "that sucks man," he said, or something like it.

It does suck, I agreed, as I began to think about his story, recounted to millions through his autobiography. I had been gifted a copy of that tome back when my father was first diagnosed with cancer, but it was many months after his death that I finally forced myself to take the book from the shelf. I didn't want to know about some other man's miraculous recovery when the man closest to me had missed the miracles. I didn't need to learn about how awful cancer and its treatment are or how brave people can be, because I had witnessed all that up close — far too close. So why did I eventually read it? Perhaps because I had seen the worst-case cancer scenario and wanted to know what it was actually like to beat the disease (and the odds). And I might also have been trying to figure out this man who had completely overshadowed the sport of cycling, attempting to discern the secret of his success. Whatever the reason for reading, the book had left me angry.

I continued to wrestle the pedals round, tried to untangle my barbed mess of thoughts and explain how pissed off with him I was — not for allegations of doping, not for the way he had "disrespected" Pantani, not for hogging the top step of the Tour podium, but because I kept thinking over something he had said about cancer being the best thing that ever happened to him. How could he have the temerity to say that? What if he hadn't beaten it, or if he had survived but the battle had left him unable to walk, let alone win the world's toughest bike race? What would he have thought about it then? Would it still have been the best thing?

"The truth is that cancer was the best thing that ever happened to me ... . Why would I want to change, even for a day, the most important and shaping event in my life?"[6.]

"Yeah, that's the quote. That's the one that gets me," I sighed, struggling to pull myself free from the literal and metaphorical melting tarmac.

Armstrong shrugged, twiddling the pedals round as if casually freewheeling on a descent.

"At this moment it seems like the most important and shaping event in *my* life so far has been my father's cancer — but I would change it. I'd do *anything* to change it. Cancer robbed me of him, robbed my sisters of their father. Worse than all that, it robbed my mother of her sweetheart, her soul-mate, her one and only true love. Cancer robbed a great man of his place on this earth, a man who did not deserve such an early nor such a gruesome demise."

My imaginary Armstrong intimated that I had misunderstood,

"When I was sick, I saw more beauty and triumph and truth in a single day than I ever did in a bike race ... ."[7]

"Oh, come off it!" I snapped. "I don't need to hear any of your bullshit. Yours reads just like a fairytale and I don't believe in fairytales."

Why couldn't *I* have a fairytale? Why couldn't there be a fantastic story in which my father still lived? God knows I had dreamt it that way so many times, woken from the warm, comforting hallucinations only to crash slap-bang into the cold, solid, all-too-grim reality. Fairytales don't happen in real life, certainly not in mine.

I wanted to know if he realised just how lucky he was. My father had fought with what the Italians call *grinta* — grit, determination — way more of it than any Grand Tour winner had ever displayed, and yet still he had died.

"I don't know why I'm still alive. I can only guess. I have a tough constitution, and my profession taught me how to compete against long odds and big obstacles ... ."[8]

"You had great treatment too, Lance. That's what you placed so much faith in." I said it as if he didn't know, as if he, in some way, should feel guilty of the fact. "If your book's to be believed, then you had doctors who enthused about your fight, vocalised their determination to get your cancer *whipped.*. My father's doctors as good as said, *step into the coffin, Mr Hansen.* There was so little positive sentiment in any of the medical staff during the entire period he was ill."

Imaginary Armstrong couldn't answer that directly but he seemed to know where I was headed, in conversation, on the bicycle and in life.

"Without belief, we would be left with nothing but an overwhelming doom ... . And it will beat you. I didn't fully see, until the cancer, how we fight every day against the creeping negatives of the world ... . Dispiritedness and disappointment, these were the real perils of life, not some sudden illness ... . I knew now why people fear cancer: because it is a slow and inevitable death, it is the very definition of cynicism and loss of spirit. So I believed."[9.]

"I *do* believe but sometimes the light fades and the darkness takes hold; it overwhelms me. Getting back can be a struggle. I have to keep reminding myself that it's still there, obscured, behind the curtains. After Dad died I told myself, told my sisters and my mother, that we would not, *could not* give up. Life is too precious. I know we have to cherish each day but it's so hard, it is just so f***ing hard. I mean, listen to those words: *cherish each day*. It just sounds like the kind of sentimental claptrap you'd find on a fridge magnet. After all the destruction I saw, all the grotesque torture that cancer put my father through, my viewpoint has become so jaded that sometimes all I can see is the slog up the mountain. All of the good involved, the summit-sense of achievement, the wondrous views, the excitement of the drop down the other side, all of it is obscured by the awful, tortuous slog to the top. No thoughts ahead to the next achievement, just bitterness, blackness, a gaping void where my spirit and purpose used to be. That's not something that fridge-magnet platitudes can easily counter."

"... you don't fly up a hill. You struggle slowly and painfully ... . Cancer is like that, too. Good strong people get cancer, and they do all the right things to beat it, and they still die. That is the essential truth that you learn. People die. And after you learn it, all other matters seem irrelevant. They just seem small."[10.]

Throughout all that my legs had somehow kept the pedals turning — not that I had given them a second thought. Imaginary Armstrong had begun to fade, a hallucination who was soft-pedalling and struggling not to tip sideways as he matched my crawl. I wanted him to go, so I could think of something else; I needed to come up through the negative cloud, to emerge into clearer skies, on this climb and all the climbs I'd ever ride. For me the trip had to be about transition as much as expedition. It was my Tour of Redemption, my journey back, from grief to life. And what a slog.

My gaze dropped back to the tarmac and caught sight of my name painted repeatedly in neat block capitals:

ROLF
ROLF
ROLF
ROLF

But it wasn't *my* name; those dedications were for team Telekom's Rolf Aldag. Then came a whole load more for "Klodi" (Aldag's teammate, Andreas Kloden) and then a couple of gallons' worth for their team leader "Ulli" (Jan Ullrich). Then we were back to the EPO-related graffiti, not aimed at any one rider, more at pro cycling in general. To begin with it kind of irritated me; to think that people would waste their time and energy travelling halfway up a mountain to paint a load of graffiti that attacked our sport (*their* sport too), but those fans (because surely they were fans, otherwise why go to all that bother?) had put that protest right under the noses of the riders, in front of the TV cameras, and they'd done so without waving placards or in any way obstructing the race. You usually have to care about something to protest and if they cared sufficiently about cycling to daub anti-doping messages then in my mind that was as good, if not better than, painting a pro-Lance or pro-Ullrich slogan.

I guess the doping-related graffiti unsettled me because it reminded me of the dreaded notion that the higher echelons of the sport I loved might well be completely saturated with cheats. What if, as I so often suspected, as Drew and I had conjectured on the Galibier, nothing much had changed since the Festina scandal of '99? What if the speculation I had read about and the "cynicism" I saw displayed on Internet forums were all actually true?

"So, Lance, you're currently suing the authors of a book that contains a load of drug-related allegations about you?"

He was fading from view but I could clearly see the rage; he looked angry, but way less angry than I felt.

"What do you think it would mean if one day the world discovered you had doped?"

He was already out of the saddle, stamping on the pedals as if Pantani *and* Ullrich had jumped up the road ahead of him. No final nugget of wisdom to help me on my way, not even a killer look over the shoulder. Imaginary Armstrong was gone.

What *would* it mean if he was one day found out, if it wasn't just all those other "lesser" riders who had resorted to doping (and been "stupid enough" to get caught)? What if the main man himself, the *patron* of the era had cheated his way to glory? It would mean that for almost a decade, maybe more, the sport of cycling had been nothing more than a fantasy. Lance's survival from cancer, his near instantaneous return to the top and his all-conquering reign: all of it one big, fat fairytale.

***

Much of the Madeleine's detail either never made it to my mind or completely disappeared, pinging straight back out, unable to stick. The negative cloud that had blown in on the lower stretches blocked all other consideration, obscuring most of the climb, from the open slopes of lower pasture and on toward the relative cover of the upper tree-line. Whilst the road reached ever higher, twisting and turning through the forest, until an eventual re-emergence in the upper pasture, the most I remembered — indeed all I could recall, even after the descent and a good while sat in the shade drinking cold water and contemplating — was a long blur of discomfort. (I'm pretty certain that at some point we climbed up through a village called Longchamp, and that there had been a short stretch of road that felt, all too briefly, like a descent. As for any other details, the exact specifics, those I am unable to provide. To find out you will have to go and meet Madeleine for yourself. I might even go back there one day, for another shot, perhaps to ride early in the morning when the air's still cool, at a time when my mood is positive and my head's screwed on straight.)

As the road escaped the trees, I was still suffering like a dog trapped in a hot car. However, I had begun to believe. Within my reach were the closing stretches of a col on the early slopes of which I had almost completely capitulated. My worst climb of the trip thus far (I hoped my worst climb, period) was close to accomplishment, a new low almost put behind me. All I had to do was haul myself over those final few kilometres.

I became sufficiently aware to notice the cars of tourists speeding by. From the rear window of one I caught the stares of a young boy, his expression an ambiguous mix of wonder and worry. My mindset emphasised the worry and I immediately stood up on the pedals, somehow pushing the pace a little higher, scrabbling around for the threads of any former finesse. With the car disappeared over the next rise, I was concerned that my poor showing might be a nail in the coffin of that boy's cycling interest. As the sound of the engine lessened, overtaken by the respiratory evidence of my effort, I hoped he would make his final decision further up the mountain, based on the sight of Drew's purist performance.

Upon eventually reaching the summit, my feelings were not of achievement, nor even of relief. Instead I felt disappointed, sorely so. Not only had I been almost utterly useless, I had been so upon the Madeleine of all climbs. Drew didn't get what all the fuss was about but still entered into the mood of dissent, complaining about a blood-sugar drop — no surprise given the speed at which he had made the ascent. I was zipping up my jacket, suggesting that we go and look at the small café's menu when he pedalled away, mumbling something about sweets. I made chase, worried that hypoglycaemia had affected his sanity. He was practically sprinting toward what appeared to be a souvenir stall pitched at the edge of the small car park. In the slipstream I could hear his faded words, something about a sweetshop and a mirage.

Sure enough, there in front of our very eyes (I eventually caught up with him) was *the* most sugary delusion either of us would ever suffer. Arranged across a series of long wooden tables lay a multi-coloured sea of pick 'n' mix delights, a rainbow of saccharine shapes and colours that left Drew drooling and jabbering with excitement, and me scratching my head in confusion. It was an extraordinary sight to behold; even more amazing when closer inspection revealed that it was all entirely real. (Confectionery at the top of the Madeleine? There went my tale of the mountain wilderness.) Whilst I pedalled off for another shot at working out which peak upon the horizon might be Mont Blanc, Drew filled a carrier bag with enough sweets to last the remainder of the trip, and another couple of weeks after that.

***

The Madeleine's descent was packed with sharp twists and turns, many more than I recalled having encountered upon the way up. Not only was I more compos mentis, the drastic hike in velocity, from crawling at around 5mph to hurtling at 50, further increased the impact of each bend. I was reminded of riding the Seven Stanes trails — a series of Forestry-Commission-developed mountain biking tracks at Glentress in the Scottish Borders. In particular, it was reminiscent of the Spooky Wood single-track, except the tight hairpins on the Madeleine didn't have the banked berms that allow you to ride fast into bends as if careering around an off-road velodrome. Instead we were hard on the brakes, throwing our weight over the back of the saddle, being extra cautious on the right-hand turns when approaching traffic forced us onto the steepest, inside line.

A small group of cars soon gathered behind as we careered down-slope. Their proximity was distracting but we felt it was always better to have any vehicles behind us on a descent, rather than for us to be sitting on their back bumpers, eyes glued to the brake lights. They tried as best they could to catch up on the straight sections, but then immediately lost contact at the tight corners — and on it went, all the way to the outskirts of La Chambre.

***

We collected the car and returned to the small water fountain to fill bottles and cleanse ourselves beneath the cold flow. I emptied bottle after bottle over my head, until I could no longer taste the salty residue of that morning's fever. It felt like days since we had last been there, already my misery on the Madeleine assigned to memory (a subconscious survival mechanism, compartmentalising the pain in order to prevent me relating it to what would follow). And my arduous ascent wasn't all we'd forgotten: we then drove back into the village with the hatchback boot wide open, our thoughts obviously with the approaching Glandon and not on matters practical. Thankfully, we were going downhill so gravity kept our bikes, shoes, helmets, etc in the back of the car.

We lunched at a small picnic site near the base of the Glandon, a location dominated by a large wooden crucifix with the number *1999* carved into its base — of what that year was significant I had no idea. We ate fruit, salads and sandwiches; I drank and drank and drank, but still could not sate my thirst. As I poured another litre of fluids down my neck, Rain Man Drew pored over the Glandon profile, assigning every metre of its potential misery to memory.

Whilst Drew wasn't about to forget the figures, during that period of recuperation we did allow ourselves the luxury of losing track of time. The day drifted by as we relished the shade, snoozing on and off. It was late afternoon when we finally revived, accepting that it was about time — almost past time — to attempt the next ascent. With an almost rest-day-sized gap between the two, we were in no way experiencing the climbs as Tour riders would. Whilst the race might peak one, descend to La Chambre and immediately start the next, we were in a different gear altogether. Shameful behaviour, I know, but at least some of the strength I'd lacked earlier in the day had been regained. Despite how unlikely it had seemed upon the Madeleine, I actually felt quite good, as near as I'd get that day to raring, just about ready to enjoy the ride.

***

The Glandon began with a steady gradient, the road quickly escaping conurbation, heading out into pasture, before as quickly again lunging into thick forest. (You might have spotted a theme to these Alpine climbs: pasture-forest-pasture-forest.) The road meandered, a few sharp kinks to its line, but generally stayed true to the adjacent river's reasonably direct flow. With gradients around the sevens and eights, it left us with a feeling of calm progression — helped by the trees, which hid all that would follow, although Drew was only too happy to provide anticipatory updates. We passed another water fountain, a beautifully presented affair, decked out with hanging baskets and a colourful of array of blooms. Bottles that had slowly simmered in the heat of the car were emptied out and refreshed with cold, spring water, my insatiable thirst still not quenched.

By then the temperature had noticeably dropped and our muscles had cooled in conjunction — that prolonged sit in the shade left our legs seriously stiffened and it would take a couple of kilometres to loosen them up. Not that Drew was willing to wait for a warm-up. He appeared to have grown accustomed to riding off the front at his own tempo, became obviously agitated each time I tried to pull up alongside. His frustration increased accordingly on the few occasions I took to the front, even if only to let a car pass us on the narrower sections of road. He'd huff, puff and pull himself ahead again, vocally expressing a dislike of riding at any tempo other than his own. No sooner was he ensconced in that advanced position and it was my turn to express frustration: back in the game, I wanted to play, to huff and puff until my wheel was the one in front. As a result of those petty antics we pretty much raced each other through the lower section of the Col, a constant competition that upped the pace with every cycle of movement.

The first 10 of the 21 kilometres were quickly covered, the village of Saint-Colomban-des-Villards upon us in no time. The road emerged from the trees and a long plateau eased us through the main street. The place was busy, a hubbub of summer living, people out and about, chatting and drinking at the café, children running, excited to be free from lessons. We passed some pétanque pistes, a group of adults paused, boules mid-swing, stopped to stare, apparently a touch bewildered by the sight of two cyclists meandering by — as if French men and women living halfway up one of the best known Tour cols had never seen one cyclist, let alone two together.

I wondered how our lives might have turned out had we got into their chosen pass-time. Had boules taken our fancy over bikes, would Drew and I each be the proud possessor of a hefty beer gut? Would we enjoy nothing more than the aroma of cigar-smoke mixed with summer-evening air? We would most certainly *not* have shaved legs. Oh, how different our lives might have been: beautiful French women at pétanque tournaments would have sat and gazed adoringly as the two fat Scottish blokes hurled their balls onto the sandy surface — what heroes, what athletes and such hairy legs beneath those kilts!

The air cooled considerably the higher we climbed, an arrestingly fresh mountain atmosphere that proved a stark contrast to the day's earlier, stifling extremes. Whereas on the Madeleine it had felt like I'd been inhaling hot sand, this new breeze was an elixir, each intake of breath verging upon a quasi-religious experience. No doubt thanks to that climatic change, the remainder of the energy I had sorely lacked that morning returned, and then some. Drew was either fatigued or had grown accustomed to the idea of my continued existence, no longer expressing the desire to be a bike-length ahead at all times. Just as well too; given half the chance I would have been down in the drops, out the saddle, doing my best Pantani impression. It was inconceivable that the climb on which I had almost thrown my bike into the valley could be part of the same day. My earlier miseries were a lifetime away, part of some distant nightmare or a horror story overheard.

We'd grown used to the lack of gradient through the village and so struggled a touch when it began to rise again — reaching 7% and staying put for the proceeding two kilometres. As it hiked heavenward, the road re-entered the trees and narrowed, pretty much down to single-track with just the occasional passing place. Perhaps the engineers had thought it unlikely that anyone would want to go any further, had laid less than half a road for those daft enough to try. From there, the Col adopted an almost apologetic traverse of the land. Its route still part-shadowed the river but that flow became increasingly convoluted (took the snake cliché and strangled it).

The trees in this section were less green and shorter than those on the lower slopes, more woodland than forest. The encroaching branches formed strange shapes and shadows. Thin fingers reached toward the road; odd, crooked figures poised menacingly on the verge. Add in the dusky, darkening skies and an eerie silence for the impression that we had stumbled onto a Tim-Burton-styled movie set. If the Headless Horseman had gambolled down the road toward us I would not have been entirely surprised, although I may well have soiled my chamois.

Swarms of flies congregated around our sweaty heads as we finally climbed out of the spooky woods and re-entered gently sloped pasture. I was back to being overwhelmingly thirsty and hunger had built on top of that. Those empty sensations led me to recall an event from childhood. Two school friends and their father had invited me, and my older sister, Katja, out on what they had billed, "a wee walk". A worryingly long car journey led to us being deposited on the edge of a forest, easily ten miles from home. It was then that we realised this wee walk was actually going to be a serious trek back to the village via the hard-going Speyside Way. Our friends and their father had stocked up and obviously prepared, with flasks of juice and plenty of rations, but Katja and I had taken nothing at all, thinking we really were just going out for a wee walk. By the end of the ordeal, the two Rae-Hansens had been reduced to drinking from streams and eating wild berries as our "friends" failed to share their supplies. I can still vividly remember lying on the kitchen floor post-trauma, Katja pouring juice into my gaping mouth with one hand and cramming custard-cream biscuits into hers with the other. Alongside the annoyance at the way those people had treated us there'd been a real sense of satisfaction: my sister and I had effectively been left on our own but had banded together and looked after one another. As I pedalled up through the dusky Alpine landscape, my stomach began to rumble but the main sensation running through me was familial love, not hunger.

The road, whilst trying to confuse with its distracted tangle, had become deceptively steep. A glance down at the small gear I was in, at my slow-motion pedals heaving round and round backed up

Rain Man Drew's suggestion that we'd been riding through a 9% section.

"It seems tough now but it's not so tough," he stuttered. "The toughest bit is right at end — it's hard then! Right at the end, up to 11%. You think it's tough now? Oh no, oh boy! 11%. *That's* tough, not this. We *were* on 9% but not now. Not now. This is only 6.2% gradient. Up there, at the end, the last two kilometres — bigger numbers, much bigger. From kilometres 19 to 21, that's gonna be tough. 11%, that's 4.8% steeper. 4.8 plus 6.2 equals 11. That's tough. Real tough."

As the woods shrank away behind us, the road pulled hard to the left, diverging from the water and clambering out onto open pasture. The river was now obviously connected to a high waterfall that crashed and splashed in the near distance. Through that roar came the sound of what I thought were wind chimes, but were actually cowbells. Their distant, dreamy calling led to a long line of Tibetan prayer flags, which had been draped, seemingly at random, alongside the road. Their colourful cotton shapes fluttered and flapped in the gentle breeze and in turn led to my worrying about the mountain spirits. Had I offended any along the way? Surely my Madeleine shambles — that ugly, laboured slog with language bluer than my legs post-Sella — had turned a few against me? I certainly didn't expect any favours, and none were obviously forthcoming. The final two kilometres, about which Drew had so studiously warned, were a series of switchbacks, signposted as a 10% gradient but feeling more like 15. Add on the cumulative fatigue from the day's exertion and the first of those brutal little ramps might as well have been half the climb again.

Whilst the Glandon's difficulty was as predicted and feared, the carrot now dangled in full view, our deliverance lying in wait around the next two bends, up the next two agonisingly steep ramps. By the top, my head was awash with the white noise of pain, lungs rasping and tight, legs shot to pieces by cramp's lactic-acid twinges. It was one hell of a way to end the climb, one hell of a way to end one hell of a day.

Drew was still expressing doubts as to the trip's purpose, seeking but unable to find the point of riding all those bloody mountains. For me, achieving the summit had brought a sudden release of tension. Breath back and eyes opened to all that lay around, I was reassured that the uphill struggle had been anything but in vain. My experience was about more than "bagging" the climbs; each one delivered a sense of understanding and a slice of joie de vivre that served to enthuse tired limbs, to cajole and lift the spirit. The exact details were still unclear to me (and I wasn't ready to express them, let alone in front of Drew) but I had a sense that the efforts expended were akin to money deposited in the bank, an investment in my fitness, my life experience, something positively indelible branded onto my soul.

We limped over to the summit sign for our snaps and on to the reward of a most magnificent view — even after all those climbs we still stood to stare agog at nature's wonders. The sun dropped from the sapphire sky, bathing the furthest mountains of the vast range in a fiery, orange glow. On the peak to our left, yet to catch alight, we saw a large black cross, the *croix* at the top of the Col de la Croix de Fer, an equally famous Tour climb. It appeared to lie within easy reach but appearances can be deceptive. We tagged it on to the list of those that would have to wait for another day, and then we turned to head downhill.

***

It's difficult to explain to a non-cyclist the feeling of self-made speed and (barely) controlled risk that comes from careering down a col like the Glandon: leaning into the corners; the noise of the tyres gripping and occasionally slipping; the oncoming rush of air, your body a bullet cutting through; the heart pounding; the heightened senses, sounds louder, colours brighter, vibrations intensified; the realisation of being fantastically alive but also on the limit. Descending at speed is a natural high that surely blows the doors off any drug, illegal or otherwise.

Within a few seconds, my grin was wider than the road was long. Out of the steep switchbacks, we were soon twisting and turning through the pasture, and then on into the trees. Swish and swoosh, the backdrop that had slowly unfurled around the ascent now trailed off behind us in a blur of colour and sound.

Thanks to the relative lateness of the hour, the road was quiet of other traffic, almost like the closed routes Tour riders enjoy. We had only encountered one car until, bombing back down through des Villards, we had to ease up for a sporty yellow Seat — which we then attempted to race. The driver clocked us in his rear-view mirror, (hard for him not to spot two bicycles sitting feet from his back bumper), and tried forthwith to lose us. He gunned his engine on the first straight beyond the village speed limits but the distance achieved was minimal and temporary. Revving top gear, legs in a blur like Roadrunner's in full flight, we plummeted down the mountain and caught the car as it was forced to slow for the first tight bend. From there we returned to that spot stupidly close to the back bumper, so proximate we were probably being sucked along in the slipstream, stuck like limpets, at times even looking for room to overtake.

I loved that descent, my muscles twitching with excitement, adrenaline pumping, in the zone and flowing. All I wanted was a return to my teenage self, the boy I had conjured to ride alongside down the Lautaret. Again I wanted not just to tell him all about it, better still to meet him at the top of the mountain so we could race each other down. I guessed my younger self was already there with me, in a crazy, String-Theory-inspired parallel-universe kind of way — who knows. One thing is for sure, the experience brought out the kid in me, the reckless part that adulthood had safely stowed away, his carefree voice drowned by worries and concerns: *you better slow down; not so fast; what if you crash?* Near the bottom of the Col I overcooked a corner, a matter of millimetres from disappearing off the edge of the road, and only then did I ease up, my boring old, adult self shocked back into the driving seat, the recklessness of youth assigned once more to memory.

Back at the car and the crucifix, an old man sat enjoying the serene sunset. As we careered noisily to a halt, he smiled calmly, in no way obviously annoyed that two pasty-faced foreigners had interrupted his evening. We chatted and he even offered us the compliment of assuming we were Italian professional riders. No, we blushed, we're far from pro-level, and don't believe the number plates, we're not even Italian (or Bri-talian). Monsieur still appeared impressed, especially that we had ridden both his town's big climbs, was almost overawed when Drew opened his bag of Madeleine confectionery to share out the sugary delights — *très bon, les bon bons!* We bid Monsieur farewell with the sad news of Goose's passing, and hit the road for wherever it was we called home.

DAY 13:
RIDE THE HELTER SKELTER

Alpe d'Huez

Start point: Bourg d'Oisans | Height: 1815m | Height climbed: 1071m | Length of climb: 13.2km | Average gradient: 8.1% Maximum gradient: 10.6%

Breakfast felt more like a science class, an hour-long experiment during which we attempted to find a formula for the perfect boiled egg. We began (as we should have the previous day) by reading the instructions on the side of the egg-boiling machine, and quickly concurred that adjusting the thermostat so that the water actually reached boiling point would be a good place to start — or so we thought. Barely quail-sized eggs, "boiling" for four minutes, and still they came out drinkable. The English family at the next table had even more trouble with the conundrum, their young daughter rushing to lop the top off her egg, then asking excitedly,

"Mummy, will I get salmonella?"

Not only were we pleased that some other idiots couldn't boil an egg, we were also impressed that a five-year-old knew what salmonella was (the family were probably related to Edwina Currie).

Several-dozen eggs (approximately half a litre) later, we said goodbye to the Dutch couple and her giant foot — which had reduced to the size of a small melon. She took great delight in telling the "doctor" that she had researched bumble bees online, was all clued-up and fully aware that she could have died. Yes, I agreed, she did indeed owe her life to my selfless actions. Old Dutch asked where our adventures would take us next, and then proceeded to make quite sure that we were privy to the full extent of *his* encyclopaedic knowledge of cycling's greatest climbs. He really wasn't at all impressed by any of *our* petty little stories, as he had already ridden every mountain there was to ride, twice and in the olden days when mountains were much, much tougher. Old

Dutch also professed to know of many different "harder" ways to ascend all the mountains we had already been up, including those, such as La Plagne, that only had one road to the top.

The headmistress was back on duty, rubbing her hands, gleeful at the thought of our imminent departure. Yet, despite that eagerness, she left us standing at the reception desk for a good (actually, they were bad) twenty minutes whilst she finished a phone call. By the time she had taken my credit card, briefly swiped it and then informed me that it was maxed-out, (which it wasn't, by several-thousand Euros; we reckoned later that she had just pressed the cancel button before it could ring through), I was sweating and teetering on the edge. I am always of the opinion that when someone is rude to me I shouldn't lower myself to their standards, but the urge to march her into the dining room and plunge her head into the egg boiler was extremely difficult to quell (the ice-cold water within would surely have shocked some sense into her). I asked her to try my card again but she point-blank refused — as far as we could tell the whole matter was just a ploy to get me to pay by cash, because she looked just as annoyed when, shown my empty wallet, I produced another card which then, strangely enough, had no problems. By the time we drove out of B.S.M., I was raging, certain that I would never return and would be as unlikely to receive such poor service from an hotelier, or headmistress, anywhere else, ever again.

***

Next stop Grenoble (quickly re-named La Glenbogle, twinned with the imaginary village in one of Scotland's most twee TV programmes). We made it there for about 2pm, to find a small city beneath a dark and foreboding sky, a thunderstorm obviously on the way. After a week of uninterrupted clear-blue and bright sunshine it was disappointing to arrive somewhere so, to use the Scottish expression, driech. If only we'd known where the Hotel du Ville was located, we might have stopped by to register a complaint.

The proximity of many of cycling's most famous mountains has led to Grenoble seeing more than its fair share of Tour de France stages. Mountains hem-in the city: to the north the Chartreuse; to the west the Vercors; to the east the Belledonne. Capital of the Isère département, Grenoble is a major scientific centre, especially in the fields of physics, computer science and applied mathematics.

It is also a city famous for walnuts, nut cracking the pastime of those insufficiently intelligent to spend their days attempting to split the atom.

Our hotel was located across the road from the main train station, a proximity that added to the neighbourhood's busy, multi-cultural feel — a huge contrast to B.S.M.'s sans-culture, ghost-town vibe. A quick walk around the block and we calculated that there were two Chinese restaurants for every man, woman and child in the city (guess what we would be having for dinner?). However, we didn't fancy munching Chinese food before a big ride and so headed further afield to find something else. That was our plan — we forgot that we were in France, a country renowned for the quality of its cuisine but distinctly uptight about dishing it out. I don't want to sound like a Euro-sceptic *Daily Mail* columnist, but why do the French only serve food at certain, very specific times of the day and night? And why don't they put signs up to explain the system, at least issue visitors with an explanatory pamphlet? We sat ourselves down at various cafés and restaurants, all of which were displaying full menus, only for waiters to appear out of the shadows, throw their heads back and flare their nostrils, emitting a sort of screechy car-alarm sound the second we tried to order food. They didn't just refuse our requests, they looked positively aghast, deeply, personally offended, as if we had asked each of them permission to punch their grandmother.

"How dare you insult me by asking for food at 3pm? Don't you know we stop serving at 2.30 and start again at 4.30? You disgusting, foreign idiots! Why would anyone in their right mind want to *eat* at 3pm? What kind of uncivilised, barbarian backward country do you come from? And you can leave my poor grand-mère out of it. Zut alors!"

The novelty of this reaction quickly wore off, was then completely washed away when the lightning cracked directly overhead and the storm eventually broke. Yes, on the Madeleine I had prayed for rain, but the deluge came too late and with a greater intensity than I had bargained for. Raindrops ricocheted off the pavement like hailstones, as Les Glenboglers ran for cover, left, right and centre. Electric-blue forks flashed to light up the dull sky, adding some colour to the grim cityscape, before further sounds like hellish heavy artillery scared us witless. We ducked into a small bakery (which, rather kindly, did allow us to buy some food), munched a croque monsieur or two and nursed mugs of comfortingly hot, sweet tea. As we started on third helpings, it appeared as if the rain was going to persist for days and we might have to seek adoption by the family that ran the shop. Trying to make it back to the hotel without a boat would only be asking for trouble, and a quick look around the shop revealed sufficient food to keep us all going for weeks on end.

"So, what do you say? Drew and I will move in and together we can start a new civilisation?"

Two seconds later, we were back in the rain and running for cover.

***

The Tour de France first ventured up to Alpe d'Huez in 1952, when race organisers were paid by a local hotelier to bring their event to the fledgling ski resort. The intention was not only to bring much-needed publicity and income but also to satisfy the race organisers' desire for a challenging new route, one sufficiently tough to shake the peloton out of a conceived post-war complacency. Given that latter objective, it is probably fitting that the legendary Fausto Coppi was first to win what would go on to become *the* marquee mountain stage.

The previous year, Coppi had ridden what, for him, was a poor Tour de France, hindered by grief from the sudden death of his brother. In 1952, he was looking to get back to winning ways, and to do so in style. The Alps, and in particular the Alpe d'Huez stage, was the place to do it. Countering an earlier attack by Jean Robic, Coppi rode away 6km from the top and eventually crossed the line almost a minute and a half clear, taking not only the stage but also the yellow jersey. It would be another twenty-four years until Alpe d'Huez was next included in the Tour itinerary but it is exceedingly unlikely that there will ever again be such a lag between visits. Winning atop the Alpe almost gains a rider as much glory and as winning the Tour overall.

Alpe d'Huez might well be the most famous Tour mountain, the one that even non-cyclists will have heard of. On the hardship stakes it also rates pretty highly, although it's by no means the toughest climb out there (not in my humble opinion, anyway). It certainly is, however, one of the most memorable and interesting to ride. When viewed from above, the road looks like an irregular zigzag laid down upon the mountainside. The 14km-long stretch is bent around twenty-one switchback turns, or *lacets* in French, and it's a combination of those bends and the altitude gained in such a short distance (the summit is over 1000 metres higher than the base) that gives the Alpe its distinct character.

The road is steep all the way, with an 8.1% average gradient, and a maximum at over 10%. Each steep, straight ramp leads into a sharp bend that throws you around 180-degrees and on again. In the corners, the road is less steep than the straights and so here the rider can gain some respite, especially if they take the wider arc around the outside of the curve. Of course that "ease" is purely relative and extremely short-lived. Slung round the corner you're onto the next long, steep ramp and right back into the grind of the climb.

For many pure climbers that constant change in gradient and direction is a godsend, allowing them to take advantage of the fluctuating rhythm. The best *grimpeurs* are renowned for their ability to stand on the pedals and power through the steepest stretches of road, when the average guy is stuck in the saddle, grovelling out a slow and steady tempo. On Alpe d'Huez it's near impossible to find one tempo, let alone stick with it until the top. The road has far too much bite, almost a life of its own, does its best to make sure you remember exactly where you are, and exactly who's the boss.

In case you're wondering why I sound like such a (self-professed) Alpe-D expert, it's because I'd ridden the climb three times before. Drew and I had visited the ski resort a few years back, (our first experience of riding real mountains) as part of an organised coach trip to watch the Tour. The winter before, Drew had been recuperating from an operation, and I had decided that he needed something positive on which to concentrate throughout the long recovery. Alpe d'Huez was the carrot I dangled at the end of the stick. Drew duly dragged himself back to full health and our coach trip finally rolled around. Over the three days we rode the climb three times, each ascent leaving us ecstatic and utterly exhausted. Then it was back on the coach for the long slog home, all the time thinking we'd probably never return to the Alpe, let alone get the chance to ride so many of its nastier neighbours and peers.

In order to allow for a warm-up we left the car about ten kilometres outside Bourg d'Oisans, the village at the foot of the climb. We parked at almost exactly the same spot the coach had deposited us for that fateful first attempt at Alpe d'Huez, and the memories came flooding back. Drew and I had asked in advance if we could pedal up to the hotel (rather than ride in the coach as planned), and the tour rep had thought it a great idea. He proceeded to ask the rest of the passengers (all cycling enthusiasts, most of whom had their bikes with them) if anyone else would like to do the same. Not a single hand raised, not even amongst the small group of lads who'd spent every spare minute of the journey boasting about their personal-best times and their expensive, lightweight bikes.

They say you always remember your first time and losing my mountain virginity is an experience I will never forget. Our nervous chatter had only been halted by dry mouths, and I lost count of how many times we each visited the tiny on-coach toilet, no denying we were seriously scared of what lay up (way up) the road. We were heading into the unknown; that giant was soon to be encountered and only feeble attempts at a positive attitude suggested we wouldn't regret getting out of the coach. We were waved off, like sons departing for war, our fellow passengers keen to catch a last glimpse before the two skinny Scotsmen headed over the top and expired upon the mountain. Cycling along that straight road, the peak on our horizon, we truly felt like men on a mission. Only much later that evening, when we entered the hotel dining room to a standing ovation, did I realise what we had achieved.

So, once again we were riding toward the Alpe like men on a mission, this time minus the farewell party to wave us off. One extremely warm warming up later and we swung into Bourg d'Oisans, still going at a rate of knots. Drew then launched himself to the front and picked up the already *up* tempo. We raced through the town, past the campsite and turned left onto the Alpe, and all the time I was thinking that we'd slow down when we hit the first ramp (a stretch of road that is less than half a kilometre long but which I remembered being brutally steep).

Instead of slowing, Drew kept at it, and the approach to the first hairpin, which we had crawled up years before, was covered in a matter of seconds. Sprinting in an attempt to get back onto Drew's wheel, I noticed that he was in 5th gear; a quick glance down at my speedo and I saw we were doing 20mph. We swung round the first hairpin (number 21) and hit the steepest part of the road. I flashed back to images of the Tour stage in 2001, when Armstrong's teammate, Jose Luis Rubiera, had sprinted off the front of the pack. Rubiera's move had taken everyone by surprise, everyone except Armstrong. They instantly opened a gap on the rest of the group and a short while later Rubiera swung aside, leaving Armstrong clear and motoring along the road to victory.

The thing is, Drew wasn't Rubiera, and I most certainly wasn't Armstrong. I panicked, worrying how much longer I'd be able to keep on his wheel, how I was going to hold that pace for two hairpins, let alone twenty-one. I was struggling for breath, snatching gulps that were entirely insufficient for such an effort. A glance down at my own gears: in third and pushing hard. I had to give myself a shake, firm instructions to calm down and not panic — I would soon find a rhythm, oh how I hoped.

My left calf began to hurt. It had been niggling me since we got out of the car and was getting steadily worse. Pedalling from a seated position caused most discomfort, so I stood up and found that position both easier and a little faster. Concentrating on the calf pain relieved me of the business of worrying about finding a rhythm, and by just after the third hairpin I realised I had settled in, or as good as it was going to get. My breathing was just about back under control and my legs had loosened. Not that I was about to tell him, but it seemed that Drew's madness, his notion to attack the climb from word go, had actually paid off. In fact, I felt much better than I had on either of my previous three ascents of the Alpe, so good that I wanted to race for the top, see what sort of time I could get, something I could compare to the likes of Herrera and Hampsten.

It wasn't long after that (and hardly came as a surprise) when Drew exploded. His legs seemed to wither beneath him, his head bowed, shoulders hunched, a man obviously paying for that insane early pace. He began to complain about feeling short of breath, and when that wasn't of concern he worried about the daylight disappearing before we got back to the car. Perversely, the more he complained, the better I felt, the more he wanted to turn back, the more I wanted to race to the top (this contrast in our conditions had become a resounding theme of the trip). I knew I couldn't speed off and leave him but it was getting to me — why couldn't we, just once, *both* be feeling tip top and excited on the same climb, and why couldn't that climb be Alpe d'Huez?

I had positive urges, what pro riders refer to as "good sensations": my legs were bursting, itching to power me up the road at full flight. I began to be overwhelmed by the idea, overcome by emotion for that twisting stretch of road — no adversary, this climb was an old friend. I had such strong memories of it, from my previous ascents, from TV and magazine pictures, that it almost felt like a favourite local rise I hadn't ridden in a while. It also felt surprisingly easy — or was it just that, physically, I felt surprisingly well? The Madeleine, despite her promise, had proved to be a cruel mistress, but Alpe d'Huez was a long-lost love, arms open to welcome me home.

By the time we reached Dutch Corner I had come to terms with the realisation that records wouldn't be broken during that particular Alpine twilight. Said bend is the Low Country's cycling equivalent of Woodstock. Much more than just a kink in a mountain road, the temporary, occasional place of pilgrimage is a living memorial to the Netherlands' passed domination of Alpe d'Huez. (Their riders won so many times that the Alpe became known as "The Dutch Mountain".) To date, Dutch riders have won eight times atop the Alpe: Joop Zoetemelk (1976 & 1979); Hennie Kuiper (1977 & 1978); Peter Winnen (1981 & 1983); Steven Rooks (1988); and Gert-Jan Theunisse (1989). Despite the fact that a Dutchman hasn't won the Alpe d'Huez stage for so long, the fans keep on coming, they keep on drinking and they keep on cheering — just there to celebrate the mountain, a geographical feature for which their homeland isn't exactly renowned. And if they can't have a mountain in their own country, they might as well make a summer pilgrimage every few years to claim one from France. Of course, it helps that the Alpe is a great excuse for a camping holiday in the sun, with lots of beer and the world's most exciting sporting event screaming passed the tent flaps. No wonder the Dutch fans cheer so loud.

They were certainly cheering when Drew and I first rode the Alpe. They were cheering, singing, blowing air horns, ringing cow bells, smoking dope and drinking beer (lots of beer), and all that the evening before the big stage. Our tyres had spun across the orange paint they'd lathered onto the road, sending us slipping and sliding, more sideways than upwards. I remember Drew being asked by a Dutchman if he wanted some water. Being extremely thirsty he had said yes, only to get a full bucket of icy mountain torrent tipped over his head.

Like the Stelvio and La Plagne, each of the hairpins on Alpe d'Huez has a numbered signpost. As well as helping addled cyclists to keep count, the Alpe's signs also act as dedications, naming their particular bend after a rider (or riders) who have won a stage atop the mountain. We noticed that quite a few people had scribbled their own names onto the signs, under and even on top of those of the victorious professionals. It might have seemed like a real wacky idea at the time for those vandals involved but in my mind such actions showed a total lack of respect — as if some idiot's name was worthy of placement alongside the likes of Hinault or Hampsten. (So I told Drew, shaming the pen back into his pocket.)

Another previous Alpe victor with a lacet dedicated to him is Giuseppe Guerini. His 1999 stage win was as glorious as them all, but only just. He had barely rounded the last bend on the road into town, was sprinting toward the resort when a spectator stepped into his path. The daft lump in question (later identified only as, Eric) had been so busy peering through the viewfinder of his camera that he forgot to step out of the way of the speeding cyclist. Guerini was knocked to the ground but thankfully remounted and raced on to the finish and his eternal, sign-posted glory.

One of my favourite Tour images is a photo, cut carefully from a magazine, which took pride of place on my childhood-bedroom wall. It's a shot of Scottish cyclist, Robert Millar, on his way up Alpe d'Huez, from sometime in the late '80s and is (to me, at any rate) not only a classic cycling image but also, being of Millar, a classic image of the cycling climber. Millar is riding into a right-hand switchback, sat in the saddle, hunched low over the bars and obviously giving his all. The bike is leaned heavily over as he gets ready to drive through the turn. His face is a picture of pure effort: eyes focused well ahead of the front wheel, picking out the road that stretches high above, as if seeing it sooner will pull him faster to it. His poise is like that of the boxer, arm pulled back, each and every muscle ready to rip and land that knockout blow. Millar will deliver on that bend, landing a sucker punch — except on Alpe d'Huez the successful fighter must land knockout blow after knockout blow, twenty-one in total. The hurt expressed upon his face is a combination of the rounds put in just to reach that climb, of the knowledge that he must roll with the punches all the way to the top. He's obviously about to strike but simultaneously appears to be on the ropes, because that's what riding those climbs, and doing so as part of a three-week race, is like. To conquer the mountain you have to push yourself dangerously close to defeat. As I ascended Alpe d'Huez I couldn't help but see that picture and, just as I had conjured Ligget's famous commentary upon the climb to La Plagne, allowed myself to imagine that Rolf Rae-Hansen was his hero incarnate, leaning in to the bend, muscles poised, eyes picking out the line further up the road, ready to deliver a knockout blow. Oh dear, and if only.

Alpe d'Huez is around an hour (nearing the three-quarter-hour mark for the best) of all-out effort. In order to maintain morale for the duration you have to concentrate on something other than the pain. Vast swathes of the road were (probably always will be) daubed with a mess of cycling-fans' graffiti. It turns a stretch of grey tarmac into something that more resembles a fun-park helter skelter. Not only are there riders' names and nicknames to discern, there are a host of languages to test and confuse an already addled mind. (Scattered incongruously amongst the sporting scribbles were an array of rather graphic depictions of genitalia, some standing proudly alone, others coupled together, usually captioned by Spanish text that I was happily unable to translate.) On my first ascent I had also attempted to sideline the pain by thinking as much as I could about each of the riders name-checked on the hairpins' signs. That technique had proved inspiring and also a little depressing, especially when huffing and puffing past the name of a pure climber like Luis Herrera (on bend 12; winner in 1984).

There are a few other distractions but none really loud enough to be heard through the pain. La Garde comes after hairpin number 16, where you might struggle to avoid the small water fountain and restaurant, its customers staring idly as you haul yourself passed their tables. You might feel like screaming when the diners neglect to applaud, but don't forget that the locals are probably sick of seeing cyclists, thousands of them, every year, groups of all sizes, individual adventurers, one and all "taming" the Alpe. The road does ease off a touch there (if you can call a 7% gradient easy), as it does a few kilometres (or 10 hairpins) later near the hamlet of Huez. If you are suffering on the climb, those are the points where you might want to resist the temptation of riding faster, when you should relax as much as possible, recover a little before the next gruelling section to come. The last part of the climb is steep (8 to 9% all the way to the summit) and only admonished by the knowledge that the pain will soon end. The road then splits in two and you should take the left fork (the road the Tour uses — remember, doing it like the pros) and come up in the front of the town. On race day this option can often be closed, forcing you to go round the back road, which is tougher and without the knowledge that you are riding on the Tour finale. That finish line is usually placed a short ride into the village, the point at which to check your jersey is zipped up, your shades are down, arms aloft as you coast in to the appreciation of the crowd — you know, the one in your head. Or is that just me?

It took us just under an hour to ride from Bourg d'Oisans to the top, and that included a few stops for photos. The slowest time recorded in the 2004 Tour de France time trial up Alpe d'Huez was 51 minutes and 13 seconds, recorded by Australian rider Matt Wilson — so we weren't doing too badly. In 1989, Laurent Fignon climbed the Alpe in 41 minutes and 50 seconds. Marco Pantani's record time for an ascent of the Alpe is 37 minutes and 35 seconds, timed on the day of his stage win in 1997, the second time he won there (and in the midst of an era when pharmacy helped to blend fact and fiction).

Photos taken in the twilight, excitement of the climb over, and while Drew began to overflow with concern about a dark descent and a even darker ride back to the car, my mind turned to food. I was suddenly overcome by hunger, not so much the bonk as a healthy urge to eat, so bad that I swore I could smell basmati rice, even though there wasn't an Indian restaurant in sight.

"Can you smell it, Drew?"

"No. It's because you're hungry, you're hallucinating."

"Can you hallucinate smells?"

"You can, I don't know about anyone else."

The drop back down Alpe d'Huez isn't exactly a screamer, the bends tight enough to keep you on the brakes *and* on your toes. Our descent was a blur of paint, a whole load of leaning this way and that, and it was pretty chilly too. The sun had almost fully ditched below the horizon, its faltering rays blocked by the giant clouds that rolled in to fill the valley like a blanket of cotton wool. With the twenty-one counted back we rolled into Bourg d'Oisans and the realisation that it was almost dark and we'd yet to cover the 10km to the car along the busy N91. Whereas Drew's concern was of the well-founded, adult variety, mine was more of the childish, giggling kind. The thrill of the climb had infused my attitude, and thoughts of riding blind and barely visible along a juggernaut-infested road brought rushes of excitement in place of the more appropriate terror. Once again I had regressed to childhood.

The whole Alpe-D experience, including that frantic sprint to the car, captured the essence of what cycling is all about for me — a youthful sense of fun and adventure. It returned me to teenage years and riding back from the local club's evening time trials. With no lights on my racing bike, I faced a mad dash along main roads in order to get home before nightfall. Ten furious miles and I'd have made it, the dark closed in around, legs wobbly from an evening's effort and covered in the little black flies that had adhered to the sticky embrocation. (I'm not sure what tired me out more, which event I put most energy into, the time trial or the ride home.) It's that kind of situation, like car tailing on the Glandon descent, that your adult brain normally disallows, even though an occasional blowing away of the sensible shackles can do a world of good (supposing you don't get crushed by a speeding juggernaut on the N91).

DAY 14:
THE BREWING STORM

Les Deux Alpes
Start point: Le Chambon | Height: 1652m | Height climbed: 608m | Length of climb: 9.82km | Average gradient: 6.2% Maximum gradient: 10.7%

We awoke to a sunny morning that was somehow greyer than the previous afternoon's storm clouds. The contrast in post-ride mood to our first time up Alpe d'Huez couldn't have been more striking. Back then we had lived off the buzz for weeks afterwards, our grins wide, egos boosted, tales as tall as the mountain. Fast-forward and the atmosphere in the camp had fallen into a slump. Drew was particularly flat, moping like we'd been up the Alpe to bury his favourite pet. In addition to the despair he was touchy, twitching, appeared to be hanging by a thread. I had no idea what was up, grew increasingly afraid to ask, back to worrying that the slightest word out of place might bring about the final snap, send him into the car and heading for the airport. It might have been paranoid to suggest that he blamed me for all his ills but there was no denying his aversion to the trip. The evidence for the prosecution had mounted: first there'd been his contempt for the "Folder of Doom"; then the postcard home and that dream of his bike in a skip; now there was huffing and puffing, his painful silences and a thunderstorm expression.

***

Hunger attacked en route to Les Deux Alpes (the hotel had dished up the second-worst breakfast of our trip so far, almost on a par with Trento's prison provisions) so we stopped off at Bourg d'Oisans and ordered the day's healthy option: hamburger, egg and chips. A sullen silence settled over the table, was only broken by our commenting on the antics of a zany-looking couple on the street outside the café (yet another French village, and yet another set of village idiots). They were "entertaining" us (and half the street) with an affected attempt at window-shopping. Madame Kooky was the least absurd of the duo; she just looked like a flamboyant middle-aged hippie. It was Monsieur who really stole the show, appearing to be a wacky hybrid of *Fistful-of-Dollars*-era Clint Eastwood and Quentin Crisp — the most camp cowboy you ever did see (Clint Go Westwood?). The odd couple entered into a bizarre yet fascinating dance that incorporated groping, French kissing and an array of extravagant hand gestures that were either freestyle-jazz-hands or a lunatic form of semaphore. I wondered: if left together for too long, would Drew and I become such a kooky couple, possibly showing hatred toward one another instead of crazy love? (More likely the mountains would do for us before it got that far.)

Besides the freak show, there were also hordes of cyclists hovering around Bourg d'Oisans, promenading through the small streets with a post-Alpe swagger.

"Do you know what I have just done?" They asked, chests puffed with pride.

Yes, we do know; you rode up the big twisty hill. You, me, him, her and the other thousand people so far this week.

***

By the time we hit the base of Les Deux Alpes the sun had returned in full force, turning the water of Lac du Chambon a deep, cobalt blue — which still wasn't quite as blue as Drew. He had driven most of the way from Bourg d'Oisans punching the steering wheel, any underlying signs of tension and stress bubbled up and fully on display. I had asked what was wrong but got a glare in response, a look that said, *do you really have to ask?* Stuck next to him in such close confines, the tension had been intimidating; I'd kept my trap well and truly shut, concerned that another word "out of place" would send him flying off the handle, purposefully crashing the car in order to end his misery.

Just as he had done the afternoon before on Alpe d'Huez, Drew started the climb at an impressive (make that ludicrous) rate of knots, practically sprinting away from the parked car. He was in the big chainring — I caught a glimpse of it just before he shot off — now venting his anger by stamping upon the pedals. Beyond the occasional grunt he still wasn't speaking, so I decided there would be nothing to lose in sitting back off his wheel (way back), settling into my own rhythm and my own, calm space. I had come to

Europe to battle mountains not moods. I knew as well as he did that at times our trip could feel like a hassle, especially so for him with all the driving. Getting bad nights' sleep in unfamiliar beds didn't help matters but it was hardly a three-week stint of water torture in Guantanamo. We could as easily have been at work, or in the pub complaining that there was nowhere decent around Edinburgh to ride our bikes. Instead of orange jumpsuits or work attire, we were sat in the saddle, riding up Les Deux Alpes, the very stretch of road upon which Pantani had cemented his 1998 Tour victory. (Okay, it's true that Marco had made the winning move long before reaching this rather nondescript climb, but he had said in post-race interviews that he'd felt determined on Les Deux Alpes, that only then had he known for sure that victory was in the bag.)

It would have been an amazing place to be that day in '98: the roadside packed with fans, a large proportion of them Pantani's compatriots, *tifosi* who had waited for hours in the rain to witness a stage that surely surpassed even their wildest expectations. They would have heard on their radios, watched on portable TVs as Marco attacked, static-crackled suggestions, rumours that main rival Ullrich had been distanced and was in trouble. When Il Pirata had finally appeared through the clouds, head down, dancing on the pedals, the whole mountain must have erupted.

I wondered idly what the climb to Les Deux Alpes had meant to Pantani, after the fact, long down the road, when the Tour glory had faded and frayed. In his final years he'd endured far tougher battles off the bike, much of which might well have obscured his view of past sporting success. When riding at his best, Pantani had exhibited an excess of grinta, but as time went on, as his troubles mounted, that strength appeared to diminish. In the grand scheme of things, the man's battles on a bicycle were nothing in comparison to his struggle with depression and drug addiction. I wondered again, a step further: now that he is cruising in the big ring, up there with the angels, does he look back down and see cycling as mere frivolity? Or does the celestial Pantani see the inherent beauty, the almost spiritual qualities of the pedal-powered experience? As I chased after Drew on the road to Les Deux Alpes, I hoped for the latter, wanted and felt (even on this relatively unremarkable road) just a little meaning in my mountain.

I caught up with my companion, attempted to enthuse. Rather

unimpressed, Drew grunted,

"There's no magic, it's just a stretch of road."

But it was *the* stretch of road that had led Pantani to his greatest glory, and then beyond, all the way to the eternal exit point — that's why we were there and not riding some other (more interesting and challenging) ascent. Pantani was Drew's cycling inspiration, watching that 1998 Tour on Eurosport had led directly to his buying a road bike. And not any old road bike, Drew had opted for a replica of Pantani's team-issue Bianchi, complemented it with the matching Mercatone Uno jersey, shorts and bandanna.

The knowledge of our hero's flourish upon that road fuelled my imagination but the same couldn't really be said of the climb itself. Like a mini, budget version of Alpe d'Huez, its ten hairpin bends were also numbered. In addition, each sign indicated how much of the ascent there was left to ride — and that really was about as exciting as it got. The road looked strangely naked after Alpe D's colourful concrete, and the challenge it presented failed to bring either of us close to stopping for a rest or even considering such heresy. (Of course, if we had preceded it with the full 189km stage raced in 1998, and in the same dreadful conditions, then Les Deux Alpes might well have been cursed as the toughest climb of our lives.) The metaphorical bar had been raised by aggressive Dolomites and insufferable Alps, and any middling mountain would struggle to make an impression, no matter its historical significance.

All that said, I still enjoyed myself. The rain had stopped, the morning cloud that had shrouded the valley broke up and drifted away, allowing the sun to burst through and take over. I relinquished Drew's wheel, dropped into second gear and absorbed views of the lake below, lounging like a bona fide tourist. Likewise, I dropped my brain down a gear or two, let the contentment wash over, cleared of concerns; no consideration of uncomfortable beds and bad sleeps, no stress over the long journeys ahead, no worry over upcoming challenges or those we'd missed — all that mattered was my short moment in the zone, lost in peace upon the climb. And then, all of a sudden, it was over. An ascent, which had probably taken around half an hour to complete, had vanished in the blink of an eye.

Les Deux Alpes itself was a deceptively large ski resort, packed with boutiques, bars, restaurants, ski and sports shops, even an outdoor climbing-wall and beach-volleyball court. We toured around looking for a summit sign that didn't exist and the place seemed to go on forever, a vast expanse of leisure developments that only existed because people like to play in the snow and sun, and are only too happy to pay for the privilege. We turned tail and descended in the manner of our ascent: Drew took off, eager to get the ride over and done with, whilst I freewheeled into his dusty cloud. (The only excitement of the downward leg was almost getting wiped out by an old idiot in a battered Renault who decided to overtake on one of the hairpins. He throttled his rust-bucket up my side of the road as I grabbed handfuls of brakes at 40mph.)

By the time I got back to the car, Drew was changed back into his civvies and ready for the drive to Carpentras. He was chatting to a French cyclist who, it transpired, had ridden the Galibier, Alpe d'Huez and then Les Deux Alpes all in one day. The adventurous Frenchman's ascent of the latter had been a far harder experience than ours, and no wonder. Monsieur's macho, all-action image was only spoiled when he called out across the car park to his rat-sized pet dog, the aggressively named *Toto*. We were soon back on the road, with only our heavily rotated selection of CDs to fill the sullen silence.

***

That next stage of our journey took the best part of two hours and led us south, away from the Rhône Alpes and down into Provence. Again we were in a transitional stage of the trip, having jumped from Italian Dolomites and Alps, onto the French Alps, and now heading to the Pyrenees, with just one (mighty) obstacle in our way. We approached Carpentras, (apparently you say, Carpent*rah*, and don't pronounce the s on the end. What a waste of a perfectly good s!), expecting to see that very obstacle looming large upon the horizon — because its reputation preceded it and because we assumed it was the only major mountain in the vicinity. Instead, the sky was again dominated by the weather. The bright blue that had surrounded the Alpine peaks was now a thick, grey soup, sliced by bolts of lightning. The tension (emotional and meteorological) was about to break, the electric anticipation adding to the air of dread and the sense of occasion. We were heading to Mont Ventoux and it didn't take a visionary to foresee that this climb wouldn't be a pushover like Les Deux Alpes.

We approached the outskirts of town, digital speedometer

reading 88mph, just like in *Back to the Future*. That velocity allowed for a moment in honour of Drew's school friend who had been obsessed with the film (as my friends had been with *Top Gun*). This lad used to run around the school shouting, "88 miles per hour, 88 miles per hour," in the vain hope that he would get struck by lightning whilst doing so and disappear into a time warp — any excuse to get a day or two off school. Braking for the traffic lights, we laughed and joined in the excited chant, "88 miles per hour, 88 miles per hour," lightning crashing around our crazy heads as if right on special-effects cue. The bad mood had broken with the weather but our smiles weren't set to last.

When it came, neither of us had ever seen rain like it, the land transformed from bone-dry to Noah's nightmare in a matter of seconds. A few minutes in and about a foot of water had collected on the road surface, leaving us worried that the car would float away before we'd even caught a glimpse of Mont Ventoux. Nevertheless, we were still laughing and smiling, the thought of drowning in the car insufficient to dampen our newly raised spirits. Then we opened the Folder of Doom and attempted to use its map to locate the hotel. The (we were about to learn, misleading) document had pinpointed our destination according to its postcode, so we assumed it would be, at least reasonably, accurate. Well, as an idiot I once worked for used to say, "when you assume, you make an ass out of *u* and *me*."

We drove around town as per the detailed map, and then around every square inch of the outskirts of town. We followed the map up a tree-lined dirt road, and round and round and back and over, and through there, and what about that road? Then back this way, round that way, let's try over there, and on we went. Pretty soon we had passed the end of our tethers, our sanity truly shredded. Then we retraced our steps and did the whole thing again for bad measure.

Eventually, we ended up in some outskirts suburb, looking for a hotel that wasn't there unless it had recently relocated to a secret underground bunker. We were in the middle of nowhere and not the exact middle of somewhere as we had wished, and thanks to the rain there wasn't a soul around we could bother for directions. We gave up and drove back into town hoping to find someone not sheltering from the storm and prepared to give two frazzled Scotsmen some guidance. That's when we stumbled upon the blatantly obvious sign, the name of our hotel printed in big block letters.

We checked in to the mysterious venue, located not within a secret bunker but round the corner from a main street the Tour de France has raced down on numerous occasions. It was nice: nice place, nice room, nice couple that owned it. It was also our first hotel with air-conditioning and typical that we had been bestowed that blessing on a night when the weather had chosen to break and drop by fifteen degrees.

***

By nightfall, the storm still hadn't passed, the rain (*Provence, the Scotland of France*), thunder and lightning persistent. Drew appeared to be taking his lead from the weather, that morning's fury blown back in for another attempt at ruining the day (and possibly the remainder of the trip). It was gone eleven when I diplomatically suggested he turn the television off and get his head down. I wasn't playing mummy to his teen tantrum; we had to get up at six in order to squeeze in breakfast, a ride up Ventoux and showers before the hotel's noon check-out time. It's not like there was anything on the box worth watching, even supposing you understood French, which Drew didn't.

I couldn't tell if he was stalling, putting off the coming day and what it held, or preparing an excuse in advance: *we can't possibly ride our bikes up that mountain after so little sleep!* Whatever the motivation, he didn't react well to my proposition. The remote control was hurled across the ever-shrinking room and he threw himself into bed. From there he made it perfectly clear that this was *his* holiday too, *his* time off and not my trip to control. His anger was more imposing than any of the mountains we'd yet encountered, including the next in line. It threatened, frightened and then in turn angered me. What kind of a friend would speak and act that way?

I could have explained that it wasn't his holiday and that neither was it mine. We'd come to Carpentras specifically to ride up Mont Ventoux — as agreed, planned, feared and dreamt. We hadn't come to France to sit up all night watching shit TV whilst grumbling about the weather — that misery was neither agreed, planned or dreamt. I could have put all that to him but I didn't. He was seething, absolutely raging, and I knew that when his temper approached boiling point the best way forward was with a backward step. Avoid further provocation (even when you haven't knowingly or obviously provoked in the first place), provide some space and hope he simmers down, blows himself out. Pride wasn't happy with that tactical retreat; pride wanted a confrontation but was to be sacrificed for the trip's greater good. Should Drew totally flip there would be a very real chance that he'd be in the car, on an autoroute heading for the airport quicker than I could say, "*au revoir Ventoux, Tourmalet, Peyresourde ... .*"

That wasn't the first time I'd fallen out with Drew but on past occasions I'd been in a position to retreat until calm returned. Now I was stuck with him, and him with me, between a Ventoux-shaped rock and a hard place, no space into which either of us could escape and regroup. So I kept my trembling trap shut, dug around in the darkness for sleep, tried to switch off my writhing, shell-shocked brain.

Drew didn't sleep much either, spent most of the night hopping out of bed to haul back the curtains and gawp incredulously at the lightning that continued to crack and flash. (Overnight, our bedroom had been like a disco, illuminated through the thin curtains by a constant strobe of lightning, sound-tracked by the thunderous beat.) A sigh to end all sighs, he'd heave the curtains across and lunge back into bed, all the while spitting profanities.

I mean, what was wrong with the man? Who wouldn't want to ride up The Mountain of Death in a lightning storm?

DAY 15:
THE MOUNTAIN OF DEATH

Mont Ventoux
Start point: Bédoin | Height: 1912m | Height climbed: 1622m
Length of climb: 22.7km | Average gradient: 7.1% | Maximum
gradient: 11%

Since its 1951 Tour début, Mont Ventoux has built an
exceptional reputation, an eminence probably unmatched by any
other climb. Alpe d'Huez may be equally famous (more so amongst
the general, non-cycling public) but is renowned for the
excitement, the colour and glamour of the stage finales to which it
plays host. An air of menace surrounds Ventoux, the dark aura of a
legend that's as much about tragedy as it is about triumph. The fact
that Drew and I had begun to refer to Mont Ventoux as *The
Mountain of Death* was not an effort to dramatise our challenge, it
was a statement of fact.

Perhaps the best-known legend in British cycling is the demise
of Tom Simpson, the original greatest-ever British cyclist. (I won't
attempt to tell here his full and amazing tale, for that you just need
to read *Put Me Back On My Bike — in Search of Tom Simpson*, by
William Fotheringham, one of the best sporting biographies you
are ever likely to read, and an unsettling mine of information on
Ventoux.) Simpson's story starts out with him as the plucky,
exceedingly talented, exceedingly hard-working British cyclist who
took on the Europeans at their own game, and won. He scored
victories in major races like Milan-San Remo, the Tour of
Lombardy, the Tour of Flanders, Bordeaux-Paris, the professional
World Championship road race, and he held the yellow jersey in
the Tour de France — the first Brit to achieve that glory. He rode
alongside, and challenged, great riders like Jacques Anquetil, the
first man to win five Tours de France, and Eddy Merckx, the next
man to achieve the jaune quintuple. That's the beginning and the
middle of the man's tale but, sadly, it's the end, one awful day on

Ventoux, that sealed Simpson's reputation and his fate.

The 1967 Tour was supposed to be a sporting success for Simpson, recompense for a disappointing and injury-blighted 1966. Riding a good race would also enable him to cash-in at the post-Tour criterium events at which most professionals of the era earned a large chunk of their annual income. On July 13th the race set out on the stage from Marseille to Carpentras, via Mont Ventoux. Temperatures were up to at least 40 degrees Celsius when the leaders hit the lower slopes, and when Julio Jiménez attacked on one of the early steeper sections Simpson was unable to react; metaphorically and literally cooked, he forced himself on, up the mountain, driving harder and harder to lesser and lesser avail. By Chalet Reynard, some 15 kilometres into the climb, he was swaying around the road, zigzagging helplessly and on the point of collapse. A short while later he did just that, but when his team mechanic came out of the following car to offer assistance, Simpson asked only for his pedal straps to be tightened, that he be helped back up in order to continue with the race. Remarkably, that's exactly what he did, but only to collapse again, for the final time. Despite the efforts of race doctor, Simpson could not be resuscitated and died right there at the roadside.

No wonder that for many cycling fans, and not just the Brits, Mont Ventoux stands alone in the rolling Provençal countryside like a massive natural monument to one of the greatest cyclists Britain has ever produced. But whilst Ventoux might sound like the villain of this piece, Simpson's untimely demise was as much the fault of his own actions as it was attributable to the mountain. In his attempts to keep within sight of the yellow jersey Simpson had taken amphetamine. At some point on the road to Carpentras he had also imbibed alcohol. (It sounds ridiculous now, but back then it really was commonplace for riders to drink wine, champagne, brandy, basically anything the domestiques could get their hands on and get up to the thirsty team leaders.) Simpson had also been suffering the after-effects of a severe stomach complaint that had left him drained and dehydrated. Those factors, his unstoppable drive, his desire to win no matter the cost, the heat and the brutal, unforgiving mountain, all combined to push him beyond the limit.

Simpson's death upon Ventoux was very nearly preceded in 1955 when a swathe of riders collapsed in the heat. French rider Jean Malléjac fell onto the verge, semi-comatose, the foot that was still strapped in continuing to pump the pedals. Medical attention saved his life but the ride up Ventoux was Malléjac's last race. Swiss rider Ferdi Kübler also suffered his final flourish that day. Only making it over the top of the climb with assistance from the fans who lined the roadside, he crashed several times on the descent due to exhaustion and eventually disappeared into a bar on the outskirts of Avignon, the stage finish town. After thirstily consuming several cold beers he stepped out into the sun and set off along the road, the wrong way. He retired from the sport that evening, telling the press, "*Ferdi has killed himself on the Ventoux.*"

The mountain has also claimed its share of non-cyclists. Winds upon the barren summit often exceed 150mph and have been known to blow loose stones around to deadly effect. Other poor souls have been lost in blizzards, and in 1994 a Tour de France spectator was killed upon Ventoux by a bolt of lightning.

So Drew and I knew a great deal about previous exploits upon Ventoux, and we also knew a lot about the climb itself. We knew that it started quite gently, slowly rising out of the small town of Bédoin, the tarmac disappearing into forest and winding upward from there. We expected that section to be difficult, not so much for its gradient (from 8% up to almost 11%) but for the heat and lack of air. The trees were said to make the rider feel imprisoned and the flies were said to gather in thick swarms, driving already insane cyclists beyond the limit. After fifteen kilometres the road would escape the trees and snake across the barren mountainside. There would then be no shelter from the sun or the wind; the experience often likened to riding in a stone furnace or upon some baking-hot "lunar" landscape. There the gradient would ease off for a bit before rising steadily toward 10%, a further six punishing kilometres until you reached the weather station at the summit.

If perhaps it's possible to know a climb too well then setting out on a stifling hot day toward Mont Ventoux could have proved the theory. Riding out on a cold, wet day, however, would take us on a journey into the unknown.

***

We somehow achieved our 6a.m. start — I made for a persistent, nagging, un-snoozable alarm clock. Nothing was said about the previous night's tantrum; Drew's upset replaced by a subdued fog of fatigue and fear. The breakfast room was deserted, the cool, settled air barely moved by our feeble attempts at cheery bravado. The back wall of the room was dominated by a laden set of bookshelves, one title in particular standing out: a well-worn copy entitled, *Les Français Torturée*.

We sat next to the open patio doors, trying to pretend it wasn't cold and damp, that the air outside wasn't thick with thunder or the buzz of lightning. I made an attempt at welcoming the inclement conditions, genuinely relieved that we'd be climbing Ventoux minus the sweltering sun. Drew wasn't convinced, as yet uncommitted to an attempt upon the Giant, growing steadily more certain that death by lightning strike was his imminent destiny. I was steadfast, unwilling to sanction his capitulation, no way I was going to miss the one mountain I most dreaded, or allow my friend to either. That would have been like turning up to your execution, then refusing to put your head through the noose. For me, Ventoux was something of the spirit of the trip. I had been inspired and emoted by the Simpson story; this Mont was to a British cyclist what Culloden battlefield is to a Highland Scot, a location where history took a drastic and tragic wrong turn. To go home without having ridden it would surely put a hex on my life, would forever be the haunting missed opportunity.

By the time we had forced cereal, fruit and bread down throats into tight, nervous stomachs, Drew had only half come round to the idea, insisting he would head out along the road and have a look, but no further if the lightning continued. His concern about being struck was valid, and so I agreed: we were only going out to take a look — and that, of course, was a little white lie. There was no way in hell I was about to reach the lower slopes just to shrug my shoulders and turn around. It would take more than a storm to stop me. Throw in a hurricane, zombies, a swarm of killer bees and a pterodactyl or two and I might just have considered abandoning the ride.

As we sipped hot, sweet coffee, I stared out into the black sky, all the while trying hard to inject a positive sentiment into everything I said, hoping in vain to lift the mood.

"Looks like it might brighten up," I tried, pathetically. "Those clouds don't look so bad now. Isn't that lightning such a beautiful colour!"

***

On the road out of Carpentras we could almost discern Ventoux through the murk. It was a deep, dark, tooth-shaped shadow and one that, strangely enough, didn't appear as high or intimidating as I had expected, (especially as I knew that it took in 1622 metres of ascent). Humming and hawing all the way, Drew was keen to turn us around, but I'd long since made up my mind. By the time we reached Bédoin, the skies looked like they might well clear, just not for a few days to come. The rain was crashing down, we were already soaked through and the cicadas sounded like thoroughly pissed-off jackdaws, squawking and hissing, wondering where on earth their summer sunshine had gone to and when all the bloody rain would leg it back to the plains of Spain, or the lowlands of Scotland.

Whilst the weather wasn't aiding my attempts to appease Drew, the road was actually quite favourable, those first few kilometres passing with relative ease, although the aptly named Rain Man Drew was well aware that there was much worse to come. The top of Ventoux was by then only occasionally glimpsed through gaps in the clouds; it looked so close, as if just a few easy kilometres distant. Is this really a climb on the scale of any of the others we have ridden? I wondered. Is this really the Giant of Provence we have heard so much about? Despite the lightning that cracked around its dark peak, Ventoux from down below looked so understated that it reminded me of a childhood training climb around the 320-metre-high Hill of Maud, by Buckie, near the Moray coast of Scotland: flat land ranging in from the sea with that solitary, nondescript peak breaking the plain. The road began to narrow and if not for the painted messages of support from recent races it would have felt like we were anywhere but the lower slopes of such a famous name.

We wended our way, almost upward, through the vineyards of the Côtes du Ventoux (a fruity, easy-to-drink red, from vines that somehow thrive in the poor limestone soil) and then on through an equally pleasant wooded section. It was there, as we had expected, that the road steepened sharply. The surface was a mess of branches, leaves, mud and other storm debris. Add in the cold and wet and it really did feel more like autumnal Scotland than summery southern France. Not that I minded the uncharacteristically miserable weather. For some bizarre reason (but just as well considering) I quite enjoy riding in the rain. As a result of that madness, and despite the increased gradient, I felt great, in fourth gear and holding back from making an attempt on

Iban Mayo's record time to the top. This Mountain of Death was proving to be utterly, unexpectedly wonderful, entirely alien to all my dreadful expectations. Absent were the baking, oppressive heat and the swarms of flies that would have pushed the bounds of my sanity; the gradient, whilst hardly easy, hadn't yet brought me even close to considering third gear, let alone first. It looked increasingly likely that our Ventoux story would be dominated by the weather, but the exact opposite of all those infernal stories we had read. It almost felt like cheating and I couldn't help but wonder: would Tom Simpson still be alive today had the weather broken on July 13th 1967?

Lance Armstrong said that Mont Ventoux is the hardest climb in France, ominously warning that,

"There is no pretending on the Ventoux."[11.]

Well, I wasn't pretending, making no attempt to psyche myself up, or the mountain out. I just felt great and if it hadn't been for the fact that Drew appeared to be feeling the opposite, I would have opened my mouth and told the Provençal spirits just how good. As it was, I couldn't express the joy that reverberated around in my head, heart and legs when said comrade was riding off the back with a face (aptly) like thunder. So I hovered just a few bike lengths ahead, constantly fearful that at any minute he might turn round in the road and shout,

"Sod this! I'm off."

I wanted Ventoux so much, wasn't going to lose it. At the very least I was going to make it to Simpson's memorial, even if the lightning scorched my tyres along the way.

At Chalet Reynard the forest ended and the rain had cleared a little, despite the sudden lack of shelter — or had my Ventoux optimism obscured the truth? If the rain had really been clearing then its replacements were dense, swirling mist and a biting wind. Through gaps in the mist we caught further glimpses of our final destination, the images of Mont Ventoux we had expected: a hair-pinned road skirting the edge of a pale and barren slope, rising steeply upwards, cruel ramp after cruel ramp.

Whilst the road had come back round to expectations, the mountain itself remained unusual. It didn't drop off at the extremity like so many we had ridden before, seeming instead to taper toward infinity, as if falling off the edge would send you gently rolling for miles on end, coming to an eventual halt in a flat field in the neighbouring department. (I imagined that but wasn't about to test the theory.) It was as if Ventoux had been created by the Mistral slowly blowing scree across the land, gathering it into a heap, the centre of which formed a peak, purely by chance, at that particular point in Provence.

Despite the misconception of many, Ventoux is not an extinct volcano but actually part of the same geological system that forms the Alps. Not that you'd know from looking. The bright, grey-white limestone really does provide an almost unearthly environment. Under normal summer conditions the bare rock is said to absorb then radiate the heat, cooking riders from ground level as the sun beats down from above. This is not a mountaintop of lush green, of wildlife, butterflies and flowers; there's little on show beyond an expanse of dry, white rock and sand. A wonder that Mont Ventoux has been classified Réserve de Biosphère by UNESCO, the summit said to be exceptionally rich in flora, with some sixty rare species — all of which must have been hiding behind a cloud for we saw no sign of them. Struggling for oxygen, all we ascertained was the cold wind cutting us through, unhindered in its sweep of a seemingly barren landscape, the two skinny white cyclists exposed and all alone.

Or so we thought, for it was around then that our concentration was interrupted by a black Labrador puppy, maybe six months old, that bounded out of the mist and straight toward us. Its tail spinning wildly in obvious delight, the tiny brute looked like it hadn't seen a human in months, and had never before seen one on a bike — exuberance to match my mood further down the road, when I had wagged at the prospect of a run off the leash. We assumed he belonged to nearby holidaymakers and had escaped from the back of a car or campervan, but there were no vehicles obviously around. A couple of laps of the bikes, a narrow miss with my front spokes, and puppy yelped and vanished back into obscurity, taking with him the edge of my excess enthusiasm. In that moment I realised that I was no longer riding at will nor turning the pedals with ease, the mountain, despite the lack of heat, beginning to take its toll. We had been climbing for over 16 kilometres and the section just entered was about to feel as long again, and far, far tougher.

The closer I got to it, the more I began to fear the approaching ramp. I could see it, shooting ninety degrees to the left, like a stern scratch across the landscape, as if warning that my previous lack of respect was due its punishment. I braced myself for the hurt but as we turned onto the dreaded section the wind hit our backs, providing yet more unexpected assistance. There I was, returned to feeling at ease when I should have been grovelling and begging for mercy. I didn't need to be a local with one hundred climbs of the Giant under my belt to know that on Ventoux easy is wrong, just plain wrong.

As if on cue, and to put an end to the ease, Drew shifted up a gear and began to sprint, suddenly deciding that grovelling off the back was less than acceptable on this climb of all climbs. He took off up the road so I duly accelerated and pulled level, expending too much puff to be able to demand an explanation. Had he been faking earlier on, psyching me out or just warming up? Either way, I wasn't about to dismiss the opportunity for a duke on the Ventoux. In turn I shifted up a gear and kicked hard, my move eliciting his mirror reaction. So we remained, locked together, front wheels edging each other out of the photo finish until the next ramp kicked right and Drew finally came off the gas. I relaxed back into the saddle, assuming the game was up, only for him to go again, three more attempts to drop me, somehow to no avail. As each ramp turned into the headwind, our hurt intensified and my satisfaction increased: pain was exactly what I wanted; pain was what the Ventoux demanded, all that it was said to be about.

The patchy mist danced abstract shapes around us, not quite ready to completely reveal the upper stretches of road, adding a spooky feel to a mountain that already had its fair share of ghosts. With each clearing we were delivered a little more of the summit's white observatory building, so close, as if we might reach out and touch it, yet still so painfully distant. That may well have been what Simpson had thought, if indeed he'd had the energy for cognition during the final few hundred metres of his life. He had died within striking distance of the top, one more turn of the pedals, one more, one more ... and then it was all over.

I was just about to give up on paying my respects, assuming we'd missed the memorial, when it appeared on our right-hand side. I nodded, doffed my cap and instantly felt self-conscious, as if the whole occasion was just a game. Was that simple, almost flippant action really sufficient to commemorate the memory of someone's husband, a lost son, father and friend? Or was it just the means to turn a bike ride into a Boy's Own adventure?

Simpson's memorial, a large chunk of granite with the raised profile of a cyclist on its polished surface, appeared much smaller than I expected, and than I thought the sacrifice deserved. Engraved with the words, "*Olympic medallist, world champion, British sporting ambassador,*" the obelisk has become something of a shrine, the custom not just to nod or doff your cap on passing, but to stop and deliver some random cycling-related artefact as offering to the two-wheeled gods. Accordingly, the plinth was obscured by an array of caps, water bottles and discarded tyres, as if leaving something of you behind showed Simpson that he had not been left alone, forgotten upon the mountain. We remembered, and then we headed on, greedily gulping our electrolyte energy drink, wishing similar potions had filled Simpson's bidon that day in place of brandy.

From there we had about a kilometre left to cover, one last, long, tiresome stretch as the road curved right and round to the summit. One grey cloud of discomfort later and we were there. Our legs empty, bodies wet-through and shivering, we pulled up outside the small gift shop and shook hands, our first mountaintop handshake since the Bonette, and a gesture full of emotion. Despite the fact that we seemed to suffer on alternate climbs, our adventure was undoubtedly a team effort. Having shared such experiences our friendship could only benefit. Or so I wanted it to be.

The tiny summit car park swarmed with tourists who'd made the ascent in the warmth of cars and coaches. They stared from under the hoods of cagoules and ponchos, as bemused, if not more so, than those non-cyclists we had encountered on any of the climbs so far. They talked in hushed tones and gave our steaming shapes a wide berth, staring intently ahead as they ducked inside to purchase a souvenir of their "slog" up the mountain.

A stand outside the shop sagged under the weight of mugs hand-painted with French names (no souvenir reference to Ventoux whatsoever) and all for nine Euros: *you rode up Mont Ventoux in a storm and all you brought me back is this lousy mug?* Mind you, if the mug had been filled with hot, sweet, tea then I would gladly have parted with nineteen Euros. I hauled the dry gilet (double-wrapped in two carrier bags) from my back pocket and put it on over my sodden jersey. Brakes tightened, helmets on, we took our bedraggled photos and headed off, down into the cloud and mist.

***

On the descent we passed a stream of cyclists who had waited for a break in the weather before beginning their ascent. Seeing our shivering, mud-streaked forms hurtling downhill probably made them feel quite superior, but I'd been to the top, read the stories, absorbed the myth. I knew full well who the foolish ones were, was much happier to have taken my chances with the cold, the rain and the lightning than to have chanced a ride up Ventoux beneath the baking sun.

There were a lot of those heat-seeking cyclists too. I had never before said hello so often and in such a short space of time. After the twentieth greeting I grew bored, began to work my way through different accents and languages, accentuating with silly waves and salutes, occasionally gurning like a well-fed baby.

At almost the exact same point that we had seen him on the way up, the puppy bounded out of nowhere, once more attempting to dive through my front spokes. I swerved, swore, briefly shut my eyes and said a prayer to the mountain gods. Skidding to a halt, I looked back over shoulder but the black dog was gone, the last straggling wisps of mist closed in to claim him. It was another near miss, and just as well too. Only the sickest twist of fate could have led to my surviving a ride up the Mountain of Death in a lightning storm to then be wiped out by a little fluffy puppy. No time to consider life's absurdities, I was already on the move, back to flying downhill, dodging storm debris and waving inanely at the oncoming cyclists. If we didn't make the hotel before check-out there'd be an angry madame waiting to finish what mountain and dog had failed to achieve.

***

We had swapped the Alps for Provence and its one big mountain, were back on the road again, heading toward the French Pyrenees and a plethora of famous ascents. We drove through further storms, by-passed others that skirted the horizon, some of which appeared to be sucking entire towns up into their giant masses of tar-black cloud. It felt as if we were also, in some way, leaving France behind, expecting a more Spanish feel from the Pyrenees, perhaps all too aware that we were inching ever closer to Barcelona, our final port of call and Drew's much anticipated flight home.

It was late afternoon by the time we arrived in Saint-Gaudens and we marked our arrival by becoming immediately lost — the icing on the cake of our Carpentras fiasco and an afternoon on the road. We toured the area in which our hotel was alleged to be located, discovered a town that was, on first impressions, somewhat reminiscent of Dalkeith, near Edinburgh — a grim wee place that surely nobody dreams of moving to, where the locals are all too busy growling at strangers to entice anybody in — and when I thought it had felt like leaving France behind, Dalkeith was not what I envisaged. (Saint-G is a Tour de France favourite destination, which is probably why I expected more from the place. It's perhaps unfair to say, but without the mountains on its doorstep the visits would surely have been less frequent.)

One more lap of the growlers and we stopped to ask directions. Our first candidate was pungently drunk, did nothing to dispel the negative image we had fostered. Despite the beery fumes, and against our better judgement, he enticed us out from the car and dragged us over to a nearby flowerbed. There, with a stick, he scratched a rough map into the dry soil, flamboyantly marking grim streets like a mad general planning his final battle. Satisfied he had put us right, and suddenly confused as to his whereabouts, The Face of Saint-Gaudens flung the stick over his shoulder and bid us a wobbly adieu.

That departure led to a debate on whether or not to trust the inebriate: was he the human equivalent of our Internet-sourced and utterly useless map? Were we once again about to end up down a dusty track on the outskirts of town, or had we stumbled upon a knowledgeable local who had been drinking to forget? We finally decided that a drunkard's directions were better than none and drove on in the bearing he had suggested. There, next to our shattered doubts and the Super U supermarket, camouflaged by a thick layer of tarpaulin-clad scaffolding, we found our hotel.

***

We checked in and once again discovered a room with a double bed. When we complained, the manager (a camp wee fellow), appeared genuinely disbelieving (*stupid gay Bri-talians*, I could almost hear him mentally muttering) and requested clarification four times over,

"So you want two beds then?"

"Yes!" We replied, four times, "we are not honeymooners, and even if we were, we would only have come to Saint-G on honeymoon by mistake."

The hotel itself looked a bit, and smelled a lot, like a dowdy retirement home. The tattered, 1970s carpets and yellowing wallpaper combined with an airless atmosphere and a musty aroma that was relaxing, in a coma-inducing kind of way. The place brought back unsettling memories from one of the worst weeks I endured during my days as a postman. The tortuous task in question comprised delivering mail to a retirement home. It wasn't just a matter of dragging the mail sack through the front door and dumping it at reception. If only. I had to deliver each letter to the innumerable and illogically numbered flats within the maze-like complex. Roger, the senior postie overseeing my probationary period, had warned me how easy it was to get lost within the home's thickly carpeted corridors, but he'd also told me not to worry: if you get lost just hop into the lift, go to the ground floor, when you come out turn left and you'll be back at reception. What he failed to tell me was that there were two lift systems, one that led to the safety of reception, and another that went up and down and led approximately nowhere. My memories of the place involve a sweat-drenched pale-blue Royal Mail shirt, panic attacks and dragging a bottomless mailbag around endless corridors in never-ending, utterly inescapable circles.

Inside our room, we discovered steel shutters in place of curtains. Drew suggested they were blast-proof, to protect us should any local decide their night out with the rocket launcher might take a detour by the hotel. When they were lowered, the room was so dark, the effect so disorientating that you couldn't tell up from down without spitting and waiting to see if it fell back down and landed on your face. Only the TV's little red standby light would stop us from waking in the night and thinking we'd gone blind.

Midnight panics had become another theme of the trip for me: sitting bolt upright in bed, mentally scrambling, wondering where the hell I was, what country I was in, what town, which door led to the toilet and which to the corridor. I wondered if that's what life is like for professional riders, away from home hundreds of days in a year, life on the road and out of a suitcase, constantly flitting from town to town, hotel to hotel. I certainly wasn't envious.

***

Shutters down, in case of nuclear attack, we headed out for dinner. Afraid to wander too far (what if there wasn't a drunkard on hand to provide directions?) we settled on a nearby restaurant with fantastic views of Saint-G's monstrous cellulose factory. It seemed to dominate the town's skyline much as the Castle dominates Edinburgh, only a whole lot less attractive. Giant plumes of steam and smoke escaped the many chimneys, a vision somewhat perverse after days on end surrounded by Mother Nature's most stunning sculpture.

"Excuse me," I wanted to confront the civil authorities, "couldn't you cover up that carbuncle, even for a day or two? It's just that we're here for mountains, not local industry. We want organic panoramas, not grim reality."

Neither had we requested a prostitute, and yet she had wandered into the restaurant's al fresco dining area and made no secret of her "desire", eyeing us up with all the grace she could muster, which, to be fair, wasn't a great deal. Unable to solicit a reaction beyond nervous laughter, she retreated to the neighbouring table, from where she pouted, repeatedly crossed and uncrossed her legs, and stared, fluttering eyes flitting between the two sunken-cheeked Scots in a vain search for interest. As we ate I felt guilt in place of any desire to purchase the woman's services: despite having no idea what pressures had forced this woman into selling herself to strangers, I had offered up derision and not compassion.

She soon enough gave up on us and attempted to infiltrate the, until then, pleasant meal of a holidaying family. So it was back to just the two us, locked in our own, strangely uncomfortable space. Drew steered the conversation away from the prostitute, over the belching factory and on toward the mountains. There he offered a dark admission: to him each, climb was just another road in a big, boring world of roads. Within his body, mind and soul there lurked not one iota of excitement over the prospect of further ascents. To him the climbs yet to come represented an extremely tiresome chore he was compelled to complete before being allowed to fly home (back to a, presumably, bike-less "freedom"; no mountains, no me, his watch back on BST, re-synchronised with his loved ones).

I was more concerned than annoyed, worried about how on earth he was going to get through the Pyrenees. As for how he was going to get back on his bike when we did fly home, when the only option would be definitively dull local roads and those inglorious, insignificant climbs — I couldn't see it, thought the bike-in-the-skip scenario more likely. He told me that on Les Deux Alpes he had attempted to motivate himself by thinking, "Pantani once raced up here," but that any vague stirrings of excitement he'd mustered had then been completely cancelled out by the subsequent thought: "Pantani had cheated and then killed himself."

I looked away, could take no more of my friend's maudlin mug, turned my gaze to the cellulose factory and a grim vista that more than matched the mood.

DAY 16:
ROBERT MILLAR DAY

Superbagnères
Start point: Bagnères de Luchon | Height: 1800m | Height climbed: 1170m | Length of climb: 18.5km | Average gradient: 6.3% | Maximum gradient: 10%

Col de Peyresourde
Start point: Bagnères de Luchon | Height: 1569m | Height climbed: 939m | Length of climb: 15.27km | Average gradient: 6.1% | Maximum gradient: 9.8%

Not only was this day to be our first in the Pyrenees, it also marked the inaugural, and thoroughly unofficial, once only, never to be repeated, Robert Millar Day. Our riding would be in tribute to the great Scot, my childhood hero (next to Fignon — I was never sure whether I wanted to be a thoroughly French cyclist or a Scots cyclist who was so atypically Scottish that he might as well have been French), and we were going to enjoy ourselves, no matter the cost. Or so my optimism suggested.

Robert Millar is the best pure climber the British Isles has ever produced. (Not that he is peculiarly a product of Britain; more, like many British greats, he is a man of his own wee island.) To me, a young lad growing up in the dour north-east of Scotland, Millar was undeniably exotic: the mullet haircut that flowed from the back of his racing cap; a prominent, sharply angled Roman nose; the perfect pure-climber's diminutive dimensions; a Scottish-French blended drawl of an accent. He was amazing, inspiring and, despite all that, somehow still a compatriot (if only by birth).

Millar was a loner (much like myself) who had turned cycling uphill (a sporting pursuit I loved and which, in my daydreams, I would one day lead the world) if not into an art form then at least into a very successful career. On top of all that he had based himself in France, a country I viewed from afar as some kind of sun-drenched, cycling-obsessed Promised Land. He was the type of idol a teenage boy *should* have, an anti-hero of the very best kind, a punk minus the inept music, the drugs and the Doc Marten boots.

The press found Millar difficult to pigeonhole, let alone interview; he didn't suffer fools and sometimes seemed as unlikely to make friends on or off the bike. Many around him in Britain were struck by his personality, never able to get round the façade and discover whether or not there was anything else to the young man — to truly appreciate his undoubted talents. Some may have decided he was deficient but that awkward attitude had undoubtedly helped him achieve the dream of becoming a highly successful professional. It must have taken a single-minded, truly resilient and wholly unconventional character to succeed in such a gruelling minority sport, then to hop across the channel and take on the French in their own backyard.

In 1979 Millar journeyed from the Shawlands district of Glasgow to Paris, where he joined the ACBB amateur club (the kick-off point in the Continental careers of other successful English-speaking riders such as Stephen Roche, Shay Elliot and Phil Anderson, to name but a few). From there he progressed to the professional ranks and on to the Tour de France. In the 1983 edition (his début) Millar grabbed a stage win in Luchon and finished the race in 14th spot overall, despite having lost 17 minutes to a first-week crash. The following year he won the stage to Guzet-Neige, claimed the mountains-classification polka-dot jersey and finished one step off the podium. When you consider that the only riders ahead of him were Laurent Fignon, Bernard Hinault and Greg Lemond, you get an idea of the company Millar was capable of keeping.

He didn't restrict his great riding to France. Wherever there were big mountains Millar was sure to succeed, finishing as runner-up once in the Giro, and twice in the Vuelta a Espana. He might well have won the 1985 Vuelta had he not come up against a Spanish Armada of riders unwilling to see a foreigner on a French team win their national tour. Millar's fifteen-year career ended in 1995, an occasion he marked by winning the British road race title — not a bad way to sign off.

A special man, and what better way to mark his special day than suffering a second dose (and my trip's worst so far) of the holiday splats. Such an affliction is bad enough when all you have to do is lie around in the sun, but when your holiday is spent cycling up huge mountains, the unpleasant condition takes on a more menacing air. I wondered if perhaps the white (and white-haired) Billy-Ocean-look-a-like waiter from the previous evening had poisoned my dinner as punishment for our behind-his-back mocking. Or had the prostitute put a hex on me for refusing her wares? Whatever the cause, the splats had come-a-knocking the moment I woke (actually, their stomach cramps had torn me from a blissful slumber), a full-on, complete evacuation that very nearly resulted in the depositing of my internal organs down the pan. (I'd wished the bathroom, and not the bedroom, had been furnished with those blast-proof shutters.) That delightful display had been encored, immediately after breakfast, by another, equally ferocious outburst. As a result, I was to start our day completely dehydrated and devoid of energy. In a window between stomach cramps, I scuttled over to the Super U to stock up on apricots, bananas and water, hoping to get and keep something, anything at all inside my fragile gut.

***

We departed Saint-G with little ceremony, headed off toward our first taste of the high Pyrenees — and did they look high. Exposure to the Dolomites and the Alps could easily have left me feeling blasé about big mountains, but this new range was more than willing and able to confound. A vast, sawtooth swathe of green peaks hung upon the horizon in a competitively impressive fashion. We'd seen Dolomites, we'd seen Alps, but we really hadn't seen it all.

Less concerned with the obstacles ahead, Drew worriedly mulled over a text message he'd received from his girlfriend (one of the few; her lack of correspondence made him miss her more, made him more anxious to be back with her, gave him yet another reason to be down on the trip), a brief communiqué which stated that the two weeks of his absence had simply flown by. He was pissed off that she might not be missing him when he was pining like Monty Python's dead parrot; even more pissed off because he felt that time was dragging as it might for an inmate serving a very, very long stretch behind bars. The more he grumbled and fretted, the more I wanted to grab his phone and hurl it through the open window.

When we finally arrived, Bagnères-de-Louchon looked to all intents and purposes like a gentile kind of place: no cellulose factory on the horizon, not a prostitute or drunken tour guide in sight. Its neat, tree-lined streets (promenades, one might say) were packed with elegant restaurants and cafés; the air smelled cleaner, the sun shone brighter than back in Saint-G. So why had we forsaken it for a stay behind the blast-proof shutters? Drew blamed me and I blamed the Internet. We had sourced and booked all of our accommodation online and, as far as we could tell, the hotels in smaller places (those outposts that were not only prettier but also far more convenient for our climbs) didn't have websites, at least none that Google had been able to find (and none that fitted our limited budget).

Not only is it a main tourist resort in the Midi-Pyrénées, Luchon is also a leading spa (hence the Bagnères, or *baths*, in its name) for the treatment of various conditions, including respiratory complaints and rheumatism (sadly, the leaflet made no mention of alleviating the holiday splats). The town also appeared to be some kind of Mecca for paragliders — either that or it was under aerial attack from a squadron of giant, multicoloured moths. They stood out against the blue sky and green slopes like a scattering of wild-flower confetti blown on the breeze, an enchanting and disconcerting mise-en-scène. Descending a mountain on a bike can be scary enough but the idea of coming down hanging from one of those overgrown kites was positively petrifying.

I had been expressing my vertiginous concerns aloud but Drew had paid no heed, was already a few hundred metres up the road, just about to take the turn toward Superbagnères. Whilst I struggled with my fear of heights, my fear of farting and my attempts to get the pedals moving, he was being dragged up-slope by a desire to get the trip and all its "monotonous mountains" over and done with. Only then would he be free to fly back home, to chuck his bike into that skip and do everything he could to stop his girlfriend's carefree life from flying by. I could almost see the dark emotional cloud hovering above his head, feel the rumbles of his mental thunder (between those of my own, far more severe, intestinal outbursts). Nothing more had been said on the matter since the previous evening's dinner diatribe but it was patently clear that Drew was not about to spend the day, let alone the remainder of the trip, with a smile plastered across his face. He now wholeheartedly viewed this as my affair, my idea, my holiday, my dream. He saw himself as the innocent victim of the piece, the unpaid driver who was being forced to chauffeur an idiot cyclist around the mountains of Europe — and worse still, then being forced to ride up the blessed mountains to which he had driven.

Despite feeling weak and listless I was determined to try and make the most of Robert Millar Day — after all, it doesn't come around too often. Those "celebrations" would kick off in a muted manner: I would take it very, *very* easy and meander my meditative way up to Superbagnères. With no fuel in my tank the climb's 15 kilometres could easily end up feeling like 50 — all that and I'd have the Peyresourde as an aperitif.

I struggled from word go — actually, from about half a kilometre before word go. The pan-flat road out of town felt like Alpe di Pampeago, into a headwind, on a penny farthing with the brakes jammed on. I hunkered down, scratched around for some kind of tempo, already in second gear, manfully resisting the urge to go straight into first. The air was thick with heat and humidity (I could have cut it with a knife had I sufficient strength to lift the blade). I gulped energy drink, forcing electrolytes, carbs and water back in to my shrivelled and knotted intestine, doing so a little less quickly than my system sweated it all back out again.

Two kilometres covered in around twenty minutes and the road decided I hadn't suffered enough already. Leaping up from around a bend, it hit me (sledgehammer style) with a gradient of almost 8%. The subsequent ten minutes felt like a full day in the saddle. Then it was up and over 10% for two or three hundred metres that might as well have been three hundred miles. Over that hurdle — somehow, just and only just — the road decided it was bad sportsmanship to toy with me, eased off sufficiently that I could concentrate on worrying about when the next super-steep section was going to appear and how the hell I was going to get over it.

Despite the tortuous noise in my head, the climb was much quieter than those we had experienced in the Dolomites and Alps, minus the roaring and screeching stream of motorbikes and campervans that had broken what little concentration I'd been able to muster. There was also a welcome absence of roadside cheese adverts, for which my crumbling sanity and shredded guts were truly grateful — small mercies and all that. These Pyrenees might actually be quite enjoyable, I thought, if only I had the energy to meet them halfway.

For the most part, the main crest of the Pyrenees constitutes the Franco-Spanish frontier, with the principality of Andorra sandwiched in between. (Our day's starting point was only a handful of miles from the Spanish border.) The Pyrenees are geologically contemporaneous with the Alps but there are major differences between the two ranges. In terms of appearance, the four conspicuous features of Pyrenean scenery are said to be: the rarity and height of the passes; the absence of great lakes, (such as those that fill Alpine valleys); the large number of mountain torrents (known locally as gaves); and the frequency with which the upper end of a valley assumes the form of a semicircle of precipitous cliffs, (known locally as a *cirque*).

Class dismissed!

Even from this cyclist's viewpoint the Pyrenees were instantly distinguishable from the Alps. From a distance, the peaks looked sharper, up close (too close) the roads steeper and more roughly surfaced. The sweltering air felt steamy and moist, a stickier, altogether harsher, more body and soul-sapping heat than the baking aridity of the Alps. The surrounding landscape was a verdant contrast, (I was sure I could hear running water, although that may just have been the sound of sweat draining from every pore in my body), as if the thick vegetation thrived by feeding off the intense heat — opposite to the man in the saddle making the observation. The only feature we had in common was the shade of green.

The Tour de France first tackled the climb to the ski station at Superbagnères in 1961, but it's the 1989 ascent that matters most to me: when man of our day, Robert Millar, won his final Tour stage. (Millar had almost achieved victory up there three years earlier, thwarted by a rampant Greg Lemond.) Indeed, that night's Tour show on Channel 4 had gifted me double reason to celebrate. Not only had my Scottish hero won the stage but my French hero, Laurent Fignon, had attacked upon the climb to take (temporary) ownership of the yellow jersey. Number 10 of the '89 edition was a dream stage from a dream Tour — the reverie only shattered when Lemond snatched victory from the jaws of a defeated Fignon with that infamous final time trial. (I have vivid memories of being crouched in front of the TV, screaming at Fignon, imploring him to go faster; then the shock of that eight-second loss haunting me for weeks after.) It might not have been my favourite race in terms of overall outcome, but it's easily the most exciting I am ever likely to see (from afar, cut and shut into a half-hour of highlights).

About six kilometres in, the road kicked again. Thankfully, it wasn't to be full-on steep from there. Instead there was another slight easing, before another stiffening, another easing, another stiffening, on and off at regular intervals all the way to the top. Just when I thought I could handle a 6%-or-so, a 10%-plus section would spring up from around a corner to wipe away my complacency. Just when I thought I was about to fart myself inside out and then expire in a puff of gas, the road would seemingly relinquish and I'd be back to manfully clinging on. I could see why big-tempo, diesel-driven riders said they preferred the steadier climbs of the Alps but in my (utterly frazzled) mind the changes in pitch were preferable to a steady slog. Whilst the excessively hard sections took me right to the edge, they also tricked my mind and body into thinking the less-hard sections were easy — they weren't, far from it; they were just less excessively hard. It wasn't much but those moments of imagined respite were the only "help" I was going to get in my struggle to the top.

Each time one of those excessively hard parts hit, the road rising steeply along with my heart rate, I'd attempt to distract by picturing Robert Millar belting by. For an instant he'd be there — there and then gone — mullet blowing back in the breeze, a pinky-blue streak of Z-Peugeot colour as he cruised to victory. Even in my foggy imaginings he looked fast. If I could travel back in time to witness any Tour stage in the flesh then it would be number 10 in '89. I've seen the race up close before (Alpe d'Huez, 2001; Armstrong won the stage) but I hadn't believed in what I was seeing, no faith, no passion invested in any of the riders. The boy Rolf would probably have exploded with excitement had he been roadside to witness first-hand just how rapidly Millar had ridden this climb, to cheer support as his countryman battled against the Spaniard, Delgado. And then, as an encore he would have had Fignon's golden-haired, yellow-snatching attack to fill the slipstream.

For three weeks each July (actually 21 multiplied by 30 minutes, minus ad breaks) the Tour came along to show me a golden world filled with triumphs and tragedies, joy and pain; a world that disappeared again as the riders rolled over the Champs-Élysées finish line for the final time. (I had no satellite TV, magazine subscriptions or Internet to keep me connected to the peloton throughout the remainder of the year. I saw no classics, no Giro, no Vuelta.) I was passionate about the Tour in the extreme way only a teenager could be. Obsessive, probably, but a healthy obsession as it made me even keener to ride my bike.

Almost two decades had passed but there I was, battling to reach the top of a Tour climb and still feeding off that teenage passion. Without it, who knows where I'd have been. Probably sat outside one of Luchon's chic cafés sipping ice-cold Perrier. (Did my passion blind me to Drew's struggle against the fatigue, the stress and homesickness? Was his problem a lack of enthusiastic energy? Perhaps, but why couldn't he tap into, and feed off, his Pantani obsession from '98? Had it died along with the inspiration?)

Drew dropped back a couple of times to enquire as to my condition (I was completely and utterly empty — no, it was worse than that. I had an inner vacuum that sucked in energy and destroyed it. It's another *jour sans* for Rae-Hansen, thanks for askin') but paid little heed to my self-pitying replies. He was irritatingly keen for me to stop moaning and hurry up so we could get it all over and done with — this climb, the next climb, and the ones after that. He eased off the gas, sat just off my front wheel, then slowly accelerated as if hoping to drag me up the slope in his slipstream — no such luck, for either of us. I was way beyond being able to even try and stick to his superior (or at least, *less inferior*) pace, tried once and gave up after half a pedal stroke.

Between those occasional distractions I fell back into my imaginings and daydreams — I wasn't *in the zone*, exactly, more lost to some deep dark place within, a mental anaesthesia that sufficiently dulled the senses and the cries for sense to prevail, in order that my body could continue working, pushing itself dangerously close to (or beyond) what I might otherwise have assumed were its limits. That total mess was similar to the state I'd been in on the Madeleine, only now I was too exhausted even to hold an imaginary conversation.

The smelling salts were eventually administered and I snapped back into life (what little remained within me). The summit had come, three lifetimes after exiting Luchon, but a little less slowly than I'd expected. It had come but perhaps not quite quick enough to satisfy Drew's impatience; definitely not quick enough to alleviate my worries about the climb ahead. It was a matter of minutes away but I couldn't, wouldn't yet consider it. Not yet. The longer I remained upright, and not down on hands and knees begging for mercy, the better.

I needed distraction and so, between electrolyte gulps, tried to envisage Millar, wobbling, exhausted but elated as he crossed the finish line, a dejected Delgado trailing in his wake. Then the wait for the yellow jersey but with Fignon coming home first, sitting up as he crossed the line, barely resisting the urge to raise his arms in a victory salute. I imagined, tried to vocalise, to enthuse, did my best to up the ante of Robert Millar Day but my sticky-mouthed spluttering wasn't fooling anybody, least of all Drew. Short of the man himself appearing with a troupe of dancers, a brass band and a crate of cold beers, the occasion wasn't about to spark into any kind of action.

The summit itself did little to lift our spirits. Apart from what I could recall or imagine, there wasn't a great deal to see. I suppose expecting too much from a Tour-free Tour finish in a snow-free ski resort is a bit like walking around in a drained Olympic pool bemoaning the lack of swimming action. A wee snack bar at the edge of the car park was somewhat overshadowed by a huge stone hotel, the aptly named Grand, and there wasn't much else of Superbagnères to catch the eye. What little man had done with the place, nature made up for in spades: mountain after mountain in every direction. It was mesmerising and, given my woeful condition, kind of frightening too, clear that one could spend months in the Pyrenees and still head home not having discovered half the climbs.

As I pondered just how many Pyrenean passes there might be, Drew broke his sullen silence to interrupt and declare, just in case I hadn't already got the message, that he was hating the trip. He reiterated the previous evening's assertion that the climbs were the world's most boring roads, and that cycling them was an act entirely devoid of enjoyment. Whilst I'd been wittering on about Millar and Fignon, gazing into the far distance wondering at the view, he'd been dreaming of being back in Scotland, "riding round the Asda car park with my brakes jammed on." Because, in his mind, that would have been preferable to "suffering" all those bloody, beautiful mountains.

Even worse:

"At least you've got your book."

"What do you mean?"

"Well, what do I get out of this? Nothing. Nothing whatsoever. But *you*, you've got your book."

He really believed that for him there wasn't a single positive to counter-balance the innumerable negatives; more ridiculous, that I would return home to the lauded life of a best-selling author. I tried to explain that just because I was scribbling my diary every evening didn't mean to say anyone was going to publish what I'd scribbled; I wasn't sure if I would even try to get it published. It was all going down onto paper for my own good, for personal posterity, a memento of a monumental experience. Never mind that it was turning into such a depressing read that *I* wouldn't want to read it, let alone attempt to foist it upon anyone else.

Drew's latest pronouncement was even more damning than the previous damnation, but I had insufficient energy to attempt an assault upon its negative stupidity, to yet again reel off that list of benefits the trip was bestowing upon us: multiple personal and sporting ambitions achieved; lifelong memories forged; fitness and climbing prowess boosted; the monotony of riding the same roads week in week out well and truly broken; five-star bragging rights created (*yup, I've ridden that one, and that one, and that ...*); a great cyclist's tan and more vitamin D absorption than would be possible from a lifetime of Scottish summers.

I could have ridden alongside him towing one of those billboard trailers, all the plus-points printed in big block-capitals. I could have had them tattooed onto his arms and legs, on the back of his eyelids. I could have hired a motivational coach to wake him up each morning by shouting the list through a megaphone, and still he would have claimed there was nothing in it for him. Anything I had to say flew clean over his head, weak words unable to penetrate the shield of cynicism. Robert Millar Day had got off to an inauspicious start and was going rapidly downhill.

***

In a metaphorical and almost literal free-fall, we descended at a steady 45mph back to Luchon. Actually, Drew was at least another 5mph faster, riding like he wanted life, let alone the climbs, over and done with. As I winced from a distance he took racing lines round blind corners, only blind luck keeping him on the right side of disaster. Our only ceremony was a pause to re-fill our bottles at a small water fountain on the outskirts of town. Otherwise it was straight on to the Peyresourde — no fuss, no fanfare and a distinct lack of enthusiasm.

The Peyresourde has a Tour de France history dating back to 1910, the year that high mountains (in the shape of the Pyrenees) were first introduced to the race. Alphonse Steinès was the man behind the decision to take the Tour to such dizzy heights, hoping to capture the public's imagination and in the process sell more copies of *L'Auto*, the newspaper for which he worked, and the commercial body behind the race. Somehow he persuaded his boss, the inimitable Tour Director, Henri Desgrange, to include the Peyresourde, the Aspin, the Tourmalet *and* the Aubisque in the race route. More amazingly he persuaded him to include them all in one monster stage. Desgrange, a man who normally thrived on pushing riders to the limit, sensed disaster, couldn't bear to look and instead sent his assistants to watch the race unfold. Despite the near-murderous intent, disaster was somehow averted; the race was a veritable epic and the Pyrenees cemented their place in the Tour's itinerary (a lunacy that opened the door for the Alps' inclusion the following year).

It's no coincidence that 1910 was also the first year of the Tour's *voiture balai*, or broom wagon — a van that follows the race to "sweep up" any riders who have fallen at the wayside and are unable to continue.

The longest Tour ever was the 1926 edition, covering a mere 5745km. Stage 10 that year was a suitably extravagant 326km, from Bayonne to Luchon, crossing the Aubisque, the Tourmalet, the Aspin and the Peyresourde — wonder why those Pyrenean routes have been referred to as The Circle of Death? Seventy-six riders left Bayonne at midnight and it was over seventeen hours later that Lucien Buysse arrived at Luchon to win the day. After an epic slog through snow, rain and fog he sat and watched the minutes tick by, waiting on the other finishers. By midnight, only 54 riders had come in and the race organisers were forced to send out cars in search of the missing men. Deservedly, Buysse won the race overall that year, not even time lost in the Alps could undo the damage inflicted by that one Pyrenean beast of a stage.

The Peyresourde was unwilling to replicate the simple start of its near neighbour Superbagnères, throwing up a 7% section in its first kilometre. I hauled myself up the road attempting to keep thoughts on celebration of Robert Millar and off the 14 kilometres yet to come, worry over my condition and Drew's pronouncement of doom. It was stage 10 of the 1983 Tour, Millar was riding his inaugural *Boucle*, and this 201-kilometre monster from Pau was that year's first venture into the mountains, taking in that Circle of Hell: the Aubisque, the Tourmalet, the Aspin and, finally, the Peyresourde. The hero of my day had attacked and dropped his breakaway partner whilst approaching the summit on the opposite side of the Col (having raced up from Arreau). He flew down the mountain and somehow held off the pursuing (make that, descending like a lunatic) Spaniard, Pedro Delgado — the same man he'd fight for the win six years later across the valley atop Superbagnères. I looked ahead, attempting to conjure Millar whizzing toward me, his white Peugeot jersey streaked against the grey tarmac backdrop. I tried to imagine what my teenage self might have hollered into Millar's slipstream as he zipped by (*allez Robert; dig in; up-up-up; go Millar; look out, here comes Delgado!*) but the more I thought of him, the more ashamed I felt at my own utterly shambolic state.

The temperature had rocketed in the hour since Super-B, further hampering my slog with a heat that fast approached Rolf Roasting Point. As we passed through a wee village called Garin, the gradient eased to about 4%, sufficient respite to allow my mind a moment or two of contemplation: I was going to empty both bottles of water over my head; I was going to turn around and freewheel back down to Luchon, throw myself into the fountain and cry for my mummy until she flew to France to pick me up. My Laurent Brochard-style bandanna/sweatband had filled to overflowing, was drip-dripping salty sweat into my eyes, into a headset top-cap bolt now rusted and ruined by days of perspiration. I dreamt of a cold sponge on the back of my neck, the way boxing trainers revive weary fighters. In fact, forget sponges, I needed an injection of something performance enhancing, preferably deep-frozen and highly, improbably illegal. With that thought I rode over a slogan daubed onto the road: *dopé salut.*

Garin made up for its lack of spring-water fountain into which I could swan dive by playing host to an automated speed trap. Attached to a warning sign, it registered your velocity on arriving into the village and flashed the result on its digital display. Upon my passing it failed to register and I wondered if the evil contraption was there to shame pathetic cyclists into speeding up, as well as to shame speeding drivers into slowing down. Shame or no shame, I was immovably lodged at a laborious crawl.

We exited the village and climbed some more (some more, some more, always some more!), passed a campsite from which further bemused tourists gawped. (If one thing is to come from this story then make it the passing of a global law that compels those observing sweaty, struggling cyclists to offer encouragement, for any gormless gawping to be punishable by an on-the-spot fine.) Beyond the campsite, the roadside trees thinned out to singles, then the line stretched until each trunk was separated by a swathe of open space. I began to panic, not at how steep the Col's upper sections were going to be, but at how little shade there would be should I ever reach them.

The only distraction from the realisation that I might be cooked alive in the saddle came with recognising this part of the climb from TV footage of the Tour. I could recall the road rising up the valley toward the horizon, the thin line swamped by a blanket of colour, massed crowds cheering the riders. In my particular memory, those spectators were a mass of orange T-shirts, supporters of the Basque Euskaltel Euskadi team. Known as *La Marea Naranja* (The Orange Tide), they come en masse to the Tour's Pyrenean stages, having only to hop across the frontier and into France.

As each of the roadside trees approached, I mimicked my Mont Cenis technique, slowed my crawl to a half-crawl in order to linger in the minimal shade. With no momentum to carry me on, I would almost come to a complete halt, forced into a track stand from which I somehow wobbled, back into the sun and on to the next tree in line. That deplorable dance lasted for about ten trees, until, suddenly repulsed by the sight of my own shadow, I made an effort to accelerate. The intention was to ride more quickly between the trees in order to spend less time in the company of that sickening shape (less time in the direct sun would also mean less cooked flesh to deal with should I actually survive the ride). It was my last shot and proved to be a wasted effort. I pushed down on the pedals, actually went a little slower and then collapsed back into the saddle.

My mind was a mess, competing with my body for the day's booby prize, no sign of the mystery anaesthetic that had dulled my senses on Superbagnères. I went from struggling to believe that the summit was within my ability, to doubting that the top of the climb even existed. I had no recollection of the upper slopes of the Col, even though I'd probably seen it many times on TV, and my worry was that if I couldn't picture it, then I couldn't ride to it. They say you should try and visualise your sporting success in advance but I couldn't in any way imagine the road upon which that "success" was supposed to occur. The crest of the valley was just about discernible, far in the distance, but I was sure the Peyresourde was more than a long, direct haul to that point. Wasn't there a series of switchbacks just before the summit? That suggestion didn't match up with the evidence before me.

Even my progress (or lack of it) was something of a mystery. I hadn't been paying attention to my cycle computer and had neglected to reset the trip distance at the base of the climb. With Drew miles up the road, the detail of his babbled briefings well out of earshot, I was clueless as to how far there was to go, and unable to judge if the dregs of strength left in my legs would cover it. There's always at least one moment on a climb when the voice at the back of my head hollers a warning — *you're not going to do this!* — but 999 times of 1,000 I push on and keep pedalling until the voice has faded. On the middle slopes of the Peyresourde I was still pedalling, just, but the voice was still hollering.

As its panicked shouts threatened to consume me, eyes slipped from the next sliver of shade and onto three tiny, coloured dots in the far distance. Squinting into the sun, those dots became cars that were switching left and right, out of the valley and on toward the top of the Col. That was the end of the road as I had expected to see it, but why did it appear to be so impossibly far away?

In the 1923 Tour, Robert Jacquinot collapsed into a ditch on the Peyresourde roadside, paying the price for the monstrous attacks he had made earlier in the day upon the Aubisque and the Tourmalet. In that ditch he is reported to have laid, entirely spent, only able to watch as those he'd left behind came pedalling by. I couldn't help thinking: if collapsing is good enough for a Tour rider then it's definitely good enough for me. That desire to keel over was heightened by the sound of water, trickling and burbling away in the ditch to my left (quite what stopped me diving in I'll never know). I guesstimated that there were probably around three miles left to ascend but from where I was supposed to find the energy for the next three hundred metres I hadn't a clue. I looked up to the ever-distant summit; the water trickled and tempted; my mind wandered. It was the closest I had come all trip to getting off the bike and giving up, something I hadn't seriously considered on any of the other climbs, not on the mighty Stelvio, not even during my awful ascent of the Madeleine. (It's possible the knowledge that I didn't even have the energy to walk was all that kept me on the bike.)

"What's three miles," I thought? "It's only about the distance I cycle to work every weekday. Surely I can manage three miles?"

It wasn't much, but for me at that moment it was everything, the be all and end all, the longest journey; a more daunting on-the-bike prospect I could not imagine. Never mind all the climbs done and the few left to come; all that mattered were those three measly miles.

Once again as I reached rock-bottom thoughts turned to my late father. I consider the final days of his illness to be my "Vietnam" experience. I was a third-party participant in a brutal war, a campaign that was fought within his body. The cancer made its cruel advance from bowel to vital organs and destroyed the man from the inside out. Its tactics were vicious and utterly barbaric, but by no means did he roll over and die; Dad resisted with the strength of one hundred men. I realised from the outset that, no matter the outcome, my life, the lives of my nearest and dearest, would be changed irrevocably. Death had ensconced itself within our family home. I smelled it, heard it evidenced in my father's waterlogged breaths, and witnessed it in his jaundiced, emaciated, slowly deteriorating body. Death was there amongst us, my mother, my sisters and I, but it was Dad who stood firm and took it on. Death grabbed hold of the only man I have ever loved, my role model, the man who had always been there to love, nurture, provide for, educate, discipline — he fought for all of us, truly raged against the dying of the light.

He endured so much and yet I have no recollection of him complaining. I have two particularly vivid memories of him during that period and in both he is smiling — at me, at a point in time when he would have been entitled to scream, shout and hurl obscenities. But he chose not to. He was dying; he knew it and he continued to set his son an example.

Now here I am cycling up a mountain. That is all I am doing, nothing more noble or heroic. I have no excuse, no need for self-pity. I am in discomfort (not pain) but the discomfort I feel is a luxury, evidence of my continued, healthy existence. So let's get things straight, Col de Peyresourde, there is no f***ing way in hell I am going to get off this bike and hand you the victory. I know which story I want to scribble into my diary and take back to Scotland, and it doesn't involve my father's son sitting at the roadside feeling sorry for himself.

I looked up to the ever-distant summit; the water trickled and tempted; my mind wandered.

In the 1922 Tour, Belgian rider Émile Masson was struggling up the Peyresourde (although climbing the opposite slope to my ascent) when he met a shepherd who suggested a short-cut along a goat track. Sadly, the rocky route up which Masson had to carry his bike proved to be something of a long-cut, and he finished the stage three and a quarter hours behind the winner. I imagined Masson struggling up that track, cursing the shepherd, horse flies attacking his spent legs. Was I even close to *that* level of suffering? I looked up to the ever-distant summit; the water trickled and tempted; my mind wandered.

Questions upon a climb inevitably lead to one main puzzle: why am I doing this to myself? What is it about forcing my body to its limits that appeals so much and keeps me coming back for further punishment, time and time again? When I considered what we had been putting ourselves through it was no wonder Drew had been feeling downbeat. As each day started, I'd glanced at the imminent climb's profile and wilfully failed to grasp how it would feel to ride one 15-mile, incredibly steep ascent, let alone two. Each day we had dragged ourselves into an extreme situation where the only things that could give were our bodies and minds. The climbs would not relent — for anyone, ever — and our bikes could not help if we could not pedal. So when pain receptors screamed at us to stop we had to push against them Jens Voigt-style, forcing bodies and minds against their will, on toward another summit. If that situation hadn't caused stress it would only have been because we were in some way mentally deficient, super-human, doped to the gills or a touch of all three. So what was it that kept us going, why was Drew continuing even though he was so obviously (and I hoped, only temporarily) stressed? Was his the same reason I didn't get off my bike, because the need for achievement was greater than that for rest? Or was a desire to avoid (self-inflicted) humiliation all that kept me out of the ditch and Drew from giving up and going home?

I was still rooting around in the mess of my mind for answers when consciousness kicked back in, revealing my position upon the switchback bends (the three cars I'd witnessed from afar long-since gone). That final stretch of the climb averaged about an 8% gradient but was made no easier by the knowledge that the end was truly in sight. I kicked and pushed, hauled and heaved, dragged myself round and over the final crest to the summit, looking to all intents and purposes like an extra from a disaster movie. On reaching the sign marking the top, I did something I had desired to do since first leaving Luchon (and hadn't done on any of the previous climbs): I got off my bike and sat on the ground.

I mustered a smile in an effort to cheer up Drew. (He had arrived a long while earlier and was killing time by idly pedalling in slow, mournful circles.) The smile wasn't returned but I didn't really care. I was mentally destroyed, bodily baked from the hot sun, soaked through with sweat, possibly sautéed. Sucking in the last drops from my bottle, I thought of Millar passing by, on his own having dropped Jiménez, Delgado about to appear in hot pursuit. I waved the flying Scotsman on his way, promised, should it ever happen again, that the next official day in his honour would be a more worthy affair.

***

During the 1998 Tour, Rudolpho Massi, winner of stage 10 from Pau to Luchon, had been clocked at over 60mph (100kph) on the Peyresourde descent. Knowledge of that feat led me to believe that the grovel up the climb would at least be exonerated by a fearsome flight back down — just the ticket to blow away the blues. The long straights and the shallow bends where I had sucked up shade on the ascent would be perfect for the speed I sought. All I had to do was whack it into top gear, pedal like fury and keep off the brakes. Sounds simple enough, but of course when Massi dropped down the mountain like a rock into the void he'd had the benefit of closed roads i.e. no traffic, and in particular, no articulated lorries blocking both lanes on the fastest stretch. I screamed round a bend, grabbed a glance at the immovable object, and quickly grabbed twin handfuls of brake. Having to emergency stop from 50-odd miles-an-hour on a skinny-tyred road bike is no fun whatsoever. Frantically feathering both brakes, I only just managed to avoid locking up completely, somehow kept the back wheel from skidding out of control. A campervan was last in line waiting to get by the obstacle, and by the time I came to a halt (performing a rather graceless endo) my nose was pressed against its back window.

Obstruction cleared, we got moving again but only to be stuck behind a convoy of cars and that close-encounter campervan. I watched the automated speed trap at Garin clock Drew, who was in front of me by then, at 55kph, a velocity limited by the traffic but a good deal faster than my non-register on the ascent. And then, within what felt like the blink of an eye, the Peyresourde was gone. The longest climb of the trip for me thus far, at least psychologically speaking, might have been over but it was branded onto my subconscious. There, in a dark recess it will forever stay, next to the Madeleine, to be recalled as an anecdote, as a nightmare or simply as a morale booster the next time I am struggling up a (lesser) hill in some other part of the world.

"You think *this* is bad?" I will ask myself in disgust. "This is *nothing* compared to that bastard of a day on the Peyresourde!"

It had been tough all right, but for some strange reason I still preferred it to riding around the Asda car park with my brakes jammed on.

DAY 17:
LIGHTNING QUICK

Col d'Aubisque
Start point: Laruns | Height: 1709m | Height climbed: 1190m
Length of climb: 16.6km | Average gradient: 7.2% | Maximum
gradient: 10%

Nestled at the northern edge of the Pyrenees, Pau is a Tour de
France regular — more than sixty visits (and counting) since
Alfredo Binda won the first stage there in 1930. The 19th-century
poet, Alphonse de Lamartine was another particularly struck by the
place. He enthused that Pau had,
*"... the most beautiful view of land, just as Naples has the most beautiful
sea view."*
I've never been to Naples but I felt inclined to take old
Alphonse's word for it. And it wasn't just the surrounding
landscape that caught the eye. Pau itself looked rather nice too,
with its château, its grand, historic buildings and pristine parks; it
was certainly less "Dalkeith" than Saint-G. (Do you think I will be
quoted on that in years to come?)

Less agreeable than the views had been our arrival in town the
previous afternoon and another vain struggle to locate a hotel.
With so many one-way streets and a crappy map to contend with
we were quickly back to being lost — a precedent set for our entire
two-night stay in Pau. The Belvedere of the Pyrenees became The
Town With No Direction, leaving us little option but to stop the
most attractive woman we could find and ask her for directions.

Ten minutes and a couple of wrong turns later, we were there,
exhausted just from navigating the town, our struggle up the slopes
of Robert Millar Day already a distant memory. The hotel wasn't
exactly exceptional, but by combining a tobacconist, a newsagent
and a bar into its bargain certainly covered many bases. We were
(grudgingly) permitted to keep our bikes in the room, despite the
manager's insistence that he knew a man who knew another man

who had a brother who happened to have a garage that had room in it for two expensive racing bikes. We politely declined the dubious offer and decided to opt for cramming everything into the cupboard-sized chambre.

Finally untangled from the one-way maze, the only suitable means of celebration our weary minds had been able to come up with was a trip back into the one-way maze in search of dinner. After my goats-cheese surprise in Briançon, I hadn't been entirely keen on diving headlong into the local-specialities menu, but we decided it would be safe to have at least one ride on the raclette before departing France.

The evening sun still warm, the air filled with an exotic summer aroma, we'd been keen to sit outdoors, were disappointed when the waitress ushered us inside, to a table at the back of the dingy restaurant. It transpired this relocation was not intended to prevent us from scaring away other potential diners, but instead to position us suitably close to an electric socket. Into said socket was plugged a small three-bar heater, not to compensate for the lack of warming sunshine, but to melt our slab of raclette cheese. Along with this wedge of disintegrating fromage came a plate of meats, some baked potatoes and a selection of pickles, complete with the world-renowned delicacy, diced pickled-carrot.

A raclette (from the verb *racler*, to scrape) is a dining experience which, like many French meals, is supposed to slowly unfold as an occasion in itself, and not to be the nourishing precursor to some other, inferior activity. However, in typically Scottish/calorie-deficient-cyclist style, we devoured the lot in fifteen minutes flat. The poor wee heater could barely keep up as we speedily scraped away layer after layer of freshly melted cheese. No sooner had the last morsel been devoured, the last cube of carrot nibbled then spat back into the bowl, and we were reaching for our wallets and demanding the bill. Our ravenous rapidity raised several eyebrows and a concerned madame was compelled to enquire as to why we so disliked her food. *Au contraire*, we reassured the beefy, muscular French wench as she reached for her club/giant pepper-mill. Our début raclette had indeed been a fantastic treat, but we'd just ridden the Semi-Circle of Death, barely survived the One-Way System of Doom and in the process built up one hell of an appetite. Okay, so we had speedily consumed sufficient melted cheese to construct two extra-large ponchos but that's because we were very, very hungry boys, and not because we desired to get the whole ghastly process over and done with. She half smiled, gracefully grasped the gist of our cobbled French just as I was about to lift my t-shirt and use a rack of protruding ribs as substantiating evidence.

***

The next morning, we arrived at Laruns just in time for the Saturday market. A stall of some kind, or a human of some other kind, occupied every inch of the village centre. The market, which appeared to sell everything from saucisson to socks, sprawled out from the main square and down the side streets like water flooding from a burst main. Within minutes we had taken a wrong turn in yet another town devoid of correct turns and become trapped somewhere deep in the mass. The experience was unnerving, akin to driving through a zombie-infested safari park. People prowled round the car, over the car, a couple of skinnier ones slid beneath, searching out bargains and morsels. They peered through the glass at the scared Scots within, nibbling on our wing mirrors and aerial as they ruminated and rummaged.

We proceeded with caution, avoiding eye contact with the wild ones as best we could. Up another side street, thinking we'd escaped, only to have our bid for freedom stalled by a minibus on a very slow drive around the village, on a mission that appeared to involve depositing an old person at each and every front door. Perhaps it was part of some French national holiday, when the old folk get mixed up in a big basket and then evenly redistributed amongst the community. Or — bear with me — had we stumbled upon a gang of ruthless and rheumatic burglars who were slowly stealing whilst the village shopped? Probably not. Whatever the truth, Laruns was quickly re-named the French Royston Vasey (another slogan I will gladly donate free of charge to the local tourist board).

As well as being home to a crowded market and an OAP re-distribution scheme, Laruns is an ideal centre for exploring the amazing mountains and valleys of the nearby National Park. An observatory offers those not observing the shopping habits of the locals the chance to cast an eye over a colony of griffon vultures — birds of prey that would no doubt soon be hovering hungrily over our heads. Laruns is also a centre of cheese making and plays host to a cheese fair, where shepherds from all over the region come to sell their wares and frighten lost tourists. The town's eponymous variety is an unpasteurised hard cheese, shaped into a flattened round loaf, with a supple texture and a mild and nutty taste. The very thought of it and the other delicacies on display in the market sparked dreams of a future when I'm too old and fat to ride up mountains, when I'll return to France on a gourmand's holiday. (Coincidentally, Laruns is also the name for the condition I was suffering on Robert Millar Day. Get it? Sorry.)

We stuck it to the little man (and woman), took our Euros to the nearest corporate supermarché to buy water and what was fast turning into my staple diet: bananas and dried apricots. On exiting the shop I dropped two of the four bottles that I'd been attempting to juggle along with the fruit. Without a free hand to pick them up, and with no offer of assistance from Drew, I had little choice but to impudently kick the strays over to the car. By the time I got there, the scowl across my face was as wide as the gulf between our overall impressions of the trip. Drew then decided to make matters worse by casting me up and down with a scolding glare. I dumped the supplies onto the roof, got into the car and slammed the door. Drew sat down in the driver's seat, calmly shut the door and then launched into a critique on "the problem with your moods". *My* moods? *My* bloody moods? I impolitely told him where to stick his opinions, suggested he took a long hard look at himself, and barely resisted the urge to smash both our heads off the dashboard. We had definitely spent too much time in one another's company. Had this trip really been the honeymoon that so many of Europe's hoteliers had assumed it to be then I'd have been on the verge of heading home to arrange an annulment.

The grey skies that had been closing in around our heads with yet another bad mood began to crack and burst, all that wishing for rain come back at me one hundred times over. Thunder and lightning ranged from storms in every direction, the valley from one end, miles and miles to the other, thick, black and actively violent — far from welcoming, but in synch with our spirits. We sat, waited and wondered: are we wasting our time here? But those ruminations failed to take hold, constantly interrupted by the stream of concerned shoppers who rushed across the car park to point out that we had four bottles of water, two bunches of bananas and four bags of dried apricots stacked upon the roof.

"Yes, thanks, we know they're up there," we forced smiles through the gloom.

"Crazy Bri-talians," they muttered, slowly backing away from the car.

Just when we thought it might be clearing, the rain turned heavier. Then it turned from rain to hailstones — giant, evil hailstones that resembled rough chunks cut from a block of ice by a maniac with a pickaxe. As they battered off the car and smashed into the tarmac, my phone bleeped with a text from my mother. When I replied and told her about the storm she asked in turn if we had brought our wet-weather gear, by which I assumed she meant a boat (or a pair of raclette-cheese ponchos).

Three further climactic changes, four bananas and half a kilo of dried apricots later, we got the bikes out the boot and set off. By then the skies were only "damp" and appeared to be clearing, the sun halfway to being halfway out (if you squinted the right way and really used your imagination).

1910 was the Tour's fateful first year on the Pyrenean passes and also its début outing on the Aubisque. Since then the Col has become a firm race favourite and features in the line-up at a rate of around once every two years. The ascent can be made from the eastern side, riding up from Argelès-Gazost, over the Col du Soulor and then onto the Aubisque itself. However, we had chosen the western side, not so we could check out the local market, but because we thought this option looked like the tougher prospect of the two — oh, the irony!

Our climb started in a very civilized fashion, rising gently through dense forest, not exceeding 6% gradient until, at four kilometres covered, it followed a steep U-turn up and round the centre of a village called Eaux Bonnes (they were being ironic about the rain, right?). Even then, as the gradient sharpened a couple of percentage points, the Aubisque did little to defeat my determined attempts at enjoyment. The experience was distinctly pleasurable, especially so in comparison to my near-collapse on the Peyresourde. The smell of fresh, wet air mingled with resin from the tall conifers that lined the roughly surfaced road to form a dose of homely aromatherapy. Once again France could have been mistaken for Scotland and I drifted, off to entertain a notion that this Pyrenean pass was in fact a favourite route along the banks of the River Spey.

Signs placed every kilometre along the roadside reminded me of our whereabouts and indicated the distance to the summit, along with the average gradient for the coming stretch. Such significant interruptions didn't particularly spoil the climb but I would definitely have preferred it without them. Just like Drew's running commentary, their updates removed much of the mystery and shattered the illusion (more like, delusion) I had constructed that we were in some way discovering the climb (and not following in the wheel-tracks of thousands, perhaps millions of others).

I twiddled a gentle gear, gazed through gaps in the trees to the neighbouring peaks and a distant lightning show that was doing its best to entertain. Bolts cracked from clouds so remote they might as well have been back in Scotland hovering over Speyside. Being at the same altitude as those storms felt oddly comfortingly, our position apparently above the chaos and providing a tangible sense of security. Each bolt was but a tiny spark, the combined display like the faraway fireworks of a neighbouring department's celebration.

Thanks to that meteorological distraction, I paid little heed to the road beneath my tyres; it certainly wasn't bothering me in any way. I felt uncommonly relaxed, under no pressure whatsoever, and the agonies of Robert Millar Day had left me feeling that I could get over pretty much any climb the Pyrenees could put in my way (my methods might not be pretty but I'd definitely get over it). We had found a window in the weather, my body was intact, re-hydrated and refuelled. What could possibly go wrong?

As I disappeared into that haze of complacency, those tiny, faraway lightning bolts grew bored of terrorising the other side of the valley and duly crept a little closer to our position. Then they added creeping to the list of things that bored them, deciding instead to race and roar up the valley toward us. I did my best to ignore it all, to remain idle inside the happy obfuscation but a subsequent backwards glance revealed lightning that was now an awful lot closer, then really rather close and, finally, far too close for comfort. Within less than a few hundred metres of ascent those tiny sparks in the distance had become giant, jagged spears of electricity. Drew pulled his cap down tighter and upped the tempo, his almost phobic fear of lightning obvious for all to see. I too shifted up a gear, moved onto his wheel and stupidly spluttered something about lightning striking the electricity cables above our heads. It was an ill-advised comment, a bit like saying to someone with arachnophobia, "hey, look at this huge hairy spider!" I tried to retract the remark but it was already on the record, its damage done.

"Don't worry," I kept on digging, "the rubber of our tyres will act as protective insulation."

I didn't believe a word of it, neither did he and our already unlikely tempo further increased.

Whilst I clung onto Drew's back wheel and chuckled at what I saw as an irrational fear, the lightning caught up and cracked directly overhead. That explosion of noise was the loudest thing I have ever heard, hopefully the loudest thing I will ever hear. The air turned bright blue as its water content sizzled to the boil. The hairs on our necks stood on end as if we'd stuck our fingers into a electric socket; those power lines I had so recently joked about hissed, buzzed and visibly jerked on their pylon mounts like a sack full of body-popping snakes — the danger I had dismissed suddenly all too real. I shifted up a gear and raced passed Drew, no longer as brave nor as forthcoming with suggestions as to what the lightning might do next. It was all too bloody obvious: we were about to be cooked alive!

On that thought the rain started up again, a deluge that threatened to douse the coals of our human barbecue and then to drown us into the bargain. I thought the downpours in Grenoble and Provence had been bad but this Pyrenean rain was on another level, forced an instant retraction of earlier comments about my keenness for riding in the rain. We rode on with our shoulders hunched and our heads pulled in, as if any of that was going to help when 30,000 amps struck our skulls and then 30,000 gallons swamped us. Then Mother Nature revealed that up until that point she had in fact been toying with us. The heavens properly opened and it actually started raining, for real. Bucketing down? I might have preferred it had the clouds literally lobbed metal pails in our direction. Two seconds under that "proper" rain and we were soaked through and shivering uncontrollably. Then came the hailstones and the parts of our bodies that weren't blue with the cold turned black and blue, bruised by the falling chunks of ice.

The 8% gradient went unnoticed as we pedalled furiously uphill, struggling to get our brains to decide upon what our bodies should do next. We wanted for nothing more than to be off the mountain, back in the car with the heater working full blast. Problem was, to turn around and ride back down into the sheets of rain and hail seemed an even less appealing, and more dangerous, prospect than continuing uphill. I suggested we find a tree to shelter under but it appeared that all the big trees had long since uprooted and run for cover. Then we rounded the corner and saw a snow tunnel up ahead, cars parked inside, their headlights barely visible through the maelstrom. The downpour was so heavy that people had considered it unsafe to drive through and there we were cycling along in lycra T-shirt and shorts. We raced up and into the shelter, squeezed passed the line of cars, oblivious to the gormless glares that came from behind the misted glass. Bikes pulled up onto the small kerb, we sat on the wall and stared out into air that was thick with water and electricity.

Twenty minutes on, the rain had eased but we were ridiculously cold, concerned that, like at the summit of the Sella, hypothermia lay around the next bend, assuming we made it that far. The extremes of temperature and weather we had been subjected to in just two summer weeks were bewildering, from the hottest conditions I'd ever experienced (the thermometer rarely breaks the 20-degrees-Celsius mark in Scotland, let alone the 40) to some of the coldest and wettest. Heading back to the car was going to involve freewheeling into the icy air, whilst uphill meant the generation of body heat. All we could think about was building up some kind of warmth and so we opted for up. The decision was easy but actually re-starting the ascent was not. Our legs were cold and stiff, blood having shifted its attention from the extremities and long since rushed to the core and those vital organs. The seemingly minimal effort required to turn an easy gear at the start of the climb was now an impossible task, made worse by the next bloody road sign and its happy proclamation: *nine kilometres of climbing to go!* What was it the over-confident idiot had said? He could handle anything the Pyrenees put in his way? *Really?* I was no longer so sure, my confidence shattered, its shards washed downhill by the rain.

The body heat we sought wasn't forthcoming despite the undoubted effort involved, and as the road turned steeper, climbed higher, the air temperature dropped another few degrees. By the time we passed through the small village of Gourette, people were once again gawping in that perplexed manner, further cementing my idea for a global anti-staring law.

"What are you looking at?" I wanted to shout. "Haven't you

ever seen such thin, blue men on bicycles? Is this the first time the clouds have parted to reveal two coughing, spluttering and shivering Scots? Believe it or not, we're humans, just like you. So why not show us some encouragement? Better still, why not bring us flasks of hot tea? We could drink some and pour the rest over our frozen, addled heads."

The higher we climbed the harder it was to believe that our bodies might ever warm up, that the sun was ever going to come out from behind the cloud. We required fortitude, a whole lot of fortitude and even greater levels of self-delusion. The only evidence of any shift in temperature came with the steam that rose from our sodden heads, backs and shoulders, an occasional chink in the gloom and the briefest glimpse of that blissful orange ball. Those moments of respite were flimsy and fleeting and I was soon slowing down to linger in the warmth much in the same way I had idled in patches of shade upon Cenis and Peyresourde. Then, with precision timing, the rain recommenced in earnest and any additional heat we had managed to produce instantly dissipated.

The road slowly diverged from the woodland, rising up and away until it eventually emerged onto open, blatantly barren mountainside. An icy breeze swept unhindered across the land, swirling to sap thermal, physical and mental energies, but never once seeming to lend a hand and push from behind. Rain Man Drew spluttered back into action to inform that we had passed the steepest 10% section and that the gradient was now "down" to around 8%. If it felt any easier then we both failed to notice. Add in the low temperature, the deteriorating and narrowing road and instead we had a sense of heading toward a new extreme. The Col's once gentle curves and bends now switched and snapped angrily back and forth, evidence that the engineers had struggled to find a way over this particular peak. To the mountainside the crumbling, potholed sliver of tarmac clung, tenacious yet apologetic, and to it we hung in there just the same.

It was so cold but I was too busy shivering to notice, far too occupied with dodging potholes and fallen rocks, with swerving to avoid the cars that descended toward us with reckless abandon. Then, staring up through the cloud toward the next crest, I suffered my trip's first (and I hoped last) hallucination. Up ahead on the verge stood a ghostly figure, a stark silhouette, like an immense Virgin Mary of the kind we had seen on so many roadside shrines — no, forget that, this vision had come from the dark side, a hooded figure, stood erect, its face obscured, scythe in one hand.

Death was waiting for us on the Aubisque.

I blinked.

Death was still there, moving down-slope toward us. I tried to lift a frozen hand from the bars to point and warn Drew but my bloodless extremity was unable to respond. Is this really it for me, for us both? Should I have listened to Drew long ago, lobbed the Folder of Doom into the nearest bin and jumped on the first flight home? I blinked again and it still looked like the Grim Reaper, but now it was almost upon us. We drew level; Death looked up, raised a hand to wave a word through the cloud.

"Bonjour," came his gruff greeting and a welcome realisation that Monsieur Reaper was in fact a French rambler disguised by a very large, very warm-looking poncho (one, judging by its dark, off-yellow hue, most likely constructed from an excess of raclette cheese).

Less than 2km from the top we passed a small hotel that I doubt very much was there when the pioneers of cycling fought their way up this road during the 1910 Tour de France. (The poor bastards would have been forgiven for abandoning their bikes to check in for the night.) On thinking of those early exploits I realised that, despite cold bones and weary legs, we were having a comparatively easy time of it. A century before, the road, although resurfaced with money provided by the Tour, would have been truly rough, and the heavy, steel-framed, fixed-gear bikes of the era were a prehistoric contrast to our carbon and aluminium steeds. Those brave souls had also faced the extra physical challenge of this climb being part of a day far longer and tougher than ours, a day which in turn had been part of a 4737-kilometre-long route around France. In addition was the mental trial, the realisation that they really were amongst the first to ride up there — whereas we knew that thousands upon thousands of others had been before to set a reassuring precedent.

On many of our previous ascents, the switchbacks near the summit had proved to be the toughest part. Thankfully, on the Col d'Aubisque that wasn't the case. The very last section of the climb was much more forgiving, almost as easy as the initial saunter out of Laruns. I couldn't help but feel that finally the mountain gods and the ghosts of Tours gone by had come around, agreeing that we had paid our penance and suffered sufficient for them to cut some slack. It helped that through our efforts we had warmed up a little, shifted some blood back out toward the pale blue extremities. Whatever the case, as Drew had said so many times before, almost any climb is bearable once you've had sight of the one-kilometre-to-go sign.

As Tour legend would have it, upon reaching the Aubisque summit in 1910, rider Octave Lapize spat the following immortal words at the men who were waiting by the roadside:

"Vous êtes des assassins! Oui, des assassins!"

His remark, (you are killers!) was aimed at the race organisers, men apparently attempting to assassinate cyclists by way of a brutally punishing parcours. Our arrival at the same spot was marked by a breathless silence. A quick browse of the souvenir shop (selling postcards, mugs and, appropriately enough, big woolly jumpers) and we idled over to take in a view of the surrounding peaks: a rainbow of colours glistened across vast surfaces of sheer, rain-soaked rock. Before us was layer upon layer of geological history, all of it laid down millennia before we pedalled up the tiny squiggle of road. To me, the 1910 Tour was an eternity ago, especially distant when I considered everything Europe had experienced since — revolutions, wars, so much political and cultural upheaval — but the history of the Tour is nothing more than the blink of an eye in the mountains' inconceivably long time-line.

As I gazed at the view and considered my own insignificance, an old woman, who looked rather like Madame Souza from *Belleville Rendezvous*, waddled over to interrupt. She rattled away in extremely fast French and left me immediately behind. I jumped into her conversational slipstream, slowed her down a tad and deciphered that she was enquiring as to which cycling team or club Drew and I belonged. Madame Souza was none too impressed when I suggested that we didn't belong to a club, that we were (distinctly amateur) privateers. She was so unimpressed that she repeated the question. Once again I chose to disappoint and asserted that we were but two lone Scottish cyclists.

"Ah oui!" She said suddenly cheered, pleased that her interrogations were making progress, "équipe Écosse!"

She continued apace and from a couple of seconds of speech I gathered that she loved cycling, loved the Tour, and even on occasion loved wearing her own little maillot jaune. At that we laughed, exchanged smiles and soaked in the shared good feeling. How unusual and how welcome it was to have positive interest in our exploits, enthusiasm instead of the commonplace complete and utter disregard. If nothing else, my shivering ego needed the boost.

A gang of walkers appeared from the other side of the valley, trudging along in a line, their bedraggled mules at the back carrying laden packs. The vision only added to the realisation that we were somewhere extreme, a place remote from civilisation (if you discounted the souvenir shop and restaurant). The walkers and their guides looked extremely well prepared, wrapped in several waterproof layers, (easily two-dozen raclette cheese-rounds per person) their four-legged domestiques weighed down with an array of provisions — a real contrast to the two shivering stick-men who barely had a waterproof and a banana between them.

***

After an unsuccessful attempt to dry off under the struggling sun, we zipped up our jackets and dropped down the mountain. Being steep, narrow and wet, the road was dangerous enough but I was also keenly aware of all the potholes, mud and rocks I'd had such a long time to observe during our slow slog to the summit. Those hazards were there but mostly hidden from view, obscured by an eerie blanket of steam that hovered above the slowly warming tarmac.

One of the most famous Tour crashes of all time was the fall of Dutchman Wim Van Est on the descent of the Aubisque during the 1951 race. He lost control, hit a small wall and went off the edge of the road, landing bruised but alive some 70 metres down. He was rescued using a makeshift rope constructed from his team's supply of spare tyres. With just a single inner tube I couldn't afford any kind of improvised rescue and, given that Drew had rocketed ahead as if his life depended solely upon a complete and utter disregard for safety, there would be no one around to do the rescuing. Safely back at the hotel, we collapsed onto our beds to watch the finale of the Clasica San Sebastian on Eurosport. Our mood had lifted, as if returning to sunny Pau was sufficient to blow away any concern, worry or stress, no matter how extreme. Even a brief battle with the one-way system hadn't put a frown on either face. I had really enjoyed the Aubisque and thought that, despite any obvious display of emotion, Drew had too. It had been tough, but once again my feelings were of success, that we had endured an epic ride and come out the other side unscathed. There was only one thing for us to do: get drunk. What else would you expect from equipe Écosse?

DAY 18:
DIVINE INSPIRATION

Col du Tourmalet
Start point: Luz-St-Sauveur | Height: 2115m | Height climbed: 1404m | Length of climb: 19km | Average gradient: 7.4% Maximum gradient: 10.2%

Just as I was hoping that the mood in the camp might be about to lift, we again started the day in a slump. The evening before we had bounced into Pau, having decided to celebrate surviving the Aubisque with a Mexican meal and some beers. An enjoyable feed (that could have trebled in size and still not satisfied our carb requirements) was followed by a pathetic attempt at a pub-crawl. Too much crawling and not enough pubbing revealed that Pau town-centre contained a grand total of three watering holes, and our night fizzled out at a wee café-bar called Spacy (which is exactly how I felt after a few beers). One consolation was that the waiter there had recognised us as Scots — not Italians, Dutch, Germans, Chinese or even English.

So far, so not bad. Then, on the walk home, Drew had interrupted my grumbling about the local lack of fish-and-chip shops to reveal that he wouldn't be able to sleep that night. Indeed, by the time we returned to the room he was utterly convinced that sleep would be impossible — so resolute that he wasn't even going to try. As I stuffed my head under the pillow, struggling not to eat it, he set about pacing around the extremely tight space. (Our room was cramped enough without having two bikes and all our kit spilled across the floor. Even the toilet was impressively minute, so small you had to stand up on the rim of the bowl just to get the door shut. The tiny closet also stunk of pee, as if previous male residents hadn't been bothered trying to squeeze in there and had simply opened the door and urinated in from outside.)

"I'll never sleep, never! And not just never tonight, or tomorrow, or this week," Drew ranted. "I'll never sleep again.

Never again, I tell you!"

I wondered what, besides alcohol, was in the rum he had been drinking, or if "rum" in French also meant liquid cocaine. The attentions of his obsessive behaviour soon turned to his mobile phone, which had been playing up since we left Italy. (When I say it had been playing up, what I mean is, it had only intermittently received text messages from Drew's girlfriend — and he had taken that lack of communication as a sign of technological, rather than interpersonal, malfunction. To make matters worse, the last text he had received kept repeating itself, re-appearing every hour or so, refusing to delete and, in Drew's mind, barring the delivery of the myriad other heartfelt missives his girlfriend had despatched.) No matter how much time — approximately thirty-six hours a day — he spent fiddling with the phone's various functions and settings, nothing resolved the issue. This further infuriated his tired and addled brain, made him pine for home ever more, and made him yet more sick of the trip.

An hour on and Drew was locked in the bathroom, attempting to smoke himself to sleep but only managing to wake himself up a little more, and to fill the bedroom with toxic fumes. Next came his "genius" idea of watching TV as a means of inducing sleep. So, on it went and off he went hopping from French channel to French channel like a lunatic, unable to understand a word, perhaps hoping the strobe effect would somehow prove soporific. Funnily enough, (actually it wasn't that amusing) it didn't. Instead it riled me to the point that we ended up having another pointless argument. Eventually, sometime around 3am, I managed to fall asleep. When I awoke later in the night, Drew was finally snoring away, TV off, cigarettes in the bathroom cabinet, mobile phone locked in a tight grip.

I had been awake and dressed for about two hours by the time he roused from that snoring slumber. He stretched and sighed from under the sheet like an exhausted ghost, rubbed bleary eyes, sat up and offered his first words to the new dawn,

"I'll never get to sleep."

***

One thing our escapade sorely required was spiritual invigoration. Where better to receive such a boost, one would think, than the holy city of Lourdes — and just as well Pau had a one-way street that pointed in the right direction. Lourdes would definitely be an experience but, given a collective lack of Christian faith, how much, if any, meaning it would hold in store was uncertain.

On arrival we set about feeding our non-spiritual hunger, and the small bakery/café we chose (the first we came to) was a tiny Christian theme park in its own right. The menu, napkins, wallpaper, even the icing on the buns sported a Virgin Mary motif. Our sandwiches vanished as quickly as an apparition might appear; we checked the waitress' hands for stigmata and bundled out into the busy street.

Up until 1858 Lourdes was an insignificant outpost at the foot of the Pyrenees. That was the year 14-year-old local girl, Bernadette Soubirous, experienced the first of a series of visions of the Virgin Mary. Since then, official recognition from the church and numerous papal visits have transformed a humble town into the holiest European destination, next to Rome itself — an incredible seven million Catholic pilgrims visit Lourdes every year.

More importantly, from my religious standpoint, Lourdes has also featured frequently in the Tour de France itinerary, often in the guise of the climb to Hautacam, which is located about ten miles south of the town. Rather fittingly, none other than the devout Gino "The Pious" Bartali won the first stage into Lourdes, en route to his second Tour win. After the stage he visited the shrine of Bernadette to pray that he wouldn't fall from his bike later in the race.

We trundled down into the town centre, not quite sure what it was that Lourdes had to offer. We discovered a long line of shops and cafés that looked to these atheist eyes like an extremely tacky tourist resort. I felt as if we had been heading to the grace and majesty of somewhere like Rome, only to take a wrong turn and end up in Blackpool — and some higher force had stolen the sea and replaced it with commercialised religion. Every square-inch of space was crammed with a multitude of plastic tat, cheap stone and distinctly non-precious metal, all "celebrating" the love of Bernadette, our Lord, their Lord and *his* Virgin mother. People milled and swilled, bumped, banged and pushed to get toward the junk, reaching for Euros in order that they might buy a sacred souvenir to save them. Pictures of Jesus, many of which looked like Jim Morrison at a fancy dress party, were plastered across everything from mugs and tea towels to T-shirts, hologram keyrings and doorstops. The items that amazed me most were the plastic holy-water containers with their badly stencilled Virgin Mary motifs. Those receptacles ranged in size from amulet, to jerry can, to enough holy water to keep a small city supplied for a year. (For a brief moment the idea of finding holy cycling bidons sent us buzzing around tacky shop number fifty-seven in a zealous frenzy.)

Amongst myriad merchandise were myriad people, all browsing and buying. I had never seen such a multi-cultured, diverse bunch in such a small space. There were folks from every corner of every continent; men and women, boys and girls, wealthy tourists, borderline-destitute back-packers, curious families, the fit and healthy, and many others who appeared, for whatever reason, be it old age or illness, to be on the verge of death. Desperate believers lugged their gallon drums of holy water back up the road from the grotto, in a rush to anoint themselves and enact a cure. A young boy in a cassock led his mother, father and sister through the throng, heading in the opposite direction, down the hill toward salvation, away from a life of sport, music, drugs, fun, laughter and love, and into a life of frugality and faith. I felt sorry for the little chap and then considered that his fate might be no worse than that of a young lad who wanted to be a professional cyclist, prepared to devote his life to the cause, putting his faith in a strict regimen.

Although we had decided Lourdes resembled Blackpool crossed with Calcutta, touched by the hand of a Made in China god, we still felt uneasy mocking the place. (That said, Drew suggested we shouldn't feel quite as bad as the shopkeepers making a monetary profit out of such devoted and often desperate people, selling them tat dressed up as religious artefact.) As much as we criticised, we also understood that Lourdes is a place where people go seeking salvation, often when they are on spiritual and physical last legs. That it was filled with hope and a positive atmosphere, despite the crass commercialisation, was testament to the pilgrims' belief. I also related to, and genuinely empathised with, those poor souls (and their families) who were clearly beyond the point of medical assistance and had now placed their final hopes in the hands of divine intervention.

We counted ourselves blessed (by god, genetics or pure good fortune) to be in such rude health, and strolled off down the road, to see where everyone else was headed. Perhaps a peek round the corner would reveal a giant inflatable Our Lord upon the cross, a

Last Supper fast-food restaurant, or an Imax cinema that projected visions of the Virgin Mary in 3-D — for all to see and believe, at 10 Euros a ticket. Instead of all that we were treated to the sight of a magnificent cathedral, a building so beautiful even two cynics stopped to stare in wonder.

The Byzantine-influenced, Romanesque-style Basilica of the Rosary is part and parcel of the vast architectural composition of the Sanctuaries of Lourdes. The immense, gleaming limestone construction fills the skyline as you enter the plaza, almost obscuring the Pyrenean peaks that lurk behind. I strolled up the white steps and ducked inside, probably the only man ever to venture in without crossing himself at the threshold.

Off to the left of the main cathedral was a small sanctum filled with rows of flickering candles. I put my two Euros in the box, selected a new candle and dipped its wick into the neighbouring flame. The gesture was symbolic, in mind of my parents, especially my mother — a light for her faith, her love for my father, for their love, that which led to my existence. Whatever I believe, I feel certain their love lives on, somehow, somewhere, not just within my mother but external and eternal. The candle was a gesture to anyone watching — whoever, wherever, in whatever form — a light in the darkness to signal the sentiment, a guide to show the way, my version of the ritual thousands of others had already performed that day. As the flame flickered into life, I felt a spark ignite within and was just as suddenly overwhelmed by a wave of emotional energy. It flowed from my feet to my head, left me dizzy, choked and fighting back the tears.

I hadn't been in any kind of church since my father's funeral and the whole event proved too much for my poor, wee, weary soul. Back outside, blinking into the sun, I felt deeply hurt but newly connected to that mystery *something* I'd been seeking — it might have been my mother's Christian faith, perhaps her and my father's love; or had I actually touched upon my own inner spirit, the deeply held reserves upon which I'd drawn during the worst moments of the Madeleine and the Peyresourde?

Lingering under the shade of a giant stone Virgin Mary, Drew was equally overcome, amazed that the moment he'd stepped inside the cathedral his phone had, "fixed itself". That single, incessant message had disappeared from his inbox, never to return, memory-space made for the subsequent flood of (actually, three) texts that whizzed in from home upon the ethereal airwaves. He took this technological epiphany as an obvious sign: his destiny was to remain in Lourdes and establish a Holy mobile-phone repair centre — open 24-hours, for true believers, and those not quite so sure.

Still struggling to come to terms with our opposite experiences, we wandered back up the road and into a small café, to shelter from the hordes and re-fuel before the day's ride (oh yeah, so there was another reason for our being there). The Italian waiter glanced at our shaved legs and asked, somewhat hopefully, if we were cyclists, concerned we might actually be part of an all-male Christian dancing troupe. Answered in the affirmative, he rattled off a stream of excited, cycling-related chat that would last until we had settled the bill, stepped back outside, and then a little longer. He took much pride in showing off the series of framed photographs that hung above the bar — a limited but extremely precious gallery dedicated to his one true love, cycling. The largest, and obviously his favourite, was a snap of Gino Bartali, taken upon the Col d'Izoard. Bartali, he insisted, was the best cyclist ever, no one will ever be as good again: "Bartali, number one." A slightly smaller frame held a similar snap of Fausto Coppi who, it transpired, was also the best *and* number one, only not quite as good as Bartali. Another, again slightly smaller but equally treasured frame, held a colour snap of Marco Pantani being received by Pope John Paul II and, you guessed right, Pantani was also the best *and* number one to boot.

Without so much as a pause for breath he enquired as to the names of our heroes and then thoughtfully answered for us, assuming that we must be fans of Millar. Robert Millar yes, he's number one, best ever, we replied, but not David Millar, he's good but not quite as good. He agreed, Robert Millar, the best, number one, and then, with even more fervour than he'd shown towards his Italian heroes, our waiter recalled a chance meeting with Irish rider Sean Kelly at a Tour stage finish in Cauterets. Kelly, rather coincidentally, was also the best ever *and* number one. Not only did he love Kelly but also Ireland itself. He had only recently visited that distant land where, he insisted, there are no trees and it is so windy that all cyclists grow up to become Kelly-esque hard men with monstrous legs.

"Ireland, the best, number one!"

An omelette and chips later (the omelette was the best, number one) we bumbled to the car, ready to miraculously transform ourselves from tourists back into cyclists.

***

The drive from Lourdes toward Luz-St-Sauveur offered up yet more stunning scenery. I couldn't help but compare the sight of such natural wonder to gazing up at the Basilica in Lourdes, my cycling-as-church analogy keen for yet another outing: the Pyrenees form their own, natural cathedrals, the giant jagged peaks as spires, a landscape of the brightest green and blue sparkling like massive stained-glass windows. As we drove along the nave, I mean, valley, I was keen to worship, whilst Drew was pensive, acting as if he had been indoctrinated against his will.

Despite having read a great deal about the Tourmalet, it was a climb of which I had formed no prior mental picture. I knew it wouldn't be multi-coloured, carpeted, air-conditioned or diamond-encrusted; I guessed it might be wooded at some points, open and windswept at others, probably have some switchbacks and a rugged, rather steep road. Some of the climbs I had known in advance, to anticipate and even dread; all I really understood of the Tourmalet, besides Rain Man Drew's stream of consciousness, was its mean reputation — not evil like the Ventoux, just miserly, unwilling to cede any inch of ease. From French its name very roughly translates as *bad trip*, so I definitely wasn't expecting to ride along, hands off the bars, singing and clapping.

It was to be our penultimate climb but the Tourmalet's unknown quantity perfectly suited the trip's intended original essence, that (since neglected or misplaced) spirit of discovery. Those personal realisations — of the climbs and of the qualities and failings within each of us — had been, for me at least (for Drew, I had no idea), the major theme of our two-and-a-bit weeks. Most British cyclists return from their European jaunts with miles in their legs, topped-up tans and a renewed vigour for the roads around their own backyard. I would return with some of that but also having learned and grown in ways not limited to the sporting side of my life. To a certain extent those mountains had matured me, kicked my life forward a step or two. At the very least I had been given time to think; stuck in the saddle, with nowhere to go but up, unable to escape into distraction, I had pedalled head-on into my grief. Of course, it hadn't been one long Oprah-style therapy session. I'd seen for myself some of the most amazing vistas, been up close and personal with the grandest of Grand Tour mountains, accepted and completed their particular physical challenge. Roads that had until recently existed solely within the mythologies of other men were now an all too tangible part of my own life story.

In with all that progress had come a fair chunk of regression — witness my reaction to the descents of the Lautaret and Glandon. I had realised childhood dreams and bathed in the waters of youthful naivety — of joie de vivre, as they say here in Franceland — that my parched life had so recently lacked. Here was evidence that I could be happy post-Dad; I'd just need to turn my wheel away from death and aim it toward life. All that from the mountains and two more still to go.

The Tourmalet is one of the monstrous cols from the Pyrenees' 1910 Tour début. It wasn't the first Pyrenean pass to be crossed by the race but it's the one big name around which the mountain mists of legend swirl. Whilst Octave Lapize was the first Tour rider over the top of the climb, the Col's cycling story, and the Tour's mountain mythology, really begins with another man: Alphonse Steinès, he who persuaded race director, Henri Desgrange, that it was a good idea to tackle the Tourmalet and the rest of the Pyrenees. As the inclusion of the mountains had been his idea, Steinès was despatched south to reconnoitre the passes and make sure his genius wasn't actually the madness Desgrange suspected it to be. In May 1910, as the Parisian and his driver set off over the Tourmalet, locals shook their heads and mocked the man's foolhardy determination. A handful of miles up the pass their car became bogged down, spluttering to a halt, stuck in a snowdrift. Undeterred, Steinès pressed on, abandoning both car and driver, who was afraid of death from exposure or between the jaws of a bear. Luckily, he stumbled upon a shepherd who guided him to the summit, and when darkness fell he carried on alone, falling back down the other side toward Baréges. He was found by a search party in the early morning and carried into town to an unlikely hero's welcome. From there he sent a telegram to Desgrange that read:

CROSSED TOURMALET STOP
PERFECTLY PASSABLE STOP
VERY GOOD ROUTE STOP

We usually reserve our thoughts for the riders, those who were first or fastest over the top of the cols. From time to time we should also remember, and show gratitude to, the man who trod the path in patent leather shoes and summer slacks, the man who risked exposure and bears in order to introduce our sport to the high mountains. It can take a moment of madness to break the mould and, as Steinès proved, sometimes the craziest ideas are also the best.

***

Despite the Tourmalet's portentous moniker, and far from fluffy heritage, I felt instantly at ease upon its slopes. My thoughts were entirely untangled, spread neatly around one particular adjective: beautiful. The road, the nature of its ascent, the overall experience, including the scenery and the clement weather — it was all just so beautiful. Each of the climbs had made its impact, many had been stunning, even awe-inspiring, but none were quite as handsome as the Tourmalet that afternoon. My reverence might have been brought on by the realisation that this was our penultimate climb — appreciate it while you can, boy. Perhaps it was the result of a dead-cat-bounce upswing (nowhere to go but up) from the low mood of the previous days. It may also have been some effect elicited by our time in Lourdes. Whatever the cause, I felt distinctly emotional, happily satisfied that we were close to completing our task, but also sad that it would all very soon be over. In a matter of days we would be back to the daily-grind, to riding around in the rain on boring old, pot-holed Scottish roads.

The lower stretches of the climb were relatively benign and smoothly surfaced, allowing me to cheerfully spin a gear (fourth) and take it all in. We drifted up the valley, following the river, through little hamlets packed with sun-burnt summer people, passed campsites overflowing with happy, holiday cheer (everyone too ensconced in play to stop and stare). Lush green farms filled the remainder of the space: fields apparently fit to burst, their harvests straining at the leash. I gulped down the vital air, soaked in the sunshine that sustained this bounty, wished we too were camped up there amongst it all and not dossed down in the middle of Aups' one-way enigma. Only when we forked away from the valley and up onto the mountainside proper did the Tourmalet bare teeth, albeit through a warm smile. The tarmac surface deteriorated accordingly but it was still no worse than any of the Edinburgh highways of which we'd tired. It was, however, a great deal higher up and far, far steeper.

With horned cattle wandering over the road and a general lack of other traffic it was easy to imagine we were somewhere closer to the rustic roads of Steinès' early Tour adventures. Of course in those days the cols would have been little more than glorified tracks, and when it rained they would have turned to thick mud. The worst we had to endure were the vibrations that transferred through our handlebars and the complicated pattern of meandering required to dodge the livestock and their piles of dung.

Our efforts certainly never shaded those suffered by the rider who holds the title of, Man Who Most Deserved to Win the Tour But Never Did. According to another of the Tour's great stories, in 1913, Eugène Christophe rode himself toward the maillot jaune with an attack upon the climb of the Tourmalet. All went well until, wait for it, disaster struck on the descent when his front forks snapped. The legend goes that, undeterred, the man the French public called either Cri-Cri or the Old Gaul, then shouldered his stricken machine and carried it down to the small village of Sainte-Marie-de-Campan. A young girl led Christophe to the local blacksmith's forge, whereupon he set about mending his broken forks. Race regulations of the time prohibited riders from taking any kind of outside assistance, so when Christophe asked a young boy to pump the bellows while he worked, the Tour official, who was then on-hand, slapped him with a ten-minute time penalty.

The thought of a modern-day rider enduring such ill luck and continuing to race is inconceivable, especially in an age when the riders are shadowed around the route by team cars carrying spare wheels, bikes and a mechanic to do the dirty work should anything go seriously wrong. (Even if most modern pros did know their anvil from their elbow, they'd have a hard time welding a snapped carbon-fibre fork back together.) But Christophe fixed his machine, accepted his punishment and raced on toward Paris, where he finished seventh overall — probably the most famous and respected seventh place in sporting history.

For years, until I switched to modern clipless pedals, I had used Zéfal's *Christophe* clips and straps, a product invented by none other than Eugène Christophe. Back then I'd known nothing of the legend, wrongly assumed that *Christophe* was just an arbitrary brand name. With every turn of the pedals I had been unwittingly relying upon a product touched by one of the Tour's all-time greats. Only years later, decades after my clips and straps had been assigned to a dusty box of spare parts, did I learn of the man's exploits.

I'm sad that I no longer have daily contact with Cri-Cri and his clips but I'm not the kind of retro-enthusiast who puts sentiment in front of common sense. Not only have modern-day cyclists benefited from mountain passes far improved from the muddy tracks of old, we also enjoy innumerable mechanical advantages. Whereas the likes of Christophe had to cover the climbs on heavy, steel-framed single-speed bikes, we benefit from aluminium alloys, carbon fibre, clipless pedals and twenty-speed derailleur gears.

Not that my bike felt like the height of technological innovation. For the past couple of days it had been emitting a series of squeaks and squeals that suggested it was in dire need of some TLC. My front tyre was only half inflated. The sweat-caused rust appeared to have spread from the headset top-cap bolt, the bearings beneath close to seizing. My left cleat squeaked even more audibly with every turn of the pedals. My chain screamed and screeched to be cleaned and oiled. Whilst, last but by no means least, a particularly distracting creak called out from around the saddle area whenever I put any pressure on the pedals, i.e. all the way up the climb. (It would later transpire that the alarm emanated from an inch-long crack in the seatpost. The noise had annoyed but I was glad the post had stayed intact and not split in two when I was hurtling downhill at 50 miles an hour.)

As on the Aubisque, the Tourmalet was punctuated by signs that indicated the altitude, distance to the summit, and the average gradient for the coming kilometre. (Only the last of them delivered any cause for concern, by concurring with Drew's suggestion that the gradient was "only" 10%, when it looked and felt much closer to 15.) A further selection of (better late than never) signs also warned that we were travelling through farmland and to beware any animals that might have strayed onto the road. By the steeper, upper slopes, flocks of sheep had come to mingle with the cattle, all scattered across the mountainside, wandering free-range without a care. (I wondered: did they require signs to warn them about cyclists and drivers?) One particular sheep had been recently shorn, the resultant look reminiscent of a 1980s Robert Millar mullet. The poor bugger didn't appear too keen on his retro image, had slumped at the verge, weary head rested on the tarmac as if hoping to commit suicide beneath the wheels of a passing car. I told him not to worry, that the '80s are always coming back into fashion, and to remember that things could be worse — at least he didn't have to ride to the top. Whilst the sheep had entertained and somehow saddened me, the cows caused concern: I thought ahead to the descent and made a note to give their long, sharp horns an exceedingly wide berth.

Gone by then was the lush greenery of the valley below, the road now back-dropped by patchy grass and swathes of scree. We were completely exposed but the warm wind didn't aversely effect us. In comparison to the shambles of two days before I felt superbly strong, that cocky attitude I'd entertained on the ride out of Laruns back for another blast. A quick look around to check for gathering storm clouds and I allowed the thought to form: no climb can faze me now, not today's, not tomorrow's, certainly none that Britain has to offer. Our end would be achieved, not even the legendary Tourmalet, the highest paved Pyrenean pass, was going to stop me.

The "bad trip" was by no means insurmountable but that didn't make it an easy climb. The usual physical signs that accompany an arduous ascent were evident: the heavy breathing; the pounding pulse; fingers wrapped tight around the bars; eyes bulging and focussed on an ever-advancing spot upon the road ahead. The difference was I found the sensations, if not enjoyable, then broadly acceptable. Rather than baulk, I relished the challenge, slipped into the zone and smoothly pedalled progress toward the summit, never going lower than second gear. On Robert Millar Day, each and every event, from turning the cranks to blinking sweat from my eye, had required utmost concentration, seemingly monstrous physical output that in turn delivered a hefty dose of discomfort. By the last three kilometres of the Tourmalet, as the road turned abruptly to a series of steep switchbacks, my jersey was unzipped, sweat poured from my chin, but in place of prostrated panic I confidently counted down the metres.

My poor bike fared less well, sounded like its condition was worsening with every turn of the pedals. Through the last kilometre, the various noises and grinding sensations built to a crescendo, so loud it almost completely distracted from the job at hand. Drew picked up on the cacophony (would have required earplugs not to), demanded to know where the hideous sounds were coming from, implored me to make them stop. I shrugged my shoulders, kept on pedalling, but my inability to order an immediate silence wasn't well received. He glared across from his side of the road, suspicious, as if he thought my bike and I were actively conspiring to psyche him out.

We finally ground — and creaked and squeaked — our way up the last few steep switchbacks for not so much an end to the effort as a break from my injured bicycle's tortured screams. Besides the obligatory summit sign (*Col du Tourmalet — altitude 2115m*) there was a monument to Jacques Goddet, director of the Tour from 1936 to 1986. Both of those were overshadowed by *Le Geant du Tourmalet*, a larger than life, silver-coloured iron sculpture depicting a cyclist mid-ascending-effort. It's a monument to Lapize and all those who have followed in his tracks, a nod to the two-wheeled deities to whom I had pretty much sacrificed my poor bike. Whatever the future holds for cycling and the Tour de France I hope that in another hundred years' time cyclists are still testing themselves on the Pyrenean passes, still remembering to doff their casquettes in honour of the peloton's pioneers.

Whilst the bike was hanging by a thread the rider on it felt like a cheat: it wasn't fitting to have pedalled to the top of the Tourmalet in so relaxed a fashion. I'd remembered to spare a thought for Lapize (even devoted a few seconds of mental effort to Steinès, the man to whom myth had accredited the blame for all this nonsense) but I'd forgotten to put on a show for them upstairs.

"What kind of cyclist is this?" They boomed from riveted leather saddles way up above the clouds. "Did he ride up in the back of an automobile? He looks far too fresh for our liking. Send him down the mountain and then order him to come straight back up again. And then he can ride on to the Aubisque!"

As we took our snaps by the summit sign, a Frenchman wandered over from the car park to ask what gear ratios we were riding. Monsieur appeared mildly impressed when I told him, then a little perturbed when I reiterated the point by angrily jabbing a finger toward my chainset.

"No f***ing triple," I barely resisted the urge to shout. "Me and him, we're doing it just like the pros! Well, kind of, not really."

It was difficult to conceive that we were loitering at our penultimate summit, that after one more ascent it would all be over — no more mountains, no more hard-fought high points or laboured lows, just the long, flat road to Barcelona and a flight home. I had no desire to relinquish the dream I was living (*my* dream; Drew's nightmare) but the urge to linger was weaker than the urge to swap the cold mountain breeze for the warm air of the valley below. I mentally leant down to tighten my toe straps, pointed my front wheel downhill and, with a squeak and a creak, we were off.

DAY 19:
PLATEAU DE BYE-BYE

Plateau de Beille
Start point: Les Cabannes | Height: 1790m | Height climbed: 1255m | Length of climb: 15.8km | Average gradient: 7.9% Maximum gradient: 10.8%

We departed Pau on a grey, rainy day, heading east toward our penultimate pit stop at Pamiers (try saying that after a few sherries). Ahead of that lay two nights in Barcelona, the chance to relax and maybe even celebrate with a cerveza or two. To reach those hard-earned beers we'd have to ride one more climb, the Plateau de Beille or, as we had taken to calling it, the Plateau de Bye-Bye.

For us it was goodbye to mountains and all that came with them. Goodbye to the mix of dread and excitement that swilled in our guts each morning. Goodbye to Rain Man Drew and his running commentaries, his incessant stream of data, warnings and worrying. Goodbye to the adrenaline-fuelled sense of achievement that came with every summit reached. Goodbye to the most magnificent scenery Europe has to offer — beautiful, breathtaking, sometimes so imposing as to be downright scary. Goodbye to moods, to negativity and bad tempers. Goodbye to bad breakfasts — the breakfast at Pau had been one tiny plastic pot of jam, one piece of rock-hard bread and a small cup of coffee. I resolved that on my first morning back in Edinburgh I would treat myself to a celebratory fry-up with bacon, eggs, sausage, black pudding, tattie scones, beans, toast, tea, some indigestion tablets, a lie-down and a heart attack. Goodbye, for a while at least, to shaving our legs. I hadn't bothered tending to my stubbly pins that morning, already succumbed to the lazy notion of growing back the leggy locks. Goodbye to lathering on sunscreen, riding in a world of heat, hallucinating water fountains, struggling, perspiring and expiring in the saddle. I would soon be back in Scotland and the sunscreen would return to the cupboard, replaced by hot embrocation, thermal longs and gloves. Goodbye to those stress-generating long drives on scary Euro motorways. Goodbye to cars coming down the mountain on our side of the road, goodbye to Dutch campervans swaying wildly in the fast lane. Goodbye to dodgy directions, deviazioni and impossible-to-find hidden hotels. It would soon be goodbye to the hire car, our rather smelly Ford Focus estate. It stunk, like a teenage boy's bedroom, minus the spunk. Dirty bikes and sweaty kit, banana skins and jam-filled croissants rotting down the back of the seats: all of it combined to make an intoxicating, sickening stench. We had driven along with the windows and boot open in an attempt to air the interior, but it proved fruitless. Not even a forest of Magic Trees could have masked the aroma. We pitied the poor person charged with collecting the car in Barcelona and driving it back to Venice; their task would be well worth the £500 danger money ("pick up fee") that we had shelled out for. It would be goodbye to our Bri-talian passport; no longer driving hopelessly, dangerously in a car with Italian plates, we would have to return to our decidedly less exciting but better informed Scottish alter egos. Driving through Pau, Drew had been forced to emergency-stop, screeching to a halt having spotted a zebra crossing just as a smart, elderly lady stepped off the kerb. She paused to cast a disdainful eye over our vehicle and then, with a quick glance at the Italian number plate, her mind was put at ease, all questions answered:

"Ah, crazy Bri-talians," she smiled, shrugged and tootled on her way.

Whilst we were heading through town, Drew received a text message from his girlfriend (hallelujah!), not to declare her undying devotion but to tell him which reprobate had won the latest edition of *Big Brother*. He didn't care, and neither did I. Besides, we were currently pre-occupied by living in our own reality show, the one where the two crazy Bri-talians, Bruno and Giuseppe, drive around all day looking for a parking space and a decent breakfast. Difference with our show was that no one was filming, or watching.

You want a really good reality show? Look no further than the Tour de France. For three weeks every July the Tour delivers the best reality show you could ever hope to watch (given my suspicions about doping I should probably place the word *reality* within inverted commas). It's a real-life sporting soap-opera that unfolds before our eyes, live and unedited. And it's not exclusively for cycling-enthusiasts; there are numerous storylines to keep even the casual viewer glued to the screen: tragedy, triumph, humour, bravery, camaraderie, selflessness, greed. You can follow the main event, that battle for the yellow jersey, or tag on to the various sub-plots: the breakaways, the points jersey, the mountains jersey, the best young rider, the lanterne rouge, the riders struggling with injury, and the doping scandals. Last year even my girlfriend, Gaby, got hooked, and she's normally as likely to watch sport on TV as I am to spend an afternoon watching chick flicks and gorging on chocolate (that's not very likely, in case you're wondering).

Having eventually located a parking spot and some breakfast, we escaped the one-way system and headed for the countryside. We passed field after field of sunflowers, their heavy golden heads drooped toward the earth, sleeping until sunlight finally burnt away the grey morning. It would be goodbye to their colourful carpeting, that favourite visual cliché of Tour de France TV coverage, goodbye to being lost upon a back road in a strange land — soon but not quite yet. We drove by two different (we assumed they were different) signs, both of which stated that we were 43 kilometres from Pamiers. The second sign was a 30-kilometre drive from the first. Goodbye to confusion? No, probably never. Had we been prematurely optimistic about succeeding in our venture and become trapped in a French traffic-hell perpetuity? More likely we had taken a wrong turn and endured an additional, unnecessary loop.

We passed through hamlets, nobody around but a few old folk who stared at us and shook their heads in disbelief.

"Crazy Bri-talians," they mouthed as we passed through, for the second time that hour.

The longer we drove, the smaller and less hospitable those outposts became. Before long it seemed that people were peering out of the shadows just to spit curses at Bruno and Giuseppe. I was glad that we were passing through in daylight; god (or *le diable*) only knew what happened in such places under the cover of darkness. Stick to the road, crazy Bri-talians, keep off the moor!

Clearly my imagination had run wild, much like the little boy we saw, no more than ten years old, dressed up like an Ali G impersonator, waving what we hoped was a replica handgun in the air like he just didn't care.

"Keep driving, Bruno! Keep driving and don't look back."

Due to our shaky mental state, the senseless signs, and despite what the map told us, we began to wonder if Pamiers even existed. Thankfully, solid, three-dimensional, undeniably Pamiers-shaped evidence appeared at the end of the long and winding road to prove that it did (and probably still does, much to the relief of its 13,000 residents). The small town is situated on the east bank of the Ariège River and, according to the local tourist information, makes an ideal stopover for the Pyrenees. (The Pyrenees, you say? Well there's an idea.) Pamiers (or Pam Ayres as we took to calling it) was so-named to commemorate a battle undertaken by crusader Roger II de Foix. The thing is, old Rodge never made it to the crusades, that was just a story to cover up the truth of his death whilst wandering the countryside in maddening circles, looking for his castle, cursing whichever idiot put up all the confusing road signs.

***

The first I had seen of Plateau de Beille, indeed the first many cycling enthusiasts had seen of it, was during stage 11 of the 1998 Tour de France (of course, skiers had been visiting in droves long before the Tour interrupted the Plateau's summer calm). Up until then, the climb to the ski station hadn't featured in any Tour route, although it had featured in a smaller race known as La Route du Sud. During that Tour stage, Pantani had used the climb as a springboard for an attack, sprinting away from the group of main contenders in a manner that suggested his right hand was gripped around a motorbike throttle (remember, this is cycling's *reality* we're talking about). Only Jan Ullrich had been able to attempt a counter move but his large diesel engine proved insufficient to overcome Pantani's nimble, petrol-driven, fuel-injected flight: Pantani never once settled, always getting out the saddle to press harder on the pedals and kick the tempo higher; another acceleration and the elastic snapped; Ullrich was dropped. Pantani caught and passed the remnants of the day's earlier breakaway, won the stage and in the process chipped almost two minutes off Ullrich's lead — and still nobody had the diminutive Italian down as a potential Tour winner. An exciting story for Pantani fans like Drew and me, but it's one of very few tales from the Plateau.

In contrast, each of the climbs from previous days — the Peyresourde, Aubisque and Tourmalet — has a cycling heritage almost as old as the Tour itself. In some respects it seemed a shame to devote our last day to an ascent with such a limited pedigree, especially when we would be leaving the Pyrenees without having tackled old-school favourites like the Aspin or Pla d'Adet. Yet it wasn't simply a case of riding Plateau de Beille because Pantani had won there. We had come to champion a new name, that of the climb itself. It represented the notion that our sport is continually evolving. Every once in a while a climb is "discovered" by race organisers, a new battleground that, in a century to come, might well have as many stories to tell as the Tourmalet does now. Whether or not P-de-B has what it takes to hang with the veterans of cycling, only time will tell.

From the minute I saw the road at Les Cabannes I was itching, eager to get going, as if the Plateau de Bye-Bye might actually be headed somewhere.

"Let's do the last one," I thought, "quick, before we wake up and this crazy dream is over."

We passed a group of rowdy teenagers carrying rackets, headed for a game of tennis in the sun, theirs more a court for hormones and horseplay than sporting glory. I was back to thinking of Pantani, having read that he had trained for hours in the hills around his parents' home on the east coast of Italy, laying the foundations for his cycling success whist his peers headed to the beach to check out the talent. From there, insecurity and shyness had driven the fragile teenager toward an even grander opponent; he had ridden away to tackle and defeat the biggest mountains, and yet even that achievement hadn't delivered sufficient confidence to sustain his life beyond the age of thirty-three.

The excitement of facing the final challenge of our campaign combined with having eaten and slept well to ensure that I was once again happily attacking a climb (happy? On two climbs in a row? Must have been something in the water at Lourdes). Even the uncomfortably rough road surface (par for the Pyrenean course) and the intense heat did little to dent my morale — the latter proving that there's a first time for everything.

Actually, the climatic conditions presented a greater challenge than the ascent itself. It wasn't sun-shining hot but the air was horrendously humid, thick, steamy and damp. The sweat poured off us like nothing we had ever experienced, perspiring more profusely than we had on Izoard or Peyresourde. Each time I tilted my head forward sweat poured from the small sponge padding beneath my helmet chinstrap, double the amount I imbibed with every gulp from my bottle. The Aubisque might have felt like Scotland but P-de-B was surely more like a South American rainforest. (Had we taken another wrong turn? Were road signs in the Ariège really *that* bad?)

No matter. As long as I wasn't suffering any illness or injury and the heat was (just) the right side of bearable then I'd definitely make it to the top of the climb. I knew how; I'd learned, completed my apprenticeship. Hands placed on the flats of the bars, elbows dropped, shoulders relaxed, I focused on the road ahead. Down in second gear, I spun the pedals as much as possible, stood to keep things moving when the gradient steepened. *Stay fluid; don't forget to drink plenty of fluids. And try not to think too far ahead. Measure your effort but don't spend the whole time worrying about making it to the top. The summit will come, rest assured.* The more you climb the better you become at climbing, and in the past two weeks I'd done quite a bit of it.

Sadly, as was almost always the case, when one of us felt good, the other was sure to suffer. Drew struggled to deal with the humidity, aghast at how much he was sweating despite the lack of direct sunlight. Where I twitched, raring to go, he was drained and crawling, a nod towards how I'd felt on Robert Millar Day. To add to his malady, the flies were keen to demonstrate just how thoroughly they enjoyed the salty steam that rose from our bodies. They swarmed around us in hungry clouds, any rhythm that Drew managed to build, any concentration he mustered, quickly wasted with futile attempts to swat them away. Reverting back to the manic misery of the Bonette, he cursed and swore, grumbled and mumbled, hands flying around his head, serving only to pique the persistent insects' interest. The one consolation was that at least the Pyrenean pests didn't bite.

The climb had started out at over 6% gradient (Drew informed me through the swatting frenzy) but by the end of the first kilometre had jumped to around 9. I could clearly picture some of the riders' excruciating grimaces from Tour TV footage. The camera rarely captures how steep a climb is, but it never fails to illustrate the anguish of those riding at their limit. Thankfully, there weren't any cameras on hand to capture my inane, sweat-steaming grin, nor Drew's obvious torment. And the higher we climbed, the more enraged he became, as if he could hear each and every fly in the swarm commenting on a buzzing loop:

"*Oh look, there's a head, let's fly round it. Oh look, there's a head, let's fly round it. Oh look, there's a head, let's fly round it. Oh look, there's a head, let's fly round it ... .*"

There was plenty of fans' graffiti painted onto the road, including *Beloki 2005* — optimistic, possibly painted by Joseba himself. There was also a deal of artwork aimed at Basque rider Iban Mayo, no-doubt daubed in advance of his spectacular Tour-demise upon the very same stretch of road. Yet again a major theme was Lance Armstrong and allegations of doping; then came a load of anti-American crap: *Go Home Yank*; a cartoon of Armstrong as a pig holding an *I love Bush* placard. I asked Drew how he would react if he found out in years to come that Armstrong had doped. He said he'd be so disappointed, so disillusioned that he would never ride his bike again. (I neglected to remind him that in his postcard from Briançon he'd already committed to a bike-less future.) I *would* ride my bike again, definitely, wouldn't stop because of anything Armstrong, or anyone else, had or hadn't done, but I'd probably steer clear of watching any bike races on TV. (To be honest, I was almost at that point anyway, had grown tired of the Texan's robotic fairytale.) I'd steer clear until I could place more trust in the drug testing, or until the punishment for a positive was a lifetime ban.

As we came up through the almost pan-flat Pas de Roland, the toughest parts of the climb were already in the bag but the conditions had one last shot at hampering our progress. The hot, steamy clouds had thickened into a pea-soup fog. We disappeared into the vapour, visibility down to a matter of feet, the anticipated views non-existent (I could barely discern my front wheel, let alone anything of the surrounding scenery). Despite the cooler air, we were still sweating buckets; hot, thirsty and now hungry too. That latter sensation grew exponentially with every metre of ascent achieved and soon replaced the flies in Drew's molten machinations. The poor, deluded fellow convinced himself (and half-convinced me) that we would find a shop at the summit, and so he began to list the items he would buy when we got there: can of Coke, two cans of Orangina, bag of peanut M&Ms, two bags of salt and vinegar crisps ... . It's possible the desire to reach that non-existent outlet was all that kept him going.

The insects had been innumerable but otherwise the road was deserted. The only person we saw during the entire climb was the driver in a car that came down the road toward us. He acknowledged our presence in the fog with a wave and a sympathetic, almost vacant gaze that suggested there was a bike in the back of the car and he knew through recent experience *exactly* how we felt. Whatever his reason, I wondered if that reflected gaze would be the legacy of our trip, that we would forever hold a slightly haunted look in our eyes, a kind of thousand-yard stare, the physical feature that scars all veterans of the great mountain conflict.

As I considered that possibility, and Drew had almost completed his shopping list, we broke through a bank of mist and realised, a bit too suddenly for my liking, that it was all over. (*That was a 15-kilometre ascent? Really? Did we take a short cut by mistake?*) The empty, nondescript car park of the summit all around us, the road crumbled to a halt beneath the ski-lifts' shadows, and the climb to Plateau de Beille was over — *all* our Euro climbing was over, and I was so completely and utterly disappointed. Our challenge was done and dusted, and despite (perhaps because of) the way I had felt upon Robert Millar Day, how I had grovelled on the Madeleine, I didn't want to stop. Like an addict who knows how much their drug is damaging, I needed one more high — just one more climb, one more! Forever one more.

I desired the fix but knew it wasn't forthcoming and the essence of the end hit me all at once. I simmered with a panicked fear of the kind that might be elicited from saying goodbye to a loved-one, only to realise, as they disappeared over the horizon, that you would never see them again. Could that really be it for me? Would I ever return to the Dolomites, Alps or Pyrenees? What about the missed Italian monsters, like Monte Zoncolan, the Gavia and the Mortirolo? Would I ever get to complete the Sella Ronda? And couldn't I ride up Alpe d'Huez just *one* more time? Never mind the fact that my Spanish experience was limited to the hills around Burgos and the climb up Sierra Nevada to Veleta. Could I really end my days knowing that I'd never even attempted the hideous gradients of L'Angliru?

Not only had I an insatiable desire for the mountains, I also had a newfound respect, a realisation that from now on the names I would champion would be those from the parcours and not the peloton. The paint on tarmac will fade to be replaced in a continual cycle of renewal but the names printed white onto brown summit signs will never desert me — always there, for all of us, and future generations too. In essence, the climbs that Drew and I had tackled were the very same routes ridden one hundred years ago, the same arduous ascents cyclists will be slogging their way up in another hundred years to come. Tourmalet, Ventoux, Galibier, Stelvio, d'Huez ... those are the sport of cycling's true legends. They feature in races (and the headlines) year in year out; they never lose form, can't retire. More importantly, in this era of doubt, the mountains won't test positive — solid as the millennia of rock upon which their roads were laid, guaranteed to never let you down.

As the fog closed in, the sun unable to penetrate, the curtain lowered upon our performance. The story of this mountain adventure had concluded and if we had not paid attention or shown appreciation when we were there, alive upon the stage, then that was just too bad. Life is not a rehearsal; it's a series of adventures.

For this particular exploit Drew and I hadn't properly rehearsed. Back home, in the safety of low-altitude Edinburgh, we had failed to consider, or dreamily dismissed, just how difficult our chosen task would be. Our original itinerary — held on record within the Folder of Doom — had optimistically pencilled us in for 33 climbs. That target had by no means been an impossible achievement but it would have required better preparatory training, better logistics, and having a driver/cook/masseur/motivational coach wouldn't have hurt either. Our original ambitions had been curtailed but the end achievement was by no means paltry. Consider that during 16 days of riding we had tackled a total of 20 Category-1-or-above ascents. Then consider that the total height we had climbed was almost 23,000 metres (or about 75,000 feet) — that's approaching three times the height of Mount Everest.

Drew was in no mood to linger, no inclination toward celebratory consideration or contemplation. Unable to locate the shop of his hungry hallucinations, he shot off down to Les Cabannes, speeding into the mist and round blind bends as if the last flight (ever) back to Scotland was in the valley and cleared for take off.

I knew roughly where the road was headed (one final unread

map within that folder) but I doubted the direction our friendship would take. Together we had achieved a hat-trick of Alpe D ascents, ridden up Europe's highest paved road, and now this. Despite our differences, I knew that I wouldn't and couldn't have done it without him. We had shared a truly extraordinary experience; I just wished it had strengthened the bond and not pushed us apart. The optimistic angel on one shoulder suggested that in decades to come Drew and I would be old codgers, a tartan rug over our knees, arguing about which climb had been the toughest. The opposing devil had other ideas, doubted that our friendship would last that long, if it did that Drew would still be mad at me for having dragged him round Europe on the *trip from hell*. I really didn't understand how we could have come to rest at such diverging viewpoints. Together we had boozily boasted of coming out here and riding all the climbs. It hadn't been *my* dream or *his* dream — indisputably it had been *our* crazy dream and somehow, despite our obvious incompetence, we had turned it into a reality. So why had he spent half the trip acting in a manner that suggested our fantasy was his nightmare? He was homesick, physically sick, stressed by the driving, I knew all the excuses but, to be honest, I was tired of trying to figure him out. (Deciphering the contents of my own head was difficult enough.) There is no exclusive true telling of any story. I just hoped that the version of events he eventually settled on had sufficient gaps in the cloud through which the sunlight could shine.

And so, on a personal level, what had our adventure done for me? To be honest, I wasn't totally sure. The only thing of which I could be certain was that it might be months, possibly years, before I'd taken it all in, come to comprehend how much of an impact the mountains had made.

As I had suspected it might, the trip had afforded me a greater understanding of my human heroes — where they had suffered so too had I. Whilst that experience should have brought me closer to the likes of Millar and Fignon, it was actually to the mountains themselves that I felt the greater connection. No two are the same; each has its own essence or aura, a truly unique spirit. Individually they had gifted, shown and taught me something — about the ascent and myself. Taken together as a whole, the mountains had irrevocably altered me, and for the better.

I already had a definite sense of having dropped the grief that had wheel-sucked my life for far too long. Now was the time to get down on the drops, fix my eyes upon the road ahead and concentrate on progressing. Had the mountains taught me that or had I known it all along? The mountains had certainly taught me that riding uphill for ten miles on the trot hurts, and hurts a lot, but it's the pain of life; I now appreciated that struggle as a gift. The mountains had also taught me that in order to reach the top you must be determined, sometimes fearless and always optimistic. Like the mountains, life has its fair share of ups and downs; it's what you make of it that counts. At some point, on the road, tilted uphill, I had come to realise that because my father had fought tooth and nail to cling on to his life I was duty-bound to cherish my own existence with a similar zeal.

Unwilling to chase after Drew, to make another futile attempt at brightening his mood, I opted instead to freewheel down at my own, rather sedate pace. I was no longer afraid of falling; my only aim was to delay the moment of letting go, like a breakaway in reverse: the slower I rode, the longer it would take to reach the finish.

The further down the mountain I got, the more glimpses of scenery made it through the mist, and the sight of those immense landscapes brought their final inspiration. Much as the Alps had enlivened the von Trapp family, I too began to sing. The self-composed, entirely improvised gem won't make it onto any soundtrack CD but the nonsense ditty was spewed forth with an outburst of emotion the intensity (if not the technical competence) of which Meat Loaf would have been proud. I sung for the last mountain, for an end to moods and exhaustion. I sung of my respect for cycling's Grand Tours, their incredible climbs and all those who had ridden up them — from geriatric tourists to pro racers (those who'd ridden clean and even the doped deniers). I sung for the heat and the cold, for the insects we'd seen and heard so much of, for the marmots we'd failed to glimpse — I even sung for the rancid goats and their repulsive fromage. I sung for myself (the future me, the current me and the teenage me), because I understood and appreciated the achievement, because no one else would sing for me.

I loved that final climb, as looking back down the road of our travels I loved them all. I loved life, the gift of it, in a way I hadn't since before my father's diagnosis, and as the joy returned, the guilt slowly dissipated. I hauled in deep breaths and the air tasted heavenly. Mountainous, majestic Mother Nature had spread her arms around me, her sky impossibly blue, her forests vibrant-green, their damp leaves sparkling in the sunlight. I let the image flood my mind, so it might form a mental souvenir, one that would last forever, of which I would take no photograph, holding it within, truly my own. As an old man on his deathbed, that moment will come to me — the most vivid, vivacious recollection — and I will smile and I will sing.

REFERENCES

1. www.pezcyclingnews.com 16/12/03

2. www.dangerousroads.org/france/300-col-du-lautaret-france.html

3. Fotheringham, William. (2003). *Put Me Back On My Bike - In Search of Tom Simpson*. London: Yellow Jersey Press. P29.

4. Kimmage, Paul. (2001). *Rough Ride*. London: Yellow Jersey Press. pp136-137.

5. Proser, Chip. *Top Gun*. Revised Final Script. April 1998. The Daily Script. 6 Dec. 2012. < http://www.imsdb.com/scripts/Top-Gun.html>.

6. Armstrong, Lance. (2000). *It's Not About the Bike — My Journey Back to Life*. London: Yellow Jersey Press. p4.

7. Ibid. p5.

8. Ibid. p3.

9. Ibid. pp117-118.

10. Ibid. p3.

11. www.autobus.cyclingnews.com/road/2004/tour04/news/?id=jun04/jun10news

BIBLIOGRAPHY

Fife, Graeme. (2002). *Inside the Peloton: Riding, Winning and Losing the Tour de France*. Edinburgh: Mainstream Publishing.

Fotheringham, William. (2003). *Put Me Back On My Bike - In Search of Tom Simpson*. London: Yellow Jersey Press.

Kimmage, Paul. (2001). *Rough Ride*. London: Yellow Jersey Press.

Moore, Richard. (2008). *In Search of Robert Millar*. London: Harper Sport.

Mulholland, Owen. (2003). *Uphill Battle - Cycling's Great Climbers*. Boulder: Velo Press.

Ronchi, Manuela., and Josti, Gianfranco. (2005). *Man on the Run - The Life and Death of Marco Pantani*. London: Robson Books.

Simpson, Joe. (1998). *Touching the Void*. London: Vintage.

Wheatcroft, Geoffrey. (2004). *Le Tour - A History of the Tour de France*. London: Pocket Books.

Woodland, Les., ed. (1999). *A Moustache, Poison and Blue Glasses - Tales of the Tour de France*. London: Bromley Books.

Woodland, Les. (2003). *The Yellow Jersey Companion to the Tour de France*. London: Yellow Jersey Press.

CLIMB DATA

The data — such as climb length, average gradient, and maximum gradient — presented in this book is in no way intended to be a definitive work of reference.

When undertaking "research" for the trip, I often came across contrasting sets of statistics for the same climb. However, whilst the various sources differed slightly (say on a climb's maximum gradient), on the bigger picture they all more or less agreed.

Much of the climb data we relied upon was from www.salite.ch and Google searches often led me to official Tour de France and Giro d'Italia climb profiles contained in articles on sites such as www.cyclingnews.com and www.pezcyclingnews.com.

At the time of publication, the one website I found to be most reliable, and valuable as a reference resource was www.climbbybike.com. Another site that I wish had been around when we were planning the trip is (perhaps it was and I missed it) www.cyclingthealps.com.

The data I have included here is pretty much that which was contained within the Folder of Doom (and is probably to this day still lodged in Rain Man Drew's subconscious). Feel free to use it as a guide, or even as an inspiration, but remember, there's no better way to find out exactly how long, steep or hard a climb is than to ride it yourself.

Printed in Great Britain
by Amazon